Including the stranger

NEW STUDIES IN BIBLICAL THEOLOGY 50

Series editor: D. A. Carson

Including the stranger

FOREIGNERS IN THE FORMER PROPHETS

David G. Firth

Aᴘᴏʟʟᴏs

Academic
An imprint of InterVarsity Press
Downers Grove, Illinois

APOLLOS (an imprint of Inter-Varsity Press, England)
36 Causton Street, London SW1P 4ST, England
Website: www.ivpbooks.com
Email: ivp@ivpbooks.com

Inter Varsity Press, USA
P.O. Box 1400, Downers Grove, IL 60515, USA
Website: www.ivpress.com
Email: email@ivpress.com

Inter-Varsity Press, England, publishes Christian books that are true to the Bible and that communicate the gospel, develop discipleship and strengthen the church for its mission in the world.

IVP originated within the Inter-Varsity Fellowship, now the Universities and Colleges Christian Fellowship, a student movement connecting Christian Unions in universities and colleges throughout Great Britain, and a member movement of the International Fellowship of Evangelical Students. That historic association is maintained, and all senior IVP staff and committee members subscribe to the UCCF Basis of Faith. Website: www.uccf.org.uk.

Inter Varsity Press®, USA, is the book-publishing division of Inter Varsity Christian Fellowship/USA® and a member movement of the International Fellowship of Evangelical Students. Website: www.intervarsity.org.

Unless stated otherwise, Scripture quotations are the author's own translation.

Quotations marked esvuk are taken from the ESV Bible (The Holy Bible, English Standard Version) Anglicized, copyright © 2001 by Crossway, a publishing ministry of Good News Publishers. Used by permission. All rights reserved.

First published 2019

Set in Monotype Times New Roman
Typeset in Great Britain by CRB Associates, Potterhanworth, Lincolnshire
Printed and bound in Great Britain by Ashford Colour Press Ltd, Gosport, Hampshire

UK ISBN: 978–1–78359–507–5 (print)
UK ISBN: 978–1–78359–508–2 (digital)

US ISBN: 978–0–8308–2919–4 (print)
US ISBN: 978–0–8308–4195–0 (digital)

British Library Cataloguing-in-Publication Data
A catalogue record for this book is available from the British Library.

Library of Congress Cataloging-in-Publication Data
A catalog record for this book is available from the Library of Congress.

For Gordon Wenham

Contents

Series preface

New Studies in Biblical Theology is a series of monographs that address key issues in the discipline of biblical theology. Contributions to the series focus on one or more of three areas: (1) the nature and status of biblical theology, including its relations with other disciplines (e.g. historical theology, exegesis, systematic theology, historical criticism, narrative theology); (2) the articulation and exposition of the structure of thought of a particular biblical writer or corpus; and (3) the delineation of a biblical theme across all or part of the biblical corpora.

Above all, these monographs are creative attempts to help thinking Christians understand their Bibles better. The series aims simultaneously to instruct and to edify, to interact with the current literature and to point the way ahead. In God's universe mind and heart should not be divorced: in this series we will try not to separate what God has joined together. While the notes interact with the best of scholarly literature, the text is uncluttered with untransliterated Greek and Hebrew, and tries to avoid too much technical jargon. The volumes are written within the framework of confessional evangelicalism, but there is always an attempt at thoughtful engagement with the sweep of the relevant literature.

In much of the world, and certainly in the Western world, foreigners are everywhere: it is no longer the case that people are born, reared, educated and then work and finally die in one country or state. We move within our home country, we visit and sometimes settle in a different country, and even the most casual exposure to the world's big cities shows them to be multicultural enclaves, overflowing with immigrants (documented and undocumented), transients, refugees and seasonal workers. Responses are hugely varied. Some delight in the diversity; others fear the loss of well-defined cultural heritage. Some welcome the stranger; others fan into flame the latent xenophobia that lurks in many a human breast. David Firth carefully traces out what can be learned of the ways in which foreigners were viewed in the Former Prophets. Along the way he draws attention to surprises: a foreign prostitute like Rahab becomes an Israelite, and an Israelite like Achan is cut off from the Israelites. Tracing the trajectories, Dr Firth opens up biblical texts that are not as widely known as some passages, and drops tantalizing hints about the ultimate canonical move to the notion of God's people drawn from every tongue, tribe, people and nation.

D. A. Carson
Trinity Evangelical Divinity School

Author's preface

This is a study that is very close to my own heart, both as someone who lives in a strange land and as someone who has spent much of this century studying the Former Prophets. At the same time, it has been intriguing to me that issues I was observing in the text about national identity and how they played out within Israel became progressively more important in political discussions in many parts of the world. I have consciously stayed away from making pronouncements about the politics of any one place today, though I do believe that these texts are an undervalued resource for thinking theologically about this vitally important topic. It is my hope that this study will contribute to discussions about national identity and how it is formed, and how the people of God live within that while also being distinct.

As always, writing a book is a communal act, one that could not be achieved without the support of others. Particular thanks should be given to my wife Lynne for her love, patience and encouragement. Words are insufficient for expressing how much this means to me. It has also been a pleasure to work on this book in the congenial setting of Trinity College, Bristol, and I need to express my thanks to my colleagues for making this such a good place to work. In particular, thanks are due to Dr Emma Ineson for making us so welcome when we moved here a few years back. Her recent departure to take up the position of Bishop of Penrith has left a significant gap that will not easily be filled. Phil Duce has shepherded this book through to publication with his normal skill, and Eldo Barkhuizen has (again) worked wonders in preparing the text for publication. Thanks too to Suzanne Mitchell for her careful checking of the text in final preparation for publication.

This book is dedicated to Dr Gordon Wenham, someone who went from being a senior scholar of whom I was in awe to being a good friend and source of encouragement (though the sense of awe has not gone away!). It was Gordon who, hearing a paper from a young scholar at Tyndale House in 2001 asked me to write the Apollos Commentary on Samuel, something that took me much deeper into the study of the Former Prophets. When we moved to the UK, I had the privilege of being secretary of the Old Testament study group of the Tyndale Fellowship while he continued as chair, before taking over the chair from him. His work on the ethics of the Old Testament, and in particular how its narrative and poetry shape us ethically, has been particularly formative for me. As one of my predecessors here at Trinity, he has also been a continuing source of encouragement. Dedicating this book to him is thus an appropriate, though ultimately inadequate, means of saying thanks for all this and more.

David Firth

Abbreviations

4QJosh^a	*First Joshua Scroll* (Dead Sea Scrolls)
4QSam^a	*First Samuel Scroll* (Dead Sea Scrolls)
AB	Anchor Bible
AcT	*Acta Theologica*
ANE	ancient Near East
Ant.	*Jewish Antiquities* (Josephus)
AOTC	Apollos Old Testament Commentary
BBR	*Bulletin for Biblical Research*
Bib	*Biblica*
BibInt	*Biblical Interpretation*
BibSac	*Bibliotheca sacra*
BRev	*Bible Review*
BST	The Bible Speaks Today
BZ	*Biblische Zeitschrift*
CBC	Cambridge Bible Commentary
CBQ	*Catholic Biblical Quarterly*
CJT	*Concordia Journal of Theology*
ESVUK	English Standard Version: Anglicized
ET	English Translation
GKC	*Gesenius' Hebrew Grammar*, ed. E. Kautzsch, rev. and tr. A. E. Cowley, Oxford: Clarendon, 1910
HBT	*Horizons in Biblical Theology*
Hebr.	Hebrew
hi.	hiphil
ICC	International Critical Commentary
Int	*Interpretation*
ITC	International Theological Commentary
JBL	*Journal of Biblical Literature*
JETS	*Journal of the Evangelical Theological Society*
JPT	*Journal of Pentecostal Theology*
JSOT	*Journal for the Study of the Old Testament*
MSS	manuscripts
MT	Masoretic Text

NAC	New American Commentary
NCBC	New Century Bible Commentary
NICOT	New International Commentary on the Old Testament
NIDOTTE	*New International Dictionary of Old Testament Theology and Exegesis*, ed. Willem A. VanGemeren, 5 vols., Grand Rapids: Zondervan, 1997
NIV	New International Version
NRSVA	New Revised Standard Version: Anglicized
OT	Old Testament
OTE	*Old Testament Essays*
OTL	Old Testament Library
OTS	*Oudtestamentische Studiën*
PNTC	Pillar New Testament Commentary
RB	*Revue biblique*
RevExp	*Review and Expositor*
SEÅ	*Svensk Exegetisk Årsbok*
SJOT	*Scandinavian Journal of the Old Testament*
STR	*Southeastern Theological Review*
TOTC	Tyndale Old Testament Commentary
TynB	*Tyndale Bulletin*
VT	*Vetus Testamentum*
WBC	Word Biblical Commentary
WO	B. K. Waltke and M. O'Connor, *An Introduction to Biblical Hebrew Syntax*, Winona Lake: Eisenbrauns, 1990
yiq.	yiqtol
ZAW	*Zeitschrift für Alttestamentliche Wissenschaft*

Chapter One

Concerning foreigners and the Former Prophets

Being a foreigner and reading the Bible

I am a foreigner. Almost any day when I speak to people I have not met before, I encounter an observation along the lines of 'You're not from around here are you?' Since many British people seem unable to distinguish between an Australian, New Zealand or South African accent I am normally happy to string them along a little – though since I sometimes struggle to identify certain regional accents within the UK in spite of the years we have spent here, it is also quite common for us to spend time in a mutual attempt to work out where the other is from.

So, although I apparently do not look foreign (whatever that might mean!), the status of 'foreigner' is one that I constantly bear and which to varying degrees shapes my interaction with my community. Often that takes the form of good-natured teasing during certain sporting events, mostly from those I know well, though that is not entirely predictable. More problematic, though, are times when I or members of my family have attended meetings or events where 'foreigners' were blamed for a variety of ills. When we point out that we are foreigners, a response is usually given along the lines of 'Oh, but you're not the kind of foreigner I mean.' Leaving aside the rather problematic concept of exactly what makes some foreigners acceptable and others not, it does indicate that host cultures are capable in some way of distinguishing between foreigners when needed, though equally that it is possible for foreigners to be treated as an undistinguished group. Extending the UK example, it is also possible to regard others as 'foreign' under some circumstances and as 'native' under others – for example, is someone English, Scottish or Welsh? Each of these can be distinct, yet, under other circumstances all these people would be 'British'. Even within England, someone might be from Yorkshire or Cornwall, and so 'not from around here', although at other times their status as English would be stressed. In short,

1

'foreignness' (however defined) depends on the attitude of a speaker to another and whether someone is defined as 'us' or 'other' and this is something that can vary.[1]

This is a non-scientific set of observations, but they form an important background to this study. It emerges out of a social context in which issues of migration and national social identity are widely discussed in the media across much of the Western world. As a migrant, I hope to bring some significant social benefits and skills to my host country. But I am always foreign, and no construction of British identity includes me just because the simple act of my speaking makes this clear. So, even though national identity within the UK can be constructed in a range of ways, some more inclusive than others, some of us cannot be included whereas others might live in a more marginal position in which they might be included under some constructions and not others.

My work as a biblical interpreter cannot be separated from this experience, perhaps because as with any reader my experience of the world makes me more aware of some themes within the Bible than others.[2] That is, my social location could well have made me more aware of some themes within the Bible than I might have recognized had I been in another, though there is no real way of testing this. However, it could be said that one of the virtues of reading as a foreigner is that I see things that the dominant culture might not see, or perhaps ask questions that might not otherwise be posed, while conversely others can make me more aware of biblical themes that I might otherwise miss. The fact is that we all bring some degree of pre-understanding to the reading of the Bible, and though the emphasis on *wissenschaftlich* (scientific/critical) interpretation that emerged out of the Enlightenment discouraged this because of its belief that the interpreter must in some way be detached from the material, the reality is that readers have consistently brought their own political situation to bear on their reading of the Bible.[3]

At the same time, it is not my contention that the position of the reader is to be absolutized such that this becomes the most important issue in interpretation. Rather, the situation of the reader and those

---

[1] Cf. Zehnder 2005: 17–20. Because of this, 'race' is not addressed here since this is a second-order construct rather than a primary marker of whether someone is foreign (cf. ibid. 34). This is not to marginalize what is a very important issue (see J. D. Hays 2003a). Rather, it recognizes that although these elements are often linked in popular discussion, there is value in addressing them separately.

[2] Cf. Massey 1994: 150.

[3] Cf. Gorringe 1998: 67–69.

questions for the Bible that emerge from a given reader's social and political context are themselves to be brought into a dialogue with the Bible. It is through interaction with the Bible that our pre-understanding can be challenged and changed through the process of reading the text.[4] This means that although I can reasonably aim for a degree of detachment as an interpreter I can never do so absolutely, and indeed to do so such that I miss certain elements of what is in the Bible is to lose the benefit that acknowledging my pre-understanding brings. At the same time, there will be points where the act of reading the Bible leads me to reassess those convictions with which I began the process of reading.

The reason for this is that although biblical studies has for some time emphasized the place of critical method in reading the Bible, there is also an important place for criticism as something also applied to the reader.[5] This idea has been helpfully explored by Briggs as he has noted the ways in which the narrative texts of the Old Testament (our focus for this study) themselves function to shape the interpretative virtues that are important for reading them well.[6] Hence, although we come as readers with certain points of pre-understanding, the process of reading these texts also shapes us as readers. This indicates that although hermeneutical reflection is important, good reading of the Bible does not require that this be the starting point.[7] Indeed, my own testimony would be that I did not recognize the importance of foreigners within these texts until I had read them several times; though I would also suggest that my status as a foreigner has made me more aware of this motif than might otherwise have been the case. In turn, it is my hope that this volume will enable other readers who might not self-identify as 'foreign' to appreciate the significance of this motif within the Former Prophets[8] and the implications this has for our understanding of the identity of the people of God in general along with the ethical challenges posed by migration today.

[4] Klein, Blomberg and Hubbard 2017: 226–243.
[5] S. I. Wright 2000: 243.
[6] Briggs 2010.
[7] Ibid. 38.
[8] Although the common scholarly parlance for these texts is the 'Deuteronomistic History', throughout this work I will refer to them by their traditional label from within the canon of the Hebrew Bible. This is not to prioritize one construal of the canon over another (though for the benefits of seeing different ways of presenting the canon with reference to Samuel, see Firth 2017a: 2–9), so much as to reflect my discomfort with some of the key ideas in the concept of the Deuteronomistic History along with the fact that this one label is used to mean rather different things. As such, 'Former Prophets' offers a less problematic term that still appreciates the coherence of this group of books.

Why the Former Prophets?

Given the goals just noted, a not unreasonable response might well be to ask if perhaps an exploration in Israel's legal texts of the foreigner might be more constructive. After all, this approach allows us to trace the main lexical data about foreigners. That is, given that the various categories of foreigner are discussed within the law, and these laws direct Israel how to respond to foreigners, might not this be a more constructive approach for considering this theme?

There are several reasons, however, why this approach is not taken here. First, a number of studies already exist that consider the issue of the foreigner in Israel's law,[9] so the relative gain in considering the same selection of texts is relatively small.

Second, there is value in a more focused study that considers the contribution of the Old Testament's narrative materials. Walter Houston[10] has pointed out that laws can change a society's behaviour only when justice is taught and not only enforced, and one of the key ways in which this teaching happens in the Old Testament is through its narrative materials.[11] The importance of the narrative materials for understanding the place of foreigners has been recognized by Fleur Houston[12] and Lau,[13] though neither has considered the Former Prophets to a significant degree.

There are, however, more fundamental reasons for turning to Israel's wider narrative traditions. One important point is that the law provides not an ethical maximum but rather a minimum. That is, law recognizes a problem that needs to be addressed, but what it provides is the least that should be done, not necessarily the ethical goal towards which a people should aspire. By contrast, Wenham has argued that the narrative texts of the Old Testament are didactic and so try 'to instil both theological truths and ethical ideals into their readers',[14] and that therefore the narratives offer a form of

---

[9] E.g. Achenbach, Albertz and Wöhrle 2011; Awabdy 2014; Carroll R. 2008: 91–112; Hoffmeier 2009: 71–96; F. S. Houston 2015: 69–79; Pitkänen 2017; van Houten 1991; Wünch 2014; Zehnder 2005: 279–385.

[10] W. J. Houston 2008: 107.

[11] This is, of course, not the only way this is done – the wisdom literature, psalms and prophets can all be consulted with profit, as W. J. Houston demonstrates in his reading of Amos (2008: 58–73) and his conclusions from a wider range of texts (227–231). As Wenham (2000: 2) also points out, the more directive nature of these texts has led to their being central to most discussions of the OT's ethics.

[12] F. S. Houston 2015: 79–92.

[13] Lau 2011 (cf. Lau and Goswell 2016: 7–10).

[14] Wenham 2000: 3.

paradigmatic ethics.[15] Understanding narrative material in this way still requires reflection on whether the narrative presents characters and their actions as exemplary in some way,[16] an issue to which we will return. But with Parry[17] it is important that the narratives we consider within the Former Prophets are placed within the larger story that the Old Testament, and indeed the New Testament, provides – which is why we reflect briefly on these themes in the New Testament in the final chapter. As we will see, this is often because the narrators in the Former Prophets tend to assume that readers are aware of other texts within the Old Testament (principally the Pentateuch); but beyond this it is an important element in a Christian reading of these texts that they are also placed within the framework of the whole canon, albeit one that takes seriously its nature as a work containing two Testaments in which the two mutually inform our reading of the other.[18] It is this awareness that enables a reading of these texts that is alert to their contribution to this theme.

Third, and more specific to the Former Prophets rather than narrative texts in general, these books contain a significant number of references to foreigners and these have not been explored in detail in a systematic way.[19] A feature that emerges from a reading of these books is a developing response to the presence of foreigners within Israel whereby foreigners who may seem unacceptable can be included within Israel even as those who are ethnically Israelite are excluded because of their failure to live out the demands of the covenant with Yahweh. For example, within the book of Joshua Rahab is the archetypal foreigner, a Canaanite prostitute, and yet she is included within Israel. By contrast, Achan effectively becomes a Canaanite and is excluded, even though he has an exemplary Israelite heritage. I shall argue that these stories are intended to make readers ask questions about the identity of Israel as the people of God. However, where Joshua is particularly concerned about those people from the land who remain among Israel, by the time we reach the book of Kings the focus is on foreigners who live outside the land and yet desire a

---

[15] Here, to some extent, following Janzen 1994. This model can be contrasted with the approach of C. J. H. Wright (2004), for which the legal material provides the principal paradigm. Wenham's model is helpfully integrated with anthropology by Rowe (2011: 69–100). See also Rowe 2012: 11–31.

[16] Wenham 2000: 3–4.

[17] Parry 2004: 83.

[18] Cf. Seitz 2011.

[19] For partial treatments, see Spina 2005: 52–93 and Zehnder 2005: 402–498.

relationship with Yahweh. These elements point to positive reasons for considering these texts.

But a more negative reason also exists for considering the Former Prophets, in particular exposing readings of them that have taken hold in popular thought but that may be contrary to what they say. There is a perception that these books point to an understanding of God that is highly ethnocentric. This understanding can be seen in both contemporary critics of the Christian faith and Christians who believe that these books have a highly negative view of foreigners. From the perspective of critics of Christian faith, Richard Dawkins speaks for many, even if they might regard his language as somewhat intemperate. But it should be noted that it is his reading of the Old Testament, and especially the Former Prophets, that leads to his (in)famous observation that

> [t]he God of the Old Testament is arguably the most unpleasant character in all fiction: jealous and proud of it; a petty, unjust, unforgiving control-freak; a vindictive, bloodthirsty ethnic cleanser; a misogynistic, homophobic, racist, infanticidal, genocidal, filicidal, pestilential, megalomaniacal, sadomasochistic, capriciously malevolent bully.[20]

Dawkins, along with his fellow 'new atheists', is usually a fairly flat-footed reader of the Bible who does not recognize the nuances of the text.[21] Nevertheless, when it comes to the book of Joshua in particular, his comments come close to those of many Christians who struggle with the violence they see in it when he observes that it is

> a text remarkable for the bloodthirsty massacres it records and the xenophobic relish with which it does so. As the charming old song exultantly has it, 'Joshua fit the battle of Jericho, and the walls came a-tumbling down . . . there's none like good old Joshuay at the battle of Jericho.' Good old Joshua didn't rest until 'they utterly destroyed all that was in the city, both man and woman, young and old, and ox, and sheep, and ass with the edge of the sword' (Josh. 6:21).[22]

Dawkins is never knowingly understated in his attacks on God and the Bible, but there is no doubt that he here addresses an issue that

---

[20] Dawkins 2006: 51.
[21] Cf. Strawn 2017: 83–102.
[22] Dawkins 2006: 280.

continues to trouble many readers of the Bible today. Operating from an expressly Christian perspective, Robert Coote expresses a similar perspective on Joshua:

> Much about the book of Joshua is repulsive, starting with the ethnic cleansing, the savage dispossession and genocide of native peoples, and the massacre of women and children – all not simply condoned but ordered by God. These features are worse than abhorrent; they are far beyond the pale.[23]

Although discussion of most of these issues can be deferred until chapter 2, the popularity of such readings means they cannot be ignored. Staying only with the example of the book of Joshua, it is evident that the way in which many Christians have dealt with the challenge is by ignoring these texts. This may or may not be intentional, but if we take the occurrences of Joshua in the lectionary as a guide, then congregations using a lectionary will almost never hear readings from Joshua on a Sunday.[24] Not all congregations follow the lectionary, but this is a guide to how unlikely it is that some Christians will encounter Joshua in any significant way – and of course it is quite possible to omit the Old Testament reading. In my experience as a teacher of the Old Testament, attitudes such as these are now commonplace among Christians, and most of my students arrive with a profound sense of discomfort, if not outright embarrassment, about features of these texts. There are some parts of the Former Prophets that they cherish – usually Sunday school favourites like the story of David and Goliath; but for most these are texts to be avoided where possible and that then receive comparatively little attention in church, effectively reinforcing the dominant views through non-use. It is my hope that a close reading of the Former Prophets will show that they have a much more positive contribution to make to understanding foreigners than such popular treatments might suggest.

Towards an ethical and theological reading of the Former Prophets

Reading a narrative text for its normative value (ethically and theologically) requires some careful reflection on the process, not least

---

[23] Coote 1998: 578; cf. Cowles 2003.
[24] See the helpful, though inevitably brief, listing in Ederer 2017: 376.

because a common feature of Old Testament narrative texts is that although they describe what happened, they very seldom offer readers any evaluative comment. So, although the narrators do have a view on what is approved or not, the poetics of narration within the Old Testament tends to discourage any direct comment so that readers may know 'the point' of the story.[25] A moment's reflection on the Jephthah story in Judges (Judg. 10:6 – 12:7) quickly illustrates this point. The issue that troubles most modern readers is probably the sacrifice of his daughter (Judg. 11:29–40), something that is reported but without any commentary at all.[26] But, as Baker argues,[27] the author of Judges does not moralize on a wide range of abuses prevalent among other peoples around Israel either, but expects that the way the story is told will speak for itself through the context provided and its aftermath. The narrator expects readers to discern why this behaviour is inappropriate without the need to make this explicit.

As Wenham has noted,[28] consideration of the theological and ethical concerns of a narrative largely means bracketing the sorts of historical and critical issues that have dominated study of the Old Testament across the last two centuries because these do not particularly have an impact on the ethical and theological norms they present. This does not make such questions unimportant,[29] but they are not of primary interest for this purpose. However, this should not result in a flat reading, because even though it is operating within the canonical form of the text (itself a problematic concept), it is still attentive to tensions within the text precisely because such tensions may well be how the narrator highlights key themes.[30] That is, the

---

[25] As an aside, while working in South Africa I was taken aside by one of my students who pointed out that when preaching narrative texts, I tended to make clear the point, but that doing so was contrary to the ways in which Sotho speakers told stories, especially in more traditional contexts. How the story was told should make this clear, but listeners expected to make the connections themselves rather than having them pointed out since to do so meant not treating them as mature participants in this process of interpretation. This, I would suggest, is analogous to the modes of narration in the OT.

[26] There is a long-standing tradition of reading Judg. 11:39 as suggesting that his daughter continued to live but never married. This, however, is hard to square with the statement in the verse that he 'did to her as he had vowed', since the only vow recorded is that he would put to death whoever came out to meet him following victory over the Ammonites.

[27] Baker 2018: 42.

[28] Wenham 2000: 5–7.

[29] For a reflection on the historical significance of the Former Prophets, see Provan, Long and Longman (2015: 190–378).

[30] Cf. McConville 2017: 28–38.

primary focus of the sort of reading considered here attends to practices of narration that can be observed in these texts, while being aware that the dominant convention within the Old Testament is to report but not to provide overt comment on meaning.

Although the narrators of the Old Testament do not provide overt comment on the significance of their narration, it is still possible to attend to the narrative and so recognize those things that are commended within it. This does mean, however, that we need to distinguish properly between those things a character within a narrative might do and say and those things of which the narrator approves. With Sternberg,[31] we can affirm that the narrators in the Old Testament are generally straightforward and reliable, meaning that it is possible to understand their values through their narration. Since narrators, in effect, take God's perspective within the narrative we can understand the point of view they develop through how they tell the story and from this recognize the theological and ethical values affirmed. However, the reliability of the narrator does need some qualification. This is because, although we can trust the facts that the narrator reports, there is no obligation on him to disclose everything.[32] It is this factor that the narrators of the Old Testament employ to retain interest in the stories they tell – after all, these texts are not statements of abstracted theological and ethical principles but rather an attempt to explore the complexities of faithfulness in a world where this is always a challenge and challenged. At the same time, the narrators need to hold the reader's attention in ways that invite further reflection on the values commended. It is the process by which narrators tell enough, but not everything, that enables them to invite readers to enter the world of the stories they tell and so reflect on the values commended.

There are, however, points where the narrators choose not to leave the narration to do all the work, perhaps because readers might reach faulty conclusions. For example, in 2 Samuel 17:14 the narrator ends the account of the conflicting counsel of Hushai and Ahithophel with the observation that Yahweh gave orders to 'thwart Ahithophel's good advice so as to bring harm to Absalom'. Such direct evaluative comments are rare, and in this case are probably because Hushai's advice seemed so much less sound, meaning readers would expect Ahithophel's advice to have been followed. But it was precisely

[31] Sternberg 1985: 25–35.
[32] Walsh 2009: 98.

because this outcome was so unexpected that the narrator needed to break cover and provide guidance so that readers could understand how Yahweh was continuing to work for David despite the king's earlier sin (2 Sam. 11). More generally, however, a narrator can provide details within the story that enable readers to recognize that which is commended, most notably through the characterization of a key figure or through things that a pivotal character says. Very rarely is this achieved through a direct reference to the Torah, but it is usually the case that there are enough allusions within the narrative that readers can identify that which is commended. What is striking, however, is that when these narratives are read carefully in the light of their allusions to the Torah, we frequently observe how what is commended goes beyond the demands of Torah, pointing to the theological and ethical surplus that these narratives contain.

This leaves the question of how to recognize those texts that refer to foreigners who are included within Israel. For this there is no single method. In general, it will not involve tracing the main terms for the foreigner, though at points this language will be important. A more important feature, though, is the use of a gentilic that identifies a character as belonging to a group that did not consider itself as Israelite, or that at least the narrators of the Former Prophets did not consider as Israelite. A gentilic is a type of adjective typically marked in Hebrew by adding the ending *î* to a noun and thus converting it to an adjective (GKC §86*h*) and that refers to a tribal or national association. Not all adjectives following this form are gentilics, and this same form can be used to refer (e.g.) to someone's home town (e.g. 'Jesse the Bethlehemite', 1 Sam. 16:1); these adjectives are typically marked in English by a form ending in 'ite' (e.g. 'Canaanite'). Characters who are identified through this form of adjective (e.g. Uriah the Hittite) are potential foreigners, though this needs to be confirmed through the wider context of the narrative. Many of the foreigners we consider in the next four chapters are identified in this way. More broadly, however, a narrator may mark characters as foreign through their social or physical location or through things they say that identify them as foreign;[33] for example, Rahab is clearly located among the Canaanites in Joshua 2, and within the narrative identifies herself as a Canaanite through her speech (Josh. 2:10–11). In the end, although there is no one method and there are some figures whose status is never entirely clear, many foreigners are mentioned in

---

[33] Similarly, Zehnder 2005: 402.

the Former Prophets, with many of these included among the people of God so that the boundaries of this people is constantly being challenged; so Israel are constantly being reformed in ways that remind them that just as they were once a foreign people in Egypt, so other foreigners can become a part of them.

Chapter Two

The book of Joshua: the identity of the people of God

Initial observations: the genre and language of Joshua

As noted already, for many readers the idea that the book of Joshua might contribute positively to a discussion about foreigners seems almost absurd.[1] This, after all, is the book that seemingly describes the destruction of the Canaanites. Making matters worse, the application of the law of *ḥērem* (understood as 'total destruction') means that something which looks suspiciously like 'genocide' is presented as a theological imperative as the Canaanites are destroyed. Read this way (as it frequently is), Joshua seemingly presents an image of Yahweh that is indefensibly violent, an image difficult (if not impossible) to reconcile with the image of God we find in the New Testament. Following this approach, Thomas Mann thus describes at least this element of Joshua as presenting an image of God that is 'unconscionable'.[2] Even evangelical readers who might otherwise be thought to have a high view of Scripture express direct concerns about Joshua and its presentation of the Canaanites, arguing that there is a fundamental discontinuity between how God is presented there and how he is to be understood in the light of the New Testament.[3] How then might Joshua contribute to a better understanding of the place of foreigners, and especially their integration within Israel?

It is important that proper consideration be given to these concerns and that they not be swept under the carpet. There are real and challenging issues in Joshua and we need a hermeneutic robust enough to address them. What is not acceptable is any approach where Joshua is largely ignored. Its challenges are not addressed when we follow the lead of the lectionary and hope that believers will not read the book. The problem this poses is immediately apparent in many contexts

---

[1] See Firth 2017c: 70.
[2] Mann 2011: 22.
[3] E.g. Cowles 2003: 16–17.

13

where the sort of reading of the book proposed by Richard Dawkins[4] is assumed to represent an at least broadly appropriate interpretation of the text. Even the use of the term 'genocide' in one popular book on this topic[5] means the discussion takes place in the sort of context Dawkins would only a little later assume (though without reference to the earlier work). Ignorance of the book's content and challenges leaves us without the resources to understand and interpret the book and thus see how it contributes to the overall message of Scripture. Moreover, as Zehnder has demonstrated,[6] even taking on board a modern term such as 'genocide' and then using it to describe events in Joshua is deeply problematic. This is not only because modern definitions of the term tend to vary, but because (as will be argued) events described in Joshua do not fit with this concept.[7] To appreciate this, it is necessary to consider Joshua's genre and how it uses language within this since it operates within an ancient mode of discourse different from those used in the modern world.[8] Failing to recognize this leads to a misreading of the text because it interprets the book in the light of modern, not ancient, conventions. Alongside this we need also to read the book in the light of its function of providing a hinge between the Pentateuch and Former Prophets, a text that simultaneously looks back to earlier times while also preparing for what follows.

Genre

The nature of genre as a literary concept is a complex one, but at heart it can be understood as the recognition of similarities between certain texts that enable readers to note patterns that help them transfer interpretative insights from one text to another.[9] Labelling various genres, especially ancient ones, is an act of description rather than prescription because any given work can transcend common genre boundaries and at various points integrate elements of multiple genres. As such, any one text can include a constellation of generic features, each of which may be particularly important at one point and not at others. The presence of certain features in a text acts as a trigger for readers that leads to a particular line of interpretation,

---

[4] Dawkins 2006: 280.

[5] Gundry 2003.

[6] Zehnder 2013: 266–267.

[7] For a more philosophical approach to this issue, though with exegetical awareness, see Copan and Flanagan 2014.

[8] Cf. Walton and Walton 2017: 7–12.

[9] Cf. Brown 2008: 120–128.

though skilful authors can play with these expectations and create an expectation of a particular genre that will only later be subverted. Most obviously, in 2 Samuel 12:1–6 Nathan's story about the rich man who took the poor man's lamb to feed a guest initially presents itself as the report of an actual case on which David must offer judgment, only for Nathan to reveal that it is a form of parable after David initially interprets it as an actual report (2 Sam. 12:7). Although Nathan never labels his story as 'parable', his declaration of David's guilt makes clear that his story was not, after all, a case report. In rereading the story, it becomes possible to see how he used one genre while masking it behind another. But in the end the genre needed to be revealed for it to have the required impact on David. David could understand what Nathan was really communicating only after he recognized the literary form being used, and until that point he misunderstood (as Nathan intended). Although Joshua does not mask its genre, modern readers who interpret Joshua along the lines of contemporary genre patterns are liable to misunderstand it.

As a complex text Joshua includes numerous genres such as spy story, conquest account, king list, boundary records and speeches. All of these are integrated into an overall work that appears to have a defined beginning and end, being built around the reports of Moses' death (Josh. 1:1–2) and the deaths of the leaders of the generation that entered the land (Josh. 24:29–33). Making the links between these boundaries stronger is the fact that Moses is initially described as 'the Servant of Yahweh' (Josh. 1:1–2), a title Joshua receives in his death and burial report (Josh. 24:29–30). There is also a discernible plot that runs through the book, reporting how Israel came to occupy the land that they did. What is perhaps less frequently noted is that the land occupied is not the land Yahweh had promised Abraham, but also includes territory given to the tribes of Reuben, Gad and east Manasseh in the region to the east of the Jordan. This theme is introduced in 1:12–18 and runs through much of the book, reaching its climax in the altar narrative of Joshua 22, integrating the promise of rest that also runs through the book with the question of the 'ambiguous status'[10] of the eastern tribes. As such, although the book reports the way Israel came to live in the land west of the Jordan, it does so with a focus on the identity of the people of Israel.

Considering this, we could describe Joshua as an example of narrated history, though this is broadly true of the whole of the

[10] Wray Beal 2017: 482.

Former Prophets. However, 'narrated' and 'history' need to be understood more particularly within the framework of Joshua. Here it is helpful to draw on the distinction between 'history' and 'historiography', with history understood as that which happened in the past (or at least at the level of genre studies, which a writer believed happened) and historiography as the selective process of writing about the past. These terms are often fused in more popular discussion, but recognizing historiography enables us to appreciate that any telling of the past is selective and can also be artistic in its presentation.[11] Although Joshua's narrative techniques are not always the same as those in the rest of the Former Prophets, there is certainly evidence within the book of the literary skill that has been deployed in its writing.[12] This means that even though there are some chapters that modern readers may find less than thrilling (e.g. Josh. 15), it is still a work of narrative art with the various components integrated into it. It is more than a bare record of the past. Rather, it reports the past through the creation of an integrated narrative in which only those elements relevant to its purpose are included.[13]

Nevertheless, Joshua does present itself as a work of history, albeit not a comprehensive history. As Long has noted,[14] works of history are constrained by the events they report and are not free to invent whole stories. Joshua shows clear evidence of such reporting, as it points to evidence that the events it reported continued to have an impact on those for whom the text was composed. This is most evident in the use of the phrase 'until this day', which occurs sixteen times in the book, always referring a later generation of readers to something that attested to events of an earlier time.[15] Joshua's historical intent, however, should always be linked with its narrative structure to see that it operates with conventions appropriate to its own time in how it tells its story and how it reports the past.

[11] V. P. Long 1994: 63.

[12] Firth 2017b; Lebhar Hall 2010; Wénin 2012.

[13] E.g. although often treated as a 'conquest', comparatively little of the book deals with this. Even those parts that do (particularly Josh. 10 – 11) deal only with selected battle reports, leaving large parts of the land where there is no record of Israel's having been present.

[14] V. P. Long 1994: 68.

[15] Not all scholars regard this as a reliable indicator of events, but at the level of genre it is still a clear marker that the composers of Joshua intended it to describe historical events. For a positive assessment of Joshua as a historical witness, see Hawkins (2013: 18–27); Provan, Long and Longman (2015: 201–212, 222–225).

Language

The importance of understanding how Joshua works within the conventions of its time comes to a point of clarity when attention is given to the language it uses and how it feeds into its genre and the conventions that would be meaningful to its audience. Most important for our purposes is the use of various terms for the removal of the Canaanite population since they are, by definition, foreign to Israel. Only when we understand how this language works within its generic context can we appreciate the possibilities that the book holds out to foreigners, including Canaanites. This means looking at how the book uses its language since this will be more important than attempting to trace its etymology.

Important work on conquest narratives from the period shows that hyperbole is an important element in the process of communication.[16] That is, a convention of the genre was to use language that was hyperbolic. This would not mislead readers of the time, since they would be aware of the convention, but it can be confusing for modern readers who see such language and assume it to be literal. Younger's work concentrated on certain literary codes that are present in the relevant parts of Joshua and comparative texts, but we can illustrate the reality of this by looking at Joshua 10:20. As traditionally translated (e.g. ESVUK), the Israelites 'wiped out'[17] a group, but we are then told of a 'remnant' who had fled to fortified cities. If the group was wiped out, there could be no survivors, but Joshua has no problem in putting these statements together. Unless we assume a very clumsy collecting of disparate sources, it must be recognized that the language here is hyperbolic, reporting a comprehensive victory but not more than that. Likewise, in Joshua 10:36–37 it is reported that Joshua 'devoted to destruction' (*ḥrm*) the city of Hebron, leaving no one alive in it. But only five years later the city was standing and needed to be recaptured (Josh. 14:6–15). Again we have either to conclude that there were different traditions about the city that have not been integrated with one another or, more probably, that the book uses hyperbolic language as a standard mode of communication.[18] None

---

[16] Younger 1990.

[17] The verb here is *tmm*, not *ḥrm*, but the point is equally true when the latter verb occurs.

[18] Douglas Earl (2010a; 2010b) has argued that it is more effective to understand Joshua through the category of 'myth', a concept partially supported by McConville (2017: 47–51). However, although this can be a helpful category if we mean 'stories told to explain current reality', it seems to underplay the historical intent of the text,

of this means that no Canaanites were killed – to claim this would go beyond recognition of an idiom to assert the opposite of what the text claims. However, careful attention to the text means that the more likely claim is that there were comprehensive victories won against those who resisted Israel, but that beyond this many Canaanites continued to live in the land with the result that a key goal for the book was to establish how it is that a community that was a mixture of Israelites and Canaanites could become the people of God going forward.[19]

Rahab and the initial entry into the land (Josh. 1 – 6)

The question of the identity of the people of God is raised almost from the book's outset. Following Moses' death, Yahweh told Joshua to meditate on the Book of the Torah, in context most likely a reference to Deuteronomy (Josh. 1:1–9). The reason for suggesting this is not only that Joshua immediately follows Deuteronomy in both the Jewish and Christian canon, forming a bridge between the Pentateuch and Former Prophets,[20] but also because God's speech to Joshua is saturated in references to Deuteronomy. For instance, the language of Joshua 1:5, with its assurance that no one will be able to resist Israel, seems to draw on Deuteronomy 7:24 and 11:25, since Psalm 5:5 is the only other place that uses this language, and it too appears to refer to Deuteronomy.[21] Hence, as Joshua meditates on the Book of the Torah, he is particularly directed to texts in Deuteronomy. These connections are made even stronger when we note that reference to the place where the Israelite[22] feet tread (Josh. 1:3) is drawn from Deuteronomy 11:24. Since the key references in Deuteronomy (apart from the report of Moses' death from Deut. 34) are associated with taking the land, these references serve the additional function of raising the expectation for readers that the book is about to describe the capture of the land and destruction of the local

(note 18 *cont.*) though his goal of understanding the significance of Joshua for Christian readers is certainly a positive one (cf. Firth 2017c: 71–73).

[19] The separate issue of Israel's right to claim the land falls outside this discussion but remains important. For some initial reflections, see Firth 2015: 21–22.

[20] Although often reduced to a link to Deuteronomy, Koorevaar (1990: 163–164) has also pointed to the distinctiveness of this passage as an introduction to the book.

[21] Cf. Firth 2017b: 423; Nelson 1997: 33.

[22] The 'you' of vv. 3–4 is plural, referring to the Israelites. From v. 5 it switches to the singular, and so speaks only of Joshua.

inhabitants.[23] Such an expectation is consistent with God's state-ment that he is giving Israel the land of the Hittites (Josh. 1:4), with the Hittites standing as a representative people from the list of the Canaanite peoples in Deuteronomy 7:1.

Expectation of immediate military action is also raised by the report of Joshua's dealings with the east-Jordan tribes (Josh. 1:10–18). Although some of the background here depends on Deuteronomy 3:18–20, the discussion also needs to be read against the background of Numbers 32 and its report of how two-and-a-half tribes came to settle outside the boundaries of the land promised to Abraham (Gen. 15:18–20), a land seemingly not included in the earlier description of the land's boundaries (Josh. 1:4). This geographic discrepancy seems unimportant here, and indeed at this point Joshua can describe it as the land Yahweh gave them (Josh. 1:15), but it becomes important in chapter 22, where the issue of whether or not a people live out-side the boundaries of the Promised Land becomes important. Its inclusion here thus prepares for subsequent parts of the book, and indeed a key element in the book's structure is that each major section (chs. 1–12, 13–21, 22–24) begins with reflection on the interaction between the eastern and western tribes and their relationship to one another.[24] It also highlights an important technique within Joshua of including information that although relevant to its immediate context discloses its full function only when a later part of the book is reached.

The more immediate concern in these verses is to remind the eastern tribes of their commitment in Numbers 32 to leave their families and possessions east of the Jordan and to cross ahead of their compatriots in military array, only returning once their compatriots have also received rest in the land of their possession (Josh. 1:13–15). The establishment of rest is also an important theme within the book, being picked up again in the conclusion to the land allocation (Josh. 21:43–45) and in introducing Joshua's first speech to the nation's leaders (Josh. 23:1).[25] At this point, however, the

---

[23] There is no one way in which allusions function, but Krause (2014: 56–58) helpfully suggests three basic categories – the allusion to the Pentateuch can appeal to, allude to or explain the earlier text.

[24] Although broadly supportive of Koorevaar's widely cited analysis of the book's structure (1990), other than seeing 5:12 as the end of a subsection, I would want to stress that chs. 1–2 and 13–14 need to be read as doubled introductions to each section, and these are matched with doubled conclusions (11:16 – 12:24; 20:1 – 21:45). On the importance of seeing Josh. 2 in its canonical position, see Stek 2002: 37.

[25] Most English versions include 'rest' in Josh. 11:23 and 14:15, but the Hebrew here is different, referring more to the absence of war than to rest as a settled life.

expectation is that the first step involved in this will be the initiation of a military campaign against the Canaanite population. By the end of Joshua 1 Canaanites as a specific group of foreigners are effectively the 'other' to Israel, a people to be defeated and dispossessed before Israel.

Accordingly, the beginning of Joshua 2 is something of a surprise. Rather than launching an invasion, Joshua sends two men to scout the land, especially Jericho. However, even in reporting this, the book is careful to establish key links with both chapter 1 and earlier texts from the Pentateuch. These links are important because they mean that rather than seeing the chapter as an independent insertion,[26] we understand it as providing a parallel but distinct narrative that is still to be understood in the light of themes in chapter 1. Most notably, the scouts' report (Josh. 2:24) provides assurance that Yahweh's promises to Joshua (Josh. 1:3–5) can be believed. That Joshua sent the scouts secretly probably means he did not tell any other Israelite,[27] but the more important point is that they were sent from Shittim, an allusion back to Numbers 25:1–5 where Israel had played the harlot with foreign women.[28] Foreign women had previously led Israel into sin – in the light of the expectations most had of Canaanites, would the same be true now?

Despite Joshua's directives, the scouts are not said to have focused specifically on the land and Jericho. Instead, they went straight to the city of Jericho and lodged in the house of a prostitute named Rahab. Despite a long history of attempts to make Rahab an innkeeper rather than a prostitute,[29] description of her as a *zōnâ* is best understood as labelling her as a 'prostitute'. This makes most sense of both the allusion back to Numbers 25:1–5 and the fact that the language of the chapter continually draws on various double entendres,[30] even if no sexual activity is described. Indeed, the nature of her response to the king of Jericho's constables requires such allusion because it plays with their expectations of why men would have gone to her house.[31]

---

[26] Cf. Boling 1982: 150.

[27] Krause 2012.

[28] Cf. Krause 2015a; Toczyski 2018: 142; contra Seebass 2012.

[29] Cf. Wiseman 1964, offering an approach that can be traced back to Josephus, *Ant.* 1.2.7.

[30] Cf. Spina 2005: 56.

[31] Josh. 2:3–5. That Rahab does not tell the truth to the constables is widely discussed, with many concluding that her behaviour here is unacceptable (see Howard 1998: 106–112), though it is notable that the narrative itself does not seem to be troubled by this, so that Rahab fits the pattern of the female trickster (cf. Prouser 1994).

All of this is a crucial part of the humour with which the story is told, and explains why the two scouts appear to be utterly incompetent as spies, while the king's constables are no better.

Despite the various expectations the narrative has developed to this point, an important flashback is introduced when it is reported that she has already hidden the men on the roof of her house (Josh. 2:6). When with the men later, she offers a confession of faith in Yahweh that exceeds what might even have been expected from an Israelite (Josh. 2:8–11). Rahab knows about the exodus and wilderness, and is fully aware of the nation that is camped across the Jordan. In presenting Rahab like this, Joshua is quite clearly putting a human face to a Canaanite.[32] Whereas at other points they can be described in general terms, meaning that readers can keep them at a distance, presenting Rahab at this point challenges this. In general, the Canaanites can be characterized as 'wicked' (Deut. 9:5), but this report about Rahab means that all Canaanites cannot be treated in stereotypical terms. Here, it seems, is someone who does not fit the reasons given in Deuteronomy 7:1–6 for putting the Canaanites under the ban. Yet her profession of faith seems to stand in contrast to her profession. After all, might not a prostitute represent precisely the sort of person who should be placed under the ban, especially if the allusion back to Numbers 25:1–5 has reminded readers of the threat of foreign women and harlotry? Rahab's presentation in Joshua 2 is thus fraught with ambiguity – she is both stereotypically someone who should be placed under the ban, and yet also someone who confesses faith in Yahweh in a way that challenges this.

The ambiguity of her presentation continues in her negotiation with the scouts, where she arranges for them to swear an oath to protect her and her family when Jericho is captured, expecting that otherwise they will all be devoted to destruction. Swearing such an oath is potentially problematic in that Deuteronomy 7:2 forbade Israel from entering any covenants with the Canaanite population. An 'oath' is not necessarily a covenant, but it is certainly a near synonym.[33] Given the extent to which Deuteronomy 7 has been alluded to in the previous chapter, readers may well conclude that the scouts have made a grave error; though, as with Rahab's lie to the constables, the

---

[32] Wray Beal (forthcoming) notes that Rahab thus expresses the faith that Joshua and Caleb expressed in Num. 14.

[33] Although some of his covenant features are out of sequence, the associations with a covenant are explored by K. M. Campbell (1972).

narrative provides no comment. Because of this ambiguity three broad lines of interpretation have developed:[34]

1 The agreement with Rahab is an example of Israelite disobedience, where Rahab has prevailed over them by tricking them into an agreement that places Israel's life in the land at risk.[35]
2 Rahab is a trickster who does what is necessary for survival both for herself and her family, and for the spies. Both sides get something of what they want.[36]
3 Rahab is a negotiated exception who shows a way in which a Canaanite can survive.[37]

Each interpretation can claim some validity from Joshua 2 for the simple reason that the narrators have been careful to refrain from providing any guidance on how to interpret the events reported.[38] By the end of the chapter readers are meant to be disorientated by the presence of a Canaanite prostitute who expresses Israel's faith with more clarity than any other, who has received an oath promising protection for both herself and her family provided they are gathered in her house with its marking of a scarlet cord in the window.[39] Rahab initially appears as a stereotypical Canaanite, a foreign woman who will be as dangerous as any who have gone before. Yet she knows and expresses Israel's faith with clarity, even knowing the correct terms to use, and acts to protect the scouts almost in spite of themselves so that they finally report with confidence to Joshua that Yahweh was indeed giving the land without having done any of the things he had asked of them. By placing Rahab's story at the beginning, Joshua thus poses questions about who can and cannot belong to Israel, leaving unresolved the question of the validity of the oath she caused the scouts to swear.[40]

Joshua leaves these questions aside to report on the crossing of the Jordan and the circumcision of Israelite males (Josh. 3:1 – 5:12) before returning to the story of Jericho and Rahab in particular

---

[34] Cf. Firth 2017b: 416–419.
[35] E.g. Hawk 1991: 59–74; 2000: 35–51; 2010: 21–41.
[36] E.g. García-Alfonso 2010: 39–62.
[37] E.g. Winther-Nielsen 1995: 105–162.
[38] Firth 2017b: 422–423, 427–429.
[39] Spina (2005: 61–63) argues that it marked the function of her house, placing it in the 'red cord district'.
[40] This complexity of presentation renders Crowell's attempt (2013) to see Rahab as part of a process of promoting suspicion of foreigners unpersuasive.

(Josh. 5:13 – 6:27). Although foreigners are not particularly in evidence in these interim chapters, there are key references at the point where Israel enters the land. The crossing of the Jordan is very much a rerun of the crossing of the Sea of Reeds to which Rahab referred (Josh. 2:10), but it ends with the establishment of a cairn at Gilgal (Josh. 4:19–24). This cairn is important as it foreshadows Achan's cairn (Josh. 7:26), preparing in part for his story as the contrast to Rahab. But the point to note here is that Joshua indicated that the cairn at Gilgal would be so that 'all the peoples of the earth might know that the hand of Yahweh is strong, so that you should continue fearing Yahweh your God'. This statement anticipates David's when he challenges Goliath (1 Sam. 17:45–47), along with key references in Kings (1 Kgs 8:60; 2 Kgs 19:19), and points to the fact that Israel's existence was meant to reveal Yahweh to all peoples, though these stones would also be a continued witness of these realities to Israel. Although Rahab is not mentioned, there is a reminder of the fact that Yahweh's choice of Israel was always with the wider reality of all peoples in view. Readers might thus wonder if Rahab (and her family) are among those who will discover this truth, and indeed if she has done so already. But Rahab's profession of faith is also echoed in the statement of 5:1 when it reports the Canaanite kings' hearts as having 'melted and there was no longer any spirit in them' (Josh. 5:1). Rahab's declaration of the effect Israel was having on Canaanites is thus affirmed, so that readers have more reason to trust her.

This developing sense of trust comes to the fore in the account of the capture of Jericho. As it happens, the mode by which it happens is unlike that anticipated in Joshua 2. But since the process for its capture is revealed only in Joshua 6:2–5 it is impossible to claim that Joshua has acted inappropriately in sending the scouts.[41] What is most remarkable about Rahab in the capture of Jericho is simply that there is apparently no theological problem posed by the rescue of her and her family, and indeed her actions for Israel (rather than the oath) are the reason Joshua gives for this (Josh. 6:17). Accordingly, the scouts can lead out Rahab and her family. We are then told that she has lived within Israel 'until this day' because of her actions in hiding the scouts (Josh. 6:25). Although this is the basis on which she has asked the scouts to swear their oath, it is her actions that are crucial, and by them this seemingly ultimate outsider becomes an enduring part of

---

[41] Contra Sherwood 2006: 51.

Israel's life.[42] Winther-Nielsen's reading of her as a 'negotiated exception'[43] is thus ultimately vindicated, though it is only possible to see this in the light of her whole story, and not Joshua 2 alone.[44] But Rahab's inclusion among Israel immediately poses questions about the nature of Israel. What sort of Israel is it when it can include not only a foreigner, but a Canaanite? And if it is possible to have a negotiated exception, how does this happen?

Achan (Josh. 7:1 – 8:29)

Immediately after Rahab's story is completed, Joshua introduces readers to another character, Achan ben Carmi. If Rahab was the quintessential outsider who has somehow become an insider, then Achan is the quintessential insider – though he is about to become an outsider. He is, indeed, presented as an immediate contrast to Rahab – she was the Canaanite who becomes (in some way) Israelite, but he is the Israelite who becomes a Canaanite. His story is embedded in the narrative, so that rather than seeing it as a discrete source, it is placed at this point because of the contrast it makes with Rahab.[45] Indeed, Joshua 6:19 had in part prepared for Achan's story through its reference to the particularly strict interpretation of the ban that Achan would break. But whereas Rahab's story used ambiguity to tease readers, with Achan we are told from the outset that 'The Israelites had acted treacherously with respect to the ban' (Josh. 7:1). The importance of Achan's insider status is emphasized by the fact that we are introduced to him through a genealogy that is traced back through three generations before noting that he is a member of the tribe of Judah. This genealogy is later traced backwards in the report of how Achan's sin was discovered, but its

---

[42] And, ultimately, though it stands outside the boundaries of this study, to a place in Jesus' genealogy (Matt. 1:5), as well as becoming an example of faith through what she has done (Heb. 11:31; Jas 2:25).

[43] Winther-Nielsen 1995: 162.

[44] More broadly, Lebhar Hall (2010: 39) highlights intertextual links to Gen. 19 to support her inclusion. This may well be correct, but such echoes are difficult to interpret with certainty.

[45] Winther-Nielsen 1995: 227–228. Spina (2005: 64) also notes that these are the only two stories in Joshua with spies. Even here there may be a deliberate reversal in the stories – the scouts who come to Rahab are utterly incompetent, bringing back no useful military information, and yet report correctly. These scouts clearly do a good job – and yet their report is of no use to Israel at all. Spina goes on to suggest that the careful placement of Achan's story relative to Rahab's suggests this may be a hermeneutical key to the book.

initial prominence is a mechanism for showing that Achan is an Israelite of the Israelites (cf. Phil. 3:5). Whatever else he may be, Achan is not a foreigner.

Despite this, readers enter this account knowing something has gone badly wrong because even before the story unfolds, Israel's treachery is announced (Josh. 7:1). For all his excellent Israelite pedigree, Achan is the problem, having taken some of the items placed under the ban. Astute readers may also note something curious about his name – for although his forebears have Israelite names, 'Achan' does not. As Hawk[46] notes, the name cannot easily be traced to any Hebrew root. Apart from this, there appears to be a play on his name in the naming of the Valley of Achor (Josh. 7:24), which represents a different root, albeit one close to the name Achan. In fact, in 1 Chronicles 2:7 his name is given as 'Achar', and this represents something consistent with the naming of the valley. Rösel[47] believes this is a secondary assimilation, but often enough the Chronicler retains the more original forms of names that some of the writers in the Former Prophets alter for rhetorical effect. For example, the authors of Samuel routinely change names with the suffix -baal to end with -bosheth.[48] This is not a consistent policy across the whole of this corpus, but it was apparently a rhetorical technique known to these writers. In this case the form of the name may have been changed sufficiently so that the link to the naming of the valley can be developed but left odd enough to raise questions. A reason for this can be seen in the fact that the consonants used to spell Achan are the same as those used in the name 'Canaan'. By the end of the chapter it will be seen that Achan has not only brought trouble onto Israel; he has in effect become a Canaanite. The distortion of his name is a subtle pointer to this, making the contrast between him and Rahab clearer.

The contrast between them is developed further in the report of Achan's breaking the ban (Josh. 7:1). It was Rahab who first mentioned

---

[46] Hawk 2010: 87.

[47] Rösel 2011: 111.

[48] E.g. Saul's son Eshbaal (1 Chr. 8:33) is called Ishbosheth (2 Sam. 2:8), where the form in Chronicles is much more likely original since the suffixed -baal could simply mean 'lord' and thus be a reference to Yahweh (as well as the Canaanite deity Baal), whereas -bosheth means 'shame' (a form of name it is unlikely a parent would give). The consistency of this pattern in Samuel means that Jerubbaal (Judg. 6:32) becomes 'Jerubbesheth' (2 Sam. 11:21), even though in context the name appears to mock Baal. If Achar is not original, the name 'Ochran' (Num. 1:13) is attested and comes from the relevant root, and so would be another possibility.

this practice of irrevocable devotion of people and things to Yahweh (Josh. 2:10).[49] For her, this practice led to a dread not of Israel but Yahweh. Achan, however, shows no dread at all since he committed an act of treachery in taking the banned items from Jericho. When he was ultimately revealed to Israel as the one responsible for this, Achan acknowledged that he had coveted a cloak, some silver and gold, seeing his act as sin. There may be a play on words here in that the verbs 'to covet' (*ḥmd*) and 'to place under the ban' (*ḥrm*) are orthographically similar,[50] a further pointer to his inversion of Yahweh's values. Achan places his own desires above those of Yahweh, suggesting that even as he confesses, there are elements in which his confession is deficient.[51] As such, he has placed all Israel under the ban, the place of the Canaanites, meaning that whereas previously their enemies fled before them (Josh. 1:5), it is now Israel who flee.[52] This, of course, has already been demonstrated in Israel's initial assault on the city (Josh. 7:2–6). Joshua's prayer (Josh. 7:7–9) may not get the facts of why Israel has been defeated right, but it allows Yahweh to set him and Israel right as to how they are to interpret these events. Quite simply, an Israel who thus transgresses the covenant can no longer live as the people of God (Josh. 7:10–12).

One final link between Achan and Rahab should be noted. After she has acted to rescue the scouts, the oath she has them swear is for the protection of her whole family. When Jericho is taken, Joshua saves both Rahab and her whole family. In effect, her actions have

---

[49] The translation of *ḥērem* is complex, and there is no one English term that suffices. For the most part in this chapter the more neutral 'place under the ban' is used, not least because 'devoted to destruction' suggests an outcome that is not always true. What is clear is that it involves an irrevocable giving over of something or someone to God (see *NIDOTTE* 2: 276–277 and Lilley 1993). It is associated with putting to death in Lev. 27:29, but there 'surely be put to death' employs judicial language, suggesting that in this case *ḥērem* refers to an execution for crime (see Sklar 2013: 331–332; Wenham 1979: 341). That judicial language is used here as well as *ḥērem* may suggest that putting to death was not intrinsic to the concept, though that would normally be the case in a military setting. As is clear from the case of Rahab, the book of Joshua treats this as a maximum penalty, not a required one, meaning that someone who joined Israel was no longer liable to this. On the conditional nature of its application, see also Zehnder 2005: 483–487; 2013: 285.

[50] Hebrew *r* and *d* are very similar and a common source of text-critical problems.

[51] Earl 2010b: 149.

[52] Achan's story also provides a further reflection on the strange encounter between Joshua and the commander of Yahweh's armies (Josh. 5:13–15). In that encounter the commander stressed that he was neither for nor against Israel. His purpose was to fight for Yahweh – and we now see that could be against Israel's enemies (as at Jericho) or against Israel when they have become Yahweh's enemies (as at Ai).

brought her whole family into the common life of Israel. After Achan is finally taken,[53] he is put to death along with his whole family and all that belongs to him. Although his execution is not explicitly said to have been an application of the ban, the fact that Yahweh earlier indicated that Israel stood under the ban (Josh. 7:12) indicates that Achan's death is to be interpreted along those lines. This interpretation becomes more probable when we recognize that Deuteronomy 13:12–18 allowed for parts of Israel to be placed under the ban as a judicial action.[54] Achan's actions have moved his family from being insiders to outsiders, effectively turning Israelites into Canaanites. The faithful action of an outsider, a Canaanite, has brought her family into Israel, while the faithless action of a pedigreed insider has moved his family into a position equivalent to the Canaanites. The stones piled up over Achan (Josh. 7:26) and those at Gilgal (Josh. 4:19–24) both continued to speak to Israel through these stories,[55] pointing to the power of Yahweh as the one who gave the land, but also as the one to be obeyed. These stones spoke first to Israel, but the contexts of the stories about them in Joshua indicate that they are meant to speak to a wider audience about the identity of Yahweh and his people.[56]

The altar on Mount Ebal and the Gibeonites (Josh. 8:30 – 12:24)

Although Joshua is often described as a book of conquest, it is notable that by the end of the story of Ai, roughly a third of the way into the book, very little in the way of 'conquest' has happened. This is not to ignore those places where battle and the destruction of various Canaanites have been described up to this point, though as noted much of this language may well be hyperbolic. Rather, we should note that considerably more space has been given to reflection on the nature of Israel – who is included and who is excluded. Accordingly, it ought not to surprise readers that the report of the covenant renewal ceremony on Mount Ebal

---

[53] Perhaps the verb *lkd*, usually translated as 'taken', should here be translated in its more common sense of 'captured', to highlight the fact that Yahweh is here engaged in a battle against sin.

[54] Cf. Mitchell 1993: 75.

[55] In addition, note that the king of Ai is also placed under a stone cairn (Josh. 8:29), again pointing to the fact that Achan is treated as a Canaanite.

[56] See Hubbard 2001.

(Josh. 8:30–35)[57] twice mentions the 'stranger' (*gēr*, Josh. 8:33, 35). What is perhaps more unusual is that in Joshua 8:33 'all Israel' seems to be defined as covering both the alien and the native. At this point in the book the only foreigners definitely part of Israel are Rahab's clan, but there is no reason that this passage has to be reported as part of a chronological sequence.[58] Indeed, nothing in what has been reported up to this point leads readers to believe Israel can have travelled as far north as Mount Ebal, something that also indicates that this passage is told out of chronological sequence. Rather, it now serves to force readers to address the question of the nature of Israel as a people who commit themselves to serve Yahweh, following the commandments of Torah (these events reflect a directive in Deut. 27). Such an interpretation also enables the links with Joshua 24 to be developed since Shechem (unmentioned in the passage, but beside Mount Ebal) is where Joshua speaks to the nation in that chapter. Both passages enable reflection on events so far, and both integrate foreigners into the account, showing that Israel is made up of those who commit themselves to Yahweh,[59] and both also focus on the theme of covenant. This element is more muted here, though the ark of the covenant is said to be present, while in Joshua 24 a covenant is initiated. But commitment to Yahweh's commands is central in both cases, with this defining the people of God. Reference to Torah in this passage provides an important link to both Yahweh's command to Joshua (Josh. 1:7–8) and the reference to the book of the Torah at the end of the Shechem report (Josh. 24:26).[60] Hence, read in its present context, the report of this covenant ceremony is a vital element within the book's reflections on the identity of the people of God, a reflection that also prepares for the more extensive covenant report in Joshua 24, and that specifically identifies commitment to the Torah, not ethnicity, as crucial.

---

[57] The exact location of this passage varies in the textual traditions. 4QJosh[a] appears to place it after Josh. 5:1, though given the fragmentary nature of this text this is not certain. However, the LXX places it after Josh. 9:2. For our purposes, it is unnecessary to resolve this since all agree it is part of the book. There is, however, much to be said for following the MT at this point (see Firth 2015: 100).

[58] Although Joshua generally reports elements in the appropriate chronological sequence, at certain points it does break with this. E.g. Josh. 11:23 reports that Joshua gave the land by tribal allotments, even though this is not reported until Josh. 14 – 19. In both cases the variance between historical sequence and narrative report are due to the rhetorical goals of the account, providing a mechanism for reflection on events to that point while preparing for a subsequent account.

[59] Cf. Firth 2018.

[60] Cf. Chambers 2015.

In the light of events to this point in Joshua, one might begin to formulate a simple rule for Israel's relationship with foreigners in which those who commit themselves to Yahweh through their faithfulness either to Israel and their function within God's purposes (Rahab) or to the Torah more generally (Mount Ebal) can be included within Israel, whereas Israelites who choose to rebel against Torah (Achan) are excluded. Although such a formula would be pleasingly simple to apply, it is something that is immediately troubled by the account of the Gibeonites (Josh. 9). Here we encounter a group that stands somewhere in the middle of this simple formulation – a people who are not necessarily *for* Yahweh and Israel, but who at least do not want to get in their way and so are not *against* them.[61] It is important to note too that although the main narrative about them is completed in chapter 9, it is their relationship with Israel that shapes the whole of chapters 9–12 since they are the trigger for a combined action against Israel in the south (Josh. 10) and a key point for reflection after the defeat of the northern kings (Josh. 11). This in turn indicates that the battle reports of Joshua 10 – 11 are not simply about Israel's defeating numerous cities (though they are that), but also part of the reflection on the identity of Israel that is central to the whole book.

The Gibeonites' story is immediately linked to the earlier crossing of the Jordan through the repetition of the language of Joshua 5:1 at Joshua 9:1–2, a repetition that recurs in both Joshua 10:1–2 and 11:1. But where Joshua 5:1 emphasized the dread experienced by the Canaanite kings following the news of Israel's crossing, now they gather to act against Israel. Achan's actions, and the resultant troubles at Ai, have thus triggered a different response, one where the Canaanite kings now see an opportunity to resist. But having mentioned this response from the kings, the narrative leaves them aside to focus instead on the Gibeonites, who have a very different reaction. Unlike the kings, regarding whom we are never told exactly what they heard, the position of the Gibeonites[62] is clear since they have heard

---

[61] As such, one might compare them with the two closely related statements of Jesus (Firth 2015: 108) – 'whoever is not with me is against me' (Luke 11:23) and 'whoever is not for us is against us' (Mark 9:40).

[62] There may be a further contrast with the Canaanite kings since the Gibeonites are never said to have a king, and the fact that Gibeon can be compared to a royal city (Josh. 10:5) can be taken as suggesting that it was not royal. As the leading city in a small coalition (Josh. 9:17), it would have been the royal base if there were a king. However, the absence of a king would have been odd within the culture of the time, though not altogether unparalleled. The Philistine leaders are not initially called kings,

about both Jericho and Ai. They knew not only of the victories won, but also of the struggles Israel initially had at Ai even if they showed no knowledge of Achan's sin. It was this that led them to begin a process of negotiating peace with Israel.

Where Rahab's approach was relatively straightforward, acting with loyalty towards the scouts and requesting the same for herself (Josh. 2:8–21), the Gibeonites took a rather different path. As with Rahab, the initial presentation of the Gibeonites is full of ambiguity, though this is rather difficult to bring out in translation. Most translations (e.g. the ESVUK) suggest that they acted with 'cunning' (Josh. 9:4), something that can be seen once the whole story has been read, but not on a first reading. It is said that they acted with *'ormâ*, a noun that can indeed mean 'craftily' (Exod. 21:14) but can also be expressed more positively as 'prudence' (Prov. 1:4). The issue here is complicated by an important text-critical variant,[63] with the main MT witnesses supporting a reading that can mean either 'disguise oneself' or 'act as an ambassador', while the main variant means 'prepare provisions'. On balance, preference should be given here to the MT on the view that the presence of a similar word in verse 12 might lead a scribe to correct the text here to agree with the latter verse, especially since the provisions become an important part of the discussion. However, there is no obvious reason why a scribe would change to the current MT, in that an orthographic uncertainty would presumably lead him to the alternative reading.[64] If so, first-time readers would not necessarily know how to interpret the Gibeonites' actions, the first clues coming only in the description of the things they brought with them for their encounter with Israel. In addition, if we are to understand the group who came to Israel as ambassadors, then we might expect them to be prudent and a little economical with the truth. The care with which this introduction is written suggests that Joshua's narrators were careful to ensure their readers did not reject the Gibeonites immediately, and in so doing place readers in the same position as the Israelites who had to deal with them. In the end, the more deceptive readings are correct, but we must read forward before we read back to resolve the ambiguity here.

(note 62 *cont.*) though by the time of David Achish could be referred to as the king of Gath (1 Sam. 27:2). Even this might simply have been following convention rather than formal structure since in 1 Sam. 29:2 they are referred to once again as 'lords' (Hebr. *seren*).

[63] The MT reads hithpael of *ṣ̣tr*, while some versions would suggest the orthographically similar *ṣ̣td*, the latter of which occurs in v. 12. Both roots are quite rare.

[64] Similarly, Nelson 1997: 121–122.

The balance of the story in Joshua 9 works out how Israel is taken in by the Gibeonites. Although they came from a site not far from Jerusalem (the strategic importance of which is important for Josh. 10), the Israelites accepted the claims of the Gibeonites about having not only come from some distance, but more specifically from some distance outside the land. On this basis they ask Israel to make a covenant with them so that something only hinted at in Rahab's story becomes explicit here. This distinction about their home area is important, because, according to Deuteronomy 20:10–18, Israel were free to make a covenant with a people who wanted peace with them and who lived outside the land, but not with people in the land. As Mitchell[65] observes, 'It is almost as though the Gibeonites have read the text in Deuteronomy.' More than that, the events to which they refer from Israel's past are like those mentioned by Rahab (Josh. 2:8–12), but most importantly include only events from before Israel's entry into the land, even though the narrator is quite clear that it is the events in the land that have triggered their decision. The Israelites were initially suspicious, wondering if the Gibeonites were telling the truth, but were taken in by trying their provisions and their reaffirmation of the claim that they were from outside the land so that a covenant of peace was made with them (Josh. 9:7–15). Crucially, the narrator notes that Israel did not ask Yahweh about this (Josh. 9:14). A first reading of this might suggest that this indicates that a different outcome would have been achieved had they done this rather than tasting the Gibeonites' food, but Joshua 11:19–20 reports that the decision of the Gibeonites not to fight was from Yahweh. If so, the note in Joshua 9:14 should be understood as indicating that the process could have been better, but perhaps the outcome for the Gibeonites might not have been quite so different.

The rest of Joshua 9 explores Israel's response once they realized they had been duped, with some wanting the Gibeonites put to death (Josh. 9:26), though the dominant view of the Israelite leadership was that they could not break the covenant they had made. Confronted by Joshua over their deception, the Gibeonites responded that they acted as they did because they had heard that Yahweh had commanded Moses that all the inhabitants of the land should be 'destroyed' (hi. *šmd*). Although the verb used here is different, there are clear echoes of Rahab's confession, except that where she acted for Israel the Gibeonites admit that they simply do not want to be destroyed.

---

[65] Mitchell 1993: 85.

Rahab's confession suggests they might have had a better outcome, though how that might have been achieved by a collection of cities, at least one of which (Gibeon) was quite large, is not clear. What is clear is that the Gibeonites ended up working in the central sanctuary for Israel (Josh. 9:27). Although cutting wood and drawing water means their role there was menial, it was important work for a sanctuary for which a plentiful supply of both was important. Although the root *ḥrm* does not occur in this chapter, they do in fact end up dedicated to Yahweh, but with their dedication resulting in their working in the sanctuary rather than being destroyed. Admittedly, they are cursed,[66] but it is a curse that enables them to continue living in Israel. Indeed, their continued life within Israel provides the key background to events in 2 Samuel 21:1–14, where Yahweh again demonstrates his commitment both to them and the covenant made with them. By Nehemiah 3:7 the men of Gibeon are as integral as any within Judah in the rebuilding of Jerusalem's walls, demonstrating their full acceptance as part of Israel, though by then they would have been a more mixed group. What is clear from this is that the Gibeonites, like Rahab, became an integrated part of Israel, and that their reaction to Yahweh (albeit one in which Yahweh was involved) was crucial to this.[67]

The importance of the Gibeonites' integration (however partial) is borne out by chapters 10 and 11. These are presented in parallel to one another,[68] with one reporting an attack against Israel by a coalition of southern kings led by Jerusalem (Josh. 10:1–5) and the other an attack led by a northern coalition led by Hazor (Josh. 11:1–5). Militarily, Hazor was the greater threat as it was a much more significant city,[69] but the narrative's focus is more directly on the south because of its direct associations with Gibeon. These associations are made explicit in Joshua 10:1, which notes that it was the covenant with the Gibeonites that led to the attack by the southern coalition, while in Joshua 10:41 Gibeon is a key marker for where Joshua had led Israel in battle. Most of chapter 10 is given over to recounting the defeat of the five southern kings who had allied themselves against Israel with the result that they, and various cities, were placed under the ban. As noted above, the language here is hyperbolic, but the more important point to note is that this indicates the outcome

---

[66] Something they share only with a potential builder of Jericho, Josh. 6:26.
[67] Cf. Ford 2015: 213–214.
[68] Cf. Nelson 1997: 151.
[69] Cf. Hawkins 2013: 111–117.

for a city that resists Yahweh's purposes. Given the emphasis upon the defeat of kings throughout these chapters, and especially the listing of kings defeated in Joshua 12:7–24, it was possible that it was particularly the royal structures of Canaan that Yahweh opposed. Chapter 11 can then report the militarily more significant account of the northern battles relatively briefly because this simply repeats the pattern of the previous chapter. Once again it is those who oppose Yahweh's purposes who are destroyed, though the destruction of the city of Hazor and the hamstringing of their horses (which would render them useless for chariots but still enable them to work) reminds Israel that they are not to put their trust elsewhere than Yahweh (cf. Ps. 20:7). Yahweh, indeed, was apparently more than willing to work with the Gibeonites, whereas the other foreigners had their hearts hardened to go against Israel into the battles where they would be destroyed (Josh. 11:19–20). This language is an obvious echo of the events of the exodus (cf. Exod. 7:13; 9:12), where at points Pharaoh hardens his own heart, while at others Yahweh does the hardening. The background suggests an integration of human and divine will, something that also seems likely here. However we interpret this feature, what is clear is that by the midpoint of the book a clear pattern has emerged in Israel's relationship with foreigners, one in which those who opposed Yahweh and his purposes were placed under the ban (though with degrees of severity), but those who were willing to work with Yahweh (or at least not against him) could become integrated into Israel's shared life. In case a reader had any concerns about this, the narrator emphasizes that Joshua had indeed done everything Yahweh had commanded through Moses (Josh. 11:15).[70] Including foreigners into Israel, it seems, is an important part of this.

Caleb, the surviving Canaanites and the cities of refuge (Josh. 13 – 21)

Caleb and his family

Readers turning from Joshua 1 to 12 might expect that the land allocation report that dominates proceedings through to Joshua 21 might have less to contribute to the theme of the place of foreigners

---

[70] As Lebhar Hall (2010: 197) points out, this is a point where Joshua exceeds even Moses, since his own failure to obey left him unable to enter the land (Num. 20:8–12).

within Israel. However, although it is true that the bulk of these chapters is given over to the listing of tribal boundaries and (often) of the towns within them that would be assigned to the tribes, concern with the inclusion of foreigners does not disappear. What emerges from a close reading of these chapters is an awareness of the fact that the Israel who receive the land are a people committed to Yahweh. Faith, not ethnicity, is the crucial issue, even as the text makes clear that Yahweh had the right to override existing political structures, and he overrides them based on faith.[71] It is not that Israel had the power to take this land, because, as the introduction to this section (Josh. 13:1–7) makes clear, much of the land remained to be taken. Rather, Israel are a people who operate from the perspective of powerlessness – something the events at Ai (Josh. 7) made clear. As such, this process is an act of faith by a people who have seen signs of how Yahweh can give them the land, but who know it is not a sign of their own power.[72] The land is divided up[73] and allotted as an act of faith – indeed, Joshua 18 – 19 shows that although much of it has not been examined in any way by Israel, it is still apportioned.

A central concern within the book is to demonstrate the integration of the tribes already settled east of the Jordan with those settling to the west. This integration was already indicated in Joshua 1:10–18, when the eastern tribes reaffirmed their commitment to seeing those settling west of the Jordan granted rest in the land, though this issue will come to a focus in Joshua 22. But here the integration of east and west is demonstrated through the listing of the allotments to the eastern tribes (Josh. 13:8–31) before the note about the lack of any allotment to this point for the tribe of Levi. This note reflects on events to that point, while also preparing for the allocation to the Levites at the end of this section (Josh. 21).[74] More broadly, restating the eastern allotment links Joshua's upcoming actions west of the Jordan with Moses' earlier ones (Num. 32), showing that Joshua is completing something Moses began. Hence all the territory occupied by Israel is theirs as a divine gift, even those sections outside the territory initially promised to Abraham. This is why the report of

---

[71] Cf. Creach 2012.

[72] Creach 2013: 114.

[73] As Koorevaar (1990: 118, 120) has noted, the verb *ḥlq* (divide) functions as the *Leitwort* for these chapters.

[74] The whole of Josh. 13 – 21 can be arranged in a broadly chiastic structure (Koorevaar 1990: 229). This should perhaps not be pressed too far, but is a pointer to the fact that this is not simply a collection of lists but rather a carefully designed stretch of text.

the allotment to Levi includes cities on both sides of the Jordan, while the cities of refuge (all of which are also Levitical) are explicitly allotted to provide access for those west (Josh. 20:7) and east (Josh. 20:8) of the Jordan. If the ethnic boundaries of Israel have been blurred by Joshua 1 – 12, the geographic ones will also be blurred in Joshua 13 – 21 even as the ethnic ones continue to be explored to demonstrate that Israel is made up of those who live out faith in Yahweh.

The importance of reflection on Israel as a people who are not defined by ethnicity was indicated by the double introduction to the book provided by Joshua 1 – 2. There the issue of geography was raised by the need for the eastern tribes to engage in the process of claiming the land for the western tribes before the ethnic issue was clearly raised by Rahab's story. But these chapters are clearly linked by their concern to demonstrate that Yahweh was indeed giving Israel the land. In these chapters Joshua 13 – 14 fulfils a similar function, again providing a double introduction. As noted, Joshua 13:8–31 has highlighted the geographic issues by repeating the allotment to the eastern tribes, something that might not have been expected given the fact that Joshua 13:1–7 concluded with a directive to Joshua that he divide the land for the western tribes. In fact, this process is not really begun until Joshua 15 when the allotment for Judah is reported. Joshua 14, however, will also explore ethnic issues and the integration of foreigners through its discussion of Caleb's personal allotment in the region of Hebron.[75]

Although Joshua 14:1–5 might lead readers to expect a report of the main western allotments, this is again deferred until Joshua 15 to examine the case of Caleb. As is well known, Caleb (along with Joshua, who also receives a personal allotment in Josh. 19:49–50) was one of the original spies whose mission is recounted in Numbers 13. Unlike the majority, he expressed confidence in Yahweh's ability to give Israel the land (Num. 13:30), though this view was not accepted by the people, resulting in the death of that generation in the wilderness (though not before some decided belatedly to attempt to enter the land after Yahweh had said they could not enter it, Num. 14:39–45). This background again reminds Israel that they operate from a position of weakness, their strength coming from Yahweh alone. Despite the failure of the wilderness generation, Caleb and

---

[75] According to Josh. 20:7, Hebron was a city of refuge, while Josh. 21:11–12 makes explicit that the city belonged to the Levites. However, the region could still be allotted to Caleb, even if the city was not finally his.

Joshua were promised that they would enter the land and possess it (Num. 14:25, 30). This account clearly lies in the background in this chapter.

However, Numbers 32 is also vital here, demonstrating the importance of reading Joshua, and especially this part of it, in the light of Numbers.[76] The combination of Numbers 13 – 14 and 32 as background will be more pronounced in Joshua 22, but here this combination provides two important elements. First, it indicates the background to Caleb's request for land that he presents to Joshua and Eleazar.[77] This is in part recounted in Numbers 14 but is also important in Numbers 32. This link is made clearer by Caleb's statement that he 'wholly followed Yahweh' (*wĕ 'ānōkî millētî 'aḥărê yhwh*, Josh. 14:8), a statement that echoes the description of Joshua and Caleb in Numbers 32:12. There the description of their loyalty was used by Moses to discourage the initial request of the eastern tribes to settle there since he saw the request as evidence of Israel's continued rebellion, although subsequent negotiations convinced him that this was an acceptable outcome. Here it functions as part of several links to that chapter, demonstrating that Caleb's loyalty had not ceased in the wilderness but had continued for a further forty-five years (Josh. 14:10), as he stood before Joshua and Eleazar to claim his land. Caleb's loyalty is stressed when the narrator points to it, using the same language (Josh. 14:14), to explain why he received his allocation. In a more immediate contrast Caleb insists that unlike the other spies, he has not caused Israel's hearts to melt – unlike Achan, where the result of his sin was that Israelite hearts melted (Josh. 7:5).

These links point to another, and for our purposes more important, link to Numbers 32. Twice in this chapter Caleb is called 'the son of Jephunneh the Kenizzite' (Josh. 14:6, 14). He is routinely called 'the son of Jephunneh' (e.g. Num. 13:6), but the additional label 'the Kenizzite' occurs elsewhere only in Numbers 32:12. In effect, therefore, the whole of Caleb's presentation in this chapter is bounded by allusions to Numbers 32:12, with the narration in between largely drawing on Numbers 13 – 14 as the point where he demonstrated his loyalty in the first place. But since Numbers 13 – 14 could demonstrate this anyway, why include the additional elements from Numbers 32?

[76] Cf. Wray Beal 2017.
[77] Num. 13 – 14 makes clear that although Moses sent the spies, the people's grumbling was against Moses and Aaron (Num. 14:1–2). As the mistakes of the past are resolved in these chapters, there is a closer interaction between their immediate successors.

The reasons behind an intertextual allusion can be difficult to discern, but the combination of these factors is probably because it provides a context for understanding the reference to Caleb as a Kenizzite. The word 'Kenizzite' is a gentilic and most likely derived from the name 'Kenaz'. Although Joshua and Numbers do not explain the meaning of this term, we should note that in Genesis 15:19–21 the Kenizzites were one of a group of peoples living in Canaan, in the territory that Yahweh was giving to Abraham's seed. Moreover, in Genesis 36:11, 15 and 42 Kenaz is mentioned as a descendant of Esau, and thus someone living in the area east of the Jordan, perhaps the area Israel will claim in Numbers 32. Numbers 32:12 and Joshua 14:6, 14 are the only two times Caleb is called 'the Kenizzite', but both do so in a context where his wholehearted loyalty to Yahweh is stressed. The importance of this appears to be that the gentilic here indicates that Caleb is not from an originally Israelite family, and though 1 Chronicles 4:13–15 will integrate him into the tribe of Judah, the gaps it leaves in his genealogy mean his background is not denied. Rather, the Chronicler most likely interprets his background as an outsider who has now become an insider.[78] Even if Caleb is not as 'foreign' as Rahab, the presentation in Joshua still makes the effort to stress this while also highlighting his wholehearted faithfulness, unlike Achan. He is the foreigner who has lived out the faith that Israel is meant to live.

If Rahab was effectively the paradigm figure for Joshua 1 – 12, demonstrating the faith that was meant to mark Israel, Caleb even more clearly fulfils this role for Joshua 13 – 21. This is clear when we recognize that his request to receive his land based on Yahweh's previous promise provides the pattern for a series of 'land grant' narratives that run through these chapters.[79] As well as Caleb's initial request, these include Achsah (Josh. 15:13–19), the daughters of Zelophehad (Josh. 17:3–6) and the Levites (Josh. 21:1–3).[80] What marks out these stories is that they are all examples of faith rooted in Yahweh's promise and claimed by those thereby entitled to receive some land. Achsah's story was quite likely originally part of Caleb's

[78] Similarly, Selman 1994: 102.
[79] Nelson 1997: 177.
[80] Nelson (ibid.) also includes the account of the Joseph tribes (Josh. 17:14–18), but there is no prior promise from Yahweh in this case, and it is possible to read Joshua's comment to them (Josh. 17:17–18) as ironic. Even if this latter point is not sustained, the form-critical distinction of the absence of prior promise should see this passage deleted from the list.

own story,[81] but it once again focuses, as an example of faith, on the actions of a family who are recognizably foreign.[82] The claim of the daughters of Zelophehad is built on Numbers 27, 36, while the Levites' claim is more broadly based. But all of them follow the path established by Caleb, a foreigner now integrated into Israel, who demonstrates the sort of faith expected of Israel.

The surviving Canaanites

Caleb, and through him his family, has demonstrated that a foreigner can be a significant figure within Israel. But they are not the only foreigners to take a significant role in these chapters. A key element in the allocation reports is a note for Judah, Joseph and Dan that various Canaanite groups continued to exist. These, however, are not all presented in the same form, and there is value in reading these statements against the pattern established in Joshua 1 – 12. If we do this, it is possible to see references to the surviving Canaanites as falling into three main groups: those who can be regarded neutrally (a possible threat, like the Gibeonites), those who can be regarded negatively (those opposed to what Yahweh is doing, like the southern and northern coalitions) and those who can be regarded more positively as peoples with whom Yahweh intends to continue working (like Rahab). Ethnicity itself is not the issue. Rather, the concern is with the possible religious impact of these peoples. As a full narrative is not provided for these groups, we need to work by inference; but there is enough evidence for this typology to develop.

The first statement refers to the continued existence of the Jebusites in Jerusalem in the report of Judah's allocation (Josh. 15:63). Their mention occurs at the end of a long list of towns,[83] a list that has been careful to avoid any mention of Jerusalem since the town as a whole will be allotted to Benjamin (Josh. 18:28); though as a border town the southern slope of the hill was allotted to Judah (Josh. 15:8). The key verse here includes the statement that Judah was 'unable to dispossess' (*lō' yākĕlû*)[84] them. Although often read as evidence of a

---

[81] There is no subject for the verb 'he gave' in 15:13 (though English Bibles usually make it Joshua). The broken syntax here suggests that we have picked up a story midstream, with a connection to Caleb's story most probable.

[82] In a slightly abbreviated form this story recurs in Judg. 1:11–15. Although often treated simply as a doublet, it has a different function in each book and will therefore be discussed there.

[83] Even longer if we accept, as seems likely, the much longer reading of the LXX at Josh. 15:59, as it is easy to understand why a scribe might have missed a group of towns.

[84] Here following Qere.

failing on Judah's part that aligns them with the northern tribes,[85] it is important to note that no reason is given for this inability. The statement is laconic and perhaps deliberately ambiguous, and although it clearly anticipates later references to the city as Jebus (Judg. 19:10–15) or as a Jebusite residence (2 Sam. 5:6–10), the absence of a reason for the inability to take the city should be allowed to stand. Readers might well choose to fill the gap, but given Yahweh's earlier decision to sustain the Gibeonites (Josh. 11:19) it is not necessarily a failure. Indeed, when read as preparation for Judges 19, a story that will show Israel's living like the worst of Canaan, there may even be something positive in their presence here, even if the city ultimately comes under David's control (2 Sam. 5:6–10).[86] These Jebusites can be a threat to Israel, but only if they become a religious threat, not an ethnic one.

A similar line of interpretation can also be followed in the statements about the Canaanites in Gezer within the territory of Ephraim (Josh. 16:10) and the various cities where Canaanites persisted in the territory of west Manasseh (Josh. 17:12), though with slightly less confidence. The language here varies slightly from that of Judah. In Ephraim's case it is said they 'did not dispossess' (wĕlō' hôrîšû) the Canaanites living in Gezer, while the statement for Manasseh integrates both that of Judah and Ephraim in saying they 'could not dispossess' (wĕlō' yākĕlû bĕnê mĕnaššeh lĕhôrîš) certain Canaanites, though in both cases the continuing Canaanites were finally put to forced labour. In the case of Gezer this might not have happened until the time of Solomon (1 Kgs 9:21), though there might have been earlier instances. The key point to note, though, is that in neither case is there a statement of failure on Israel's part, that no reason is given for their inability to dispossess these Canaanites. It could indeed be a failure on their part but given the continued existence of the Gibeonites within Israel this is not a necessary interpretation.

A more positive reference to continuing Canaanites occurs in the report of the boundaries for the Joseph tribes (Ephraim and west Manasseh, Josh. 16:2–3). This boundary line traces the southern border of Joseph, a line that will be replicated when Benjamin's northern border is reported (Josh. 18:12–13). In Ephraim's case the line reaches Ataroth, a town that unfortunately cannot now be

---

[85] E.g. Hawk 2000: 203.

[86] Note, though, that even then Jebusites continued to have an important part in its life; cf. 2 Sam. 24:18–25.

located. At this point, though, it has reached the territory[87] of the Archites before also moving through to the territory of the Japhletites and that of Lower Beth Horon. The latter is clearly a city located in the Valley of Aijalon, and here defines the Japhletite territory. However, both the Archites and Japhletites are peoples who are already recognized as being in the land; that is, they are Canaanites. The Japhletites are not mentioned elsewhere, but it is likely that the Archites are included in the descendants of Canaan mentioned in Genesis 10:17.[88] The implication of this boundary line seems to be that these two Canaanite groups would continue to be recognized even after the allotment of the land was completed, not least because they are the only Canaanite peoples mentioned in the boundary reports that otherwise focus on towns. Their territory would be incorporated into the Joseph tribes, much perhaps as Caleb's clan had been incorporated into Judah's, but their distinctiveness would continue to be recognized even though they were Canaanite. As will be noted when looking at foreigners in Samuel, David's key advisor, Hushai, is consistently called 'the Archite' (e.g. 2 Sam. 15:32)[89] and emerges as one of several key foreigners who sustain David at his lowest ebb. Although the implications for the continued existence of the Archites and Japhletites are not developed within Joshua, in the case of the Archites at least the positive possibilities of their existence are later picked up.

A more negative example of the continued existence of other peoples in the land is found in the case of Dan. Following the list of the cities of their allotment, we are then told of their move to the far north, outside the boundaries of the land promised, after they lost the land (Josh. 19:47). This short note receives a fuller treatment in Judges 1:34–36 and 18:1–31 and will therefore receive more comment in the next chapter. This note, however, seems to come from a different source from that behind Judges 18, and so represents an independent witness to these events.[90] The material in Judges is indisputably

[87] Hebr. *gĕbûl* can mean either 'border' or 'territory'. Here it clearly marks off a distinct territory.

[88] There is a spelling variation – in Gen. 10:17 they are *'arqî*, while here they are *'arkî*, but interchange between *q* and *k* and general inconsistency in spelling within the OT (especially of non-Israelite terms – there are several different spellings of the Jebusite name Araunah in 2 Sam. 24 alone) means this is not a major problem.

[89] The spelling here is consistent with that of Joshua.

[90] It calls the city Dan would capture 'Leshem', whereas in Judg. 18:27 it is called Laish. Although there is often variation in the spelling of non-Israelite names, the variation here is sufficient to suggest a different source. However, the note in Judg. 1:34–36 could simply be a comment on this passage or an independent witness.

negative towards Dan and the fact that they settled outside the Promised Land. The issue within Joshua is not so much that Dan settled outside the land (something that will become clear in Josh. 22) as the fact that Dan failed to settle in the land Yahweh had allotted to them. It is the fact they took possession of Leshem themselves that is problematic in Joshua because it indicates actions they took apart from Yahweh. Nevertheless, although there is evidently some criticism of Dan here, there is no observation on the actions of the people of the land. That they prevented a tribe in Israel from taking up their land could mean they were viewed negatively, but the more pressing concern in Joshua is to note Dan's failure.

Within the land allocation reports, therefore, the continued existence of various Canaanite groups might provide a critique of the relevant tribes, though this is reasonably explicit only in the case of Dan. But the continued existence of these groups can also be seen more positively in some cases, where it prepares for the introduction of important figures whose own foreign background does not prevent them from being figures through whom Yahweh works. There is thus a parallel to be drawn between these groups and those highlighted in Joshua 1 – 12.

The cities of refuge

There is one final reference to foreigners in the land allocation, and this is the note that the cities of refuge listed in Joshua 20 are for both the Israelite and the 'resident foreigner' (*gēr*, Josh. 20:9). These cities were scattered around the whole of Israel, with three on each side of the Jordan. The list here assumes the background of Numbers 35:9–34 and the fact that Moses already established three cities of refuge east of the Jordan (Deut. 4:41–43), so that, as with the rest of the land allocation, Joshua is again completing the work begun by Moses. Mention of the *gēr* here is important, not only because it shows that Joshua has fulfilled the requirement of Numbers 35:15, but also because this is the first time the *gēr* has been mentioned since the Mount Ebal ceremony (Josh. 8:30–35). That passage served as a key mechanism for understanding Israel as they entered the land, showing that they were those who committed themselves to Yahweh. Mention of them here, at a key point in the Levitical material that closes the land allocation, shows that everyone who committed themselves to Yahweh could expect the same standards of justice in Israel. There may also be an allusion to Caleb's claiming the region of Hebron (Josh. 14:6–15) since it too is listed as a city of refuge, meaning that one of the cities was in a region assigned to a clan that was originally foreign. There is an inclusive vision at work here,[91] and this means that justice is available to all, irrespective of ethnicity.[92] The whole of the land allocation narratives, therefore, are consistent with the themes noted in Joshua 1 – 12, where ethnicity (even Canaanite ethnicity) is not necessarily problematic. Those who fully commit themselves to Yahweh, like Caleb, may enjoy the blessing of life in the land, but that blessing is also open to various foreigners, including some Canaanites.

The altar on the Jordan (Josh. 22)

The issue of foreigners continues to be important in the closing three chapters of Joshua. As always, they can be a threat, but there is also the possibility of their inclusion. This possibility becomes particularly important in Joshua 24, but the place of foreigners and the wider question of exactly who Israel is remain central throughout. Indeed, questions of identity are important in the story of the altar on the Jordan (Josh. 22). Central to this chapter is the issue of the relationship of the tribes on either side of the Jordan, a theme that was intimated in Joshua 1:10–18 and then developed further in Joshua 13 – 14 and 20 – 21. It is thus placed strategically at the start of each major section of the book, as well as providing closure to the land allocation reports. That the theme should again be important as we enter the final major section of the book is no surprise, pointing to the care with which the book has been constructed, even if from rather disparate materials, to emphasize the importance of the theme of the identity of Israel.

The chapter divides into two main sections that also, to some extent, reflect the main divisions in the book. Joshua's opening speech and the brief report of the return of the eastern tribes (Josh. 22:1–9) draws heavily on the language of Deuteronomy, while also making explicit key connections to Joshua 1. The second half, which focuses on the conflict over the altar, draws most heavily on themes from Numbers[93] even as it also integrates elements from earlier in the book. This broadly matches the pattern where Joshua 1 – 12 draws heavily on Deuteronomy but much less on Numbers, whereas Joshua 13 – 21 draws heavily on Numbers but much less on Deuteronomy. This

---

[91] Cf. Howard 1998: 387.
[92] Laha 2012: 195.
[93] Cf. Wray Beal 2017: 477–478.

pattern becomes an important mechanism by which this chapter draws on previous themes about Israel's identity, and does so by referencing the whole book to this point. Joshua's speech (Josh. 22:1–8) is also the first of a series of three farewell speeches to parts of Israel, following Moses' pattern through Deuteronomy, each of which is roughly twice the length of its predecessor (Josh. 23:1–16; 24:1–28), meaning that the issues of national identity that are important here are carried through to the subsequent chapters. Joshua 22 is thus pivotal for the issue of who is, or is not, a foreigner, and thus for the message of the book.

The theme of the rest that Yahweh is giving to his people is another important motif for the book, and it too is drawn on here. In the book's opening speech to the eastern tribes (Josh. 1:10–18) Joshua stressed the pivotal role that the eastern tribes would play in gaining 'rest' (*nûaḥ*) for the western tribes that matched what Yahweh had already given them (Josh. 1:13–15). In the summary of Yahweh's faithfulness that closed the land allocation, the reality of this rest is stressed (Josh. 21:43), and it is this rest that enables Joshua to tell the eastern tribes that they can now return to their possession east of the Jordan (Josh. 22:4). Rest is thus something Yahweh has granted for all Israel, though as the book has shown to this point, the Israel who have received this rest are a mixed people, made up of those who commit themselves to Yahweh, or at least choose not to oppose him. That a faithful relationship to Yahweh is of most importance is made clear by Joshua when he charges the eastern tribes to take care to keep the Torah (Josh. 22:5), a charge that means that these tribes are reminded that they take on the same responsibility as Joshua himself (Josh. 1:7). It is this commitment that is crucial, and it was this commitment by which Joshua himself was previously assessed (Josh. 11:15). Faithfulness to Yahweh is the key marker for Israel's identity. With this and a blessing from Joshua the eastern tribes return to their home (Josh. 22:6).

Although all seems well at this point, the narrator includes a note about Manasseh as a tribe that lives on both sides of the Jordan, one that received some land through both Moses and Joshua. In mentioning this, the narrator includes the note that they received land with their 'kin' (*'āḥ*) west of the Jordan, a term that echoes Joshua's speech to the eastern tribes (Josh. 22:3). All Israel can be understood as kin, but in this Manasseh can be particularly noted as a 'bridge people'.[94] Only

---

[94] Nelson 1997: 247.

at the end of the dismissal of the eastern tribes are we told that this took place at Shiloh, but this brief note is also important for understanding this chapter because Shiloh was the place where the sanctuary was established once the land was subdued before Israel (Josh. 18:1), even if not all of it was claimed at that point (Josh. 18:2–10). Crucially, at this point in Israel's story the one place of worship to which Deuteronomy 12 refers is at Shiloh. The question that therefore echoes through the balance of this chapter is whether the eastern tribes will indeed honour this, and whether Manasseh will function as the bridge between the tribes. Perhaps more curiously, Shiloh is said to be in the land of Canaan, a term that appears to be chosen because of the importance of identifying Israel while leaving open the issue of whether Israel is to be identified with a particular place.

The rest Israel therefore achieves to this point is suddenly placed under threat when the eastern tribes depart and build an altar in the region of the Jordan (Josh. 22:10). It is important to note that at this point in the chapter the narrative not only changes its main point of Pentateuchal reflection; it also changes its mode of narration such that the events are reported but no comment is provided to guide readers as to their interpretation.[95] The effect of this is that as readers we experience the same shock as both the eastern and western tribes throughout – the western tribes when they see the altar and know that it is somewhere other than the one sanctuary in Shiloh, and the eastern tribes when they encounter a hostile response to it from the western tribes. What is clear is that the altar was meant to be seen since it is said to have been an altar of 'great size'. Perhaps more importantly, it is said that it was built 'in the land of Canaan' (Josh. 22:10). Exactly where the altar was built remains, however, unclear – it is by the Jordan, but the statement that it is *'el mûl* Canaan could mean that it was 'opposite' Canaan, and thus east of the Jordan, or 'at the front of', and thus conceivably west of the river. None of the terms used to describe the altar's location ever resolve this.[96]

Confusion about Israel's identity is then compounded by the note of Joshua 22:12 when it states that the Israelites heard about this (itself an echo of Josh. 9:1–2; 10:1; 11:1). In this context 'Israelite' refers only to the western tribes, something made clear when it is

---

[95] Technically, the switch is from zero focalization in which narrative omniscience means the narrator reports both what happens and provides assessment of it, to external focalization in which events are reported but no guidance is provided for their interpretation. See Genette 1980: 185–198.

[96] Cf. Hawk 2000: 237.

reported that the Israelites gathered for war against the eastern tribes (Josh. 22:12), though before this the Israelites had sent a group led by Eleazar's son Phinehas. Consistent with the narrative technique here, we are not told why Phinehas is chosen, though his background may well suggest a preference for violence (cf. Num. 25:10–18). Certainly, his speech to the eastern tribes begins aggressively as it accuses them of treachery, an echo of Achan's sin (Josh. 7) that he ultimately makes explicit (Josh. 22:16–20), as well as pointing back to the earlier sin at Shittim (Num. 25:1–9). But this same story has already been alluded to in Rahab's story (Josh. 2), so readers know that association with foreign women is not necessarily problematic (though it can be). But the Achan story may be considered more problematic since there an Israelite does, in effect, become a Canaanite. Although ethnicity is not mentioned directly, it lies behind the conflict, at least as Phinehas represents it. But it is also linked to the question of the land, with Phinehas suggesting that the territory of the eastern tribes may be unclean (Josh. 22:19).[97] As a result of the altar, the western tribes have claimed the label 'Israel' for themselves, implying in effect that only those living in Canaan can truly be Israel – though readers of Joshua also know that many still in Canaan are not ethnically Israelite.

Having held back any statement on why the altar was constructed, there is an important switch introduced in Joshua 22:21–29, so that readers now see events from the perspective of the eastern tribes. They are shocked (or at least present themselves as such) by the accusations of the western tribes and deny any treachery on their part. Indeed, they make the remarkable claim this was not an altar for making any sort of offering (Josh. 22:23). Such a statement is particularly odd in Hebrew since the word translated 'altar' (*mizbēaḥ*) comes from the same root as the verb meaning 'to sacrifice' (*zbḥ*). Some have therefore doubted their claim,[98] but the extensive denial, and the subsequent acceptance of their claim by Phinehas's delegation (Josh. 22:30–31), means we are probably to accept their claim that the altar was intended as a replica that would witness to the future that the eastern tribes would continue to have with Yahweh (Josh. 22:26–29). It is notable that this concern is expressed at this point only by Reuben and Gad – Manasseh's bridging status apparently meant they were not as affected by this, though they had participated in the altar's

[97] This comment ignores the earlier observation that Yahweh gave them their land through Moses (Josh. 22:9).

[98] E.g. Snaith 1978: 331.

construction. Israel cannot therefore be divided by the Jordan – geography cannot limit those who will be the people of God. This does not mean that certain people might well be excluded, as seems to be suggested for Dan in Judges 18, but the issue there is in fact unorthodox worship. On the other hand, this prepares for a theme that will become important in Kings, where people outside any recognizably Israelite territory are indeed able to have a portion in Yahweh.

That Israel can be united through faithful worship – a theme crucial to Joshua's initial charge – comes into focus in the response of Phinehas's delegation to the statement from the eastern tribes. It can be said that Yahweh's presence can be recognized because there is no breach of faith, and therefore this has 'delivered the Israelites from Yahweh's hand' (Josh. 22:31). But who are 'the Israelites' here? Although the statement acknowledges that it was the eastern tribes who wrought the delivery, the Israelites here must be those on both sides of the Jordan. Although the subsequent references to Israel (Josh. 22:32–33) include only the western tribes, it is because they can now be clarified as those in Canaan. All Israel has been delivered from the hand of Yahweh because the altar signifies their unity, however much it was previously misunderstood. This conclusion therefore holds out hope for the future, reminding Israel that geographic separation will not remove them from being part of the people of Israel. Only false worship will do that because it is ultimately faithful worship that identifies God's people. On both sides of the Jordan this covers both those who are ethnically Israelite and those who are not.

The threat of all and an invitation to all (Josh. 23 – 24)

The issue of foreigners continues to be important in Joshua's final two speeches.[99] These speeches both pick up on elements in the initial charge to the eastern tribes (Josh. 22:1–9). Most importantly, both speeches are addressed to all Israel (Josh. 23:2; 24:1–2), and this must now include those on either side of the Jordan and those foreigners who have now been integrated (or at least begun to be integrated) into

---

[99] The relationship between these two chapters has been much discussed, often on the basis that the book does not need both, with scholars divided over which was the original. For convenient discussions, see Römer 2006 and Krause 2015b, or more comprehensively Koopmans 1990: 1–164.

Israel. Beyond this, the editorial note in Joshua 23:1 also refers to the rest that Yahweh gave, something already picked up in Joshua 22:4; though the more direct allusion here is to Joshua 21:43–45. In terms of the internal links between these chapters, both Joshua 22 and 23 point to illegitimate worship, with its ultimate resolution found in Joshua 24.[100] While the altar at the Jordan was intended as a witness that Yahweh was God (Josh. 22:34), it is the stone that Joshua set up at Shechem that was a witness to the people's commitment to faithful worship. Finally, where Joshua 23 focuses on the threat foreigners can be when they lead Israel away from the faithful worship of Yahweh, Joshua 24 develops a covenant in which all people may worship, even while acknowledging that all worship is ultimately limited.

Joshua 23 opens by recalling Joshua 13:1–7, noting Joshua's advanced age, though this time it is Joshua himself, not Yahweh, who notes this point after it has been noted by the narrator. Having summoned all Israel, a term that by this point covers a mixed people ethnically, his speech focuses on Yahweh's faithfulness in fighting for Israel against 'all these nations'. Given that the audience includes Israelites from both sides of the Jordan, 'these nations' is therefore more than just the Canaanites, though it certainly includes them. Within the framework of the book the nations against whom Yahweh has fought are those who have opposed his purposes, something already in evidence in the events leading up to the allotment of the land to the eastern tribes in Numbers 32. Foreigners may indeed set themselves against Yahweh; but provided he fights for Israel, then no other nation can resist them. However, Joshua then observes that he has allotted these remaining nations as an inheritance for Israel's tribes. In that the territory of the more northerly tribes has not really been occupied at this point, there are naturally various nations still present. But, as noted above, even in territory that Israel has claimed to this point there are various Canaanite groups still present, and these peoples can be said to have been allotted to Israel's tribes. Joshua can reassure the Israelites that Yahweh will continue to force these people back[101] and so enable God's people to possess the land. The focus here is on those who continue to resist what Yahweh is doing rather than on addressing the exceptions like Rahab or the Gibeonites. When there is resistance, Israel can be assured that Yahweh will continue to grant them the land.

---

[100] Mitchell 1993: 115.
[101] The verb *hdp* here is unique for Joshua.

However, it quickly becomes apparent that ethnicity itself is not the issue here, because the summons to Israel is that they remain faithful to Torah, and that their worship be focused on Yahweh alone, something that prepares for mention of foreign gods in Joshua 24. This becomes clear when Joshua insists that Israel's successes to date are because of their absolute loyalty to Yahweh and that this therefore is the reason Yahweh has fought for them (Josh. 23:8–10). Within the book Achan provides a counterexample, not so much because of the worship of Canaanite deities but because he placed his own desires above those of Yahweh. That this could be understood as worship directed to someone other than Yahweh or as a form of non-orthodox Yahweh worship was made clear in Joshua 22, so that within the book anything that supplants the ultimacy of Yahweh has already begun to move into a Canaanite pattern of worship. Achan is not mentioned here, but he stands in the background to Joshua's warnings about associating with the remaining nations (Josh. 23:12–16). The concern here seems to focus on the problem of intermarriage and sexual relationships with the remnant of the nations, so that this leads to the worship of other gods. Although the initial reference to this deals only with these relationships (Josh. 23:12–13), that the concern is ultimately with false worship soon becomes clear (Josh. 23:16). An Israel that does this will be destroyed – like Achan, they will have made themselves a people other than the people of God, and so will be destroyed.

Joshua 23 has therefore highlighted the possible threat posed by foreign nations, though it has made clear that the issue is one of worship rather than ethnicity. It has, though, shown that an Israel that becomes indistinguishable from the nations is no longer the people of God. An alternative is perhaps implied there, but the positive alternative is not developed. For that we need Joshua's final speech (Josh. 24:1–28). This time all Israel's tribes are gathered to Shechem, close to Mount Ebal, where there was an earlier covenant ceremony (Josh. 8:30–35)[102] that defined Israel as both foreigner and native born. This understanding of Israel is important for Joshua 24.

As the people are gathered, Joshua begins with a recital of what Yahweh has done for Israel up to this point (Josh. 24:1–13). Strikingly,

---

[102] At least in narrative terms. In that Josh. 8:30–35 sits in no clear chronological relationship to the text around it, it is not impossible that the ceremony happened at the same time as these events. However, this is not a necessary interpretation, and does not justify the radical textual surgery of Soggin (1972: 221) of moving it to this point in the book, since the narrative structure of the book needs to be respected.

Joshua speaks as a prophet and reaches back to the time of Terah, Abraham's father, noting that they were a people who once served other gods. Moreover, they were from 'across the river', a phrase that in Joshua always points to outsider status.[103] Yet, despite this, Yahweh called Abraham from this context of the worship of other gods and brought him through Canaan. At this point such a clear reference back to Genesis 12 – 25 is a relatively new thing for the book since apart from some allusions to Genesis 15 the main Pentateuchal allusions have been to Numbers and Deuteronomy. But the important point here is that Joshua goes back to Terah, before there was a definable people of God who would identify themselves with Abraham, to stress that Yahweh called someone from within a clearly polytheistic context. The point of this reference is that Abraham left such a context and served Yahweh, and Yahweh's purposes were then worked out through his descendants Isaac and Jacob. Yahweh's control over the nations is indicated by his gift of Seir to Esau (Josh. 24:4), whereas Jacob's family went to Egypt. This journey ended with the exodus.

Up to this point Joshua has distinguished between the experience of his audience and those who have gone before. But from this point he deliberately conflates the experience of the wilderness generation and those who stand before him, so that although Yahweh brought their ancestors out from Egypt, it was Joshua's audience who came to the Sea (Josh. 24:6). Historically, this is clearly not correct, because the wilderness generation died, but to focus on this is to miss the rhetorical point in this collapsing of generations through the balance of the historical recital. Those gathered at Shechem experience the benefits of these great acts of Yahweh and so, rhetorically at least, can be said to experience these events. But Joshua is also aware that this collapsing of generations is taking place so that the experience of his audience is joined with what has gone before. At one level this is a typical liturgical act, one picked up in more modern terms in the American spiritual 'Were You There When They Crucified My Lord?' But rhetorically it allows Joshua to join this people to events they have not experienced.

The reason for this approach becomes clear in Joshua's famous challenge to his audience that they choose the deity they will serve, though Joshua and his family will serve Yahweh. The reason this challenge is required is seen in the directive to worship Yahweh truly

---

[103] Hawk 2000: 269.

and faithfully, something that will be marked by the removal of the gods their ancestors had served across the river and in Egypt. Narratively, this statement comes as a surprise because there has been no reference to other gods before Joshua 23 apart from the oblique observation that 'Yahweh is God of gods' (Josh. 22:22).[104] Certainly, no one has previously been said to have worshipped any other deity, but if those gathered there have other gods they worship then they are already at risk in the light of the warnings of Joshua 23:14–16. The people's initial response suggests that the problem does not exist, denying that they will serve other gods, and even recounting their own story of how Yahweh acted (Josh. 24:16–18).

Despite the initial positive response, Joshua insists that they are unable to serve Yahweh because of his holiness, something that here points to his absolute claim on his people.[105] Joshua suggests that the people's actions are contrary to the reality of Yahweh's holiness. Returning to the theme of the gods the people have with them, there is an important shift in terminology, describing these as 'foreign gods' (*'ĕlōhê nēkār*, Josh. 24:20), and it is only from this point that the encounter can move towards a resolution as the people commit themselves to serve Yahweh. As a result, a covenant was made at Shechem, the details of which were apparently included as some form of appendix to the book of the Torah, while a stone at the sanctuary there was a continued witness to this commitment (cf. Josh. 22:34).

Given the absence of reference to foreign deities earlier in the book, we are bound to ask why such gods should be present. Considering the themes traced through the book to this point the answer must be because the Israel present at this event is not made up only of those who can claim to be ethnically Israelite. There are many Canaanites and others who have now become part of the people of God, and the act of forswearing the worship of any god to serve Yahweh alone is how Yahweh's great acts in history become theirs too. Within Joshua Israel is formed as a worshipping community, one that cannot be divided by either geography or ethnicity, and this covenant ceremony is how all can be included, without denying the threat other nations can pose when they oppose Yahweh's purposes. Yet even the closing burial reports show that God's purposes for his people can be worked out among the peoples (Josh. 24:32). Foreignness itself is not a

---

[104] This may simply be a superlative that points to Yahweh's incomparability (cf. ESVUK), but the grammatical form allows for the existence of other gods.
[105] Routledge 2008: 105–106.

problem – it becomes problematic only when it leads away from sincere and faithful worship of Yahweh.

Conclusions: Joshua as the formation of the people of God

Although Joshua has often been read as a problematic book because of its attitude to foreigners, the evidence covered here indicates that when read in terms of its particular witness and with attention to its own modes of narration, it is far more positive than this more dominant approach suggests. One cannot, of course, set aside the realities of war that we find within the book, but it is important to note that it gives far more attention to the inclusion of foreigners, especially Canaanites, than it does to their exclusion. When we read the book through and see Joshua 24 as an intentional climax to all that has come before, it becomes clear that the identity of Israel as a people going forward is of far more importance than the theme of war.[106] At the end of the book Israel can look forward with hope, not because of their ethnic purity but because they have understood that they act only against those peoples who oppose what Yahweh is doing. For others, as they commit themselves to Yahweh, there is the possibility of something richer. Within the book this possibility is demonstrated most clearly in two foreigners, Rahab and Caleb, and it is as Israelites follow their lead that they begin to enjoy the full blessing Yahweh intends. Nevertheless, the book also ends on a note of warning even as it commends Israel, observing that this Israel, a truly mixed community, served Yahweh all the days of Joshua and the elders who outlived him (Josh. 24:31). The inclusion of many foreigners to this point is not a problem, but the issue of loyalty to Yahweh will be. The implications of this observation will be worked out in Judges.

---

[106] Cf. Zehnder 2005: 490.

Chapter Three

The book of Judges: the people through whom Yahweh works

Initial orientation

A key theme running through Joshua was the fact that the people of God could not be reduced to something defined by ethnicity. Rather, God's people were those who either committed themselves to Yahweh, or at least chose not to oppose what Yahweh was doing. There is no doubt that Joshua regards the first option as the better choice, but it still allows for the other. But having established that Israel were primarily a faith community rather than an ethnic one, even if for much of the time they could be recognized on the basis of ethnicity, we are still left with an important question: Does Yahweh work equally through all? That is, are foreigners who have been integrated into Israel exceptions who have received a special dispensation not to be destroyed, or are they fully members of the people of God? Without leaving the issues of national identity that were important for Joshua, it is this second question that we begin to explore through the book of Judges.

There are, however, some important differences in the perspective on foreigners developed in Judges that reflect the very different context it assumes. Where Joshua recounts Israel's origins in Canaan and explores their implications, Judges now assumes that Israel is in the land. Accordingly, where Joshua begins with the land as something to be claimed from foreigners already in the land, Judges predominantly looks at Israel's interaction with foreigners from the perspective of their being peoples who are outside the land. This division is not absolute – the Philistines with whom Samson interacts (Judg. 13 – 16) are living on the coastal plain of land that Israel will not fully occupy in this period – but is still generally true. This means that Israel's interaction with these peoples reflects on different elements in the Torah, and, rather than Deuteronomy 7 and 20 being primary points of reflection, the statement of covenant blessing and curses in Deuteronomy 28 will be more prominent.[1] The reason for this is that much of Judges explores the implications of Israel's sin and therefore why they did not continue to enjoy the rest with which Joshua had concluded. In this setting Deuteronomy 28:25 is important because it indicates that a key curse for a disobedient Israel is being defeated by their enemies, whereas Deuteronomy 28:7 promised victory for an obedient people. So Judges spends much of its time exploring this issue, meaning that many foreigners encountered by Israel within the book are those who are there as part of Yahweh's punishment for Israel's sin (cf. Judg. 2:11–15). The Philistines are a people who are never expelled, while others are those who enter Israel's territory (on both sides of the Jordan) as an expression of Yahweh's disciplining Israel. One result of this is that Judges gives considerably less space than Joshua to the question of how foreigners are integrated into Israel as the people of God. However, given the main concerns of the book, this does not mean this issue is set aside. Rather, Judges largely takes the issues explored in Joshua as part of its point of departure in demonstrating that foreigners can be the key figures through whom Yahweh works.

Along with this, Judges continues to demonstrate another feature noted in Joshua, which is that a sinful Israel easily places itself in the same place as Canaanites. Indeed, it is notable that the issue of Canaanites who continue in the land is something that holds together both the book's introduction (Judg. 1:1 – 3:6)[2] and conclusion (Judg. 17 – 21).[3] There are, indeed, numerous issues that bind these parts of the book together around its central section (Judg. 3:7 – 16:31) in which the stories of the various deliverer figures traditionally called 'judges' are reported.[4] Wong[5] points to five major themes that bind

[1] Similarly, Martin 2008b: 96–101.

[2] With Lilley (1967: 96–97) it will be seen that although Judg. 1:1 – 2:5 is often treated as unrelated to Judg. 2:6 – 3:6, these sections are complementary, because the problem is not so much the continuation of Canaanites in the land, but rather of Canaanite religion. Theology, not ethnicity, remains the problem. Such an approach allows us to consider the whole of the introduction, rather than focusing on 2:11–19 as Gillmayr-Bucher (2009) does.

[3] On this as a generally agreed outline of the book, see Beldman 2017: 50–51 and Martin 2008b: 80–91.

[4] Apart from six occurrences of *šōpĕṭîm* (judges) in Judg. 2:16–19, which provides a summary of what follows, none of the judges is called a 'judge'. Normally, a verbal form is used to indicate that they 'judged Israel' for a designated period, the only variant being Deborah (Judg. 4:4), for whom a participle is used. Othniel (Judg. 3:9) and Ehud (Judg. 3:15) are called *môšîa'* (deliverer), but there is otherwise no standard term for them.

[5] Wong 2006: 29–46.

together the introduction and conclusion of the book,[6] demonstrating through this the value in reading the book as a distinct unit. This contrasts with the dominant view, where the book is read as part of the Deuteronomistic History, which has tended to result in the value of the introduction and conclusion being diminished. By contrast, the model proposed by Wong means that much more attention is given to Joshua since it is in the conclusion that the links to Joshua are strongest.[7] We should also note, as Oeste[8] has pointed out, that the breakdown in kinship seen in Judges' conclusion is in fact drawing together key elements developed through the book, again demonstrating the need to read it as an integrated text.

The links to Joshua in the introduction and conclusion are important. Judges 1:1 sets up the link to Joshua as crucial, its opening 'After the death of Joshua' (*wayyĕhî 'aḥărê môt yĕhōšua'*) exactly mirroring the opening of Joshua save for the change of name from Moses (Josh. 1:1). Given that Joshua also ended with the deaths of Joshua and his key colleagues (Josh. 24:29–33), it seems obvious that we are meant to read Judges in the light of Joshua, though it also quickly becomes clear that circumstances have changed. This is apparent in the opening enquiry made to Yahweh, asking who should go up and lead the battle against the Canaanites. Joshua had been clear that much of the land remained to be taken (Josh. 13:1–7), and even though all the land was allocated (Josh. 13 – 21; meaning the eastern tribes could return to their possession, Josh. 22), nothing was reported in Joshua to mean that the untaken land had been captured. Yahweh had granted rest from Israel's enemies all around (Josh. 21:43–45), but this does not mean that all the internal problems had been resolved; indeed, Joshua 23 – 24 is clear that many such problems remained. Within the introduction the second section (2:6 – 3:6) also begins with reference to Joshua, but this time to the book's conclusion. Chronologically, this reference must be earlier than that in Judges 1:1 since Joshua is still alive, but canonically it allows the two segments of the introduction to Judges to reference the whole of Joshua in its current form, even while demonstrating that circumstances have changed radically.[9] It may also have the additional function of demonstrating that the book as a whole is structured in

---

[6] These are the Jebusite threat, oracular consultations, related military action, diminishing national fortune, appropriately and inappropriately arranged marriages.

[7] Wong 2006: 27–28.

[8] Oeste 2011a.

[9] Cf. Butler 2009: lviii; Hamley 2019: 90.

a dischronologized manner so that key themes and motifs can be traced.[10]

The book's opening verse does more than simply provide a link to Joshua. The variations it introduces to Joshua's opening also enables the book to establish the main issues that will be explored through Judges: How will the generation that succeeds Joshua survive in the land, most obviously in their key relationships with Yahweh and with the remaining Canaanites?[11] This in turn links into the discussion of the various deliverers who will work in Israel since they become the means by which Yahweh's order is sustained in the land. Beyond this there are also numerous links between the Samson narrative (Judg. 13 – 16) and the book's conclusion, most obviously the fact that Samson's story reflects on the experience of the tribe of Dan while they were trying to settle on the coastal plain, whereas the conclusion opens with the story of how Dan ultimately migrated to the region north of the land (Judg. 17 – 18). The conclusion in turn is carefully tied together so that the story of Dan's migration is rooted in an account about a Levite from Bethlehem in Judah who sojourned in Ephraim (Judg. 17:7–8), whereas the tale of the rape and murder of the concubine and the subsequent civil war is rooted in the tale of a Levite from Ephraim who came to Bethlehem in Judah (Judg. 19:1–2). For all its diverse materials, Judges is intended to be read as an integrated text, one that deliberately uses the end of Joshua as its starting point while also signalling its key points of difference.[12] Building on this, a key goal of this chapter is to demonstrate that at least one key theme that can be traced across this book in an integrated manner is concern with foreigners, and in particular how it is that they can be the people through whom Yahweh works. Foreigners are not only 'others' through whom punishment is worked out (something widely recognized in Judges' scholarship), but those who are integrated into Israel can also be the ones through whom Yahweh brings deliverance for his people. In this respect, it is important to note the pattern noted in the previous chapter, where Israelites like Achan who act religiously as Canaanites will also be treated like them, again showing the importance of Israel as a faith community.

[10] Gunn (1974: 293) notes that this mode of narration is not unknown in the OT, but believes it is 'rarely successful', because chronological narration is normal. I would contend that the problem lies with the expectation of modern readers; because if this is a standard variation available within the poetics of OT narrative, then we need to learn how to work with it. For other examples, see Firth 2005c; 2007.

[11] Cf. Klein 1989: 23.

[12] Cf. Wong 2006: 74–77.

After Joshua: Judges 1:1 – 3:6

A league of tribes: Judges 1:1 – 2:5

As noted, the introduction to Judges contains two sections, each of which consciously places Judges into a dialogue with Joshua. The focus of the introduction is to direct readers to Joshua, even if the major function of these chapters is to demonstrate that things are not as they were in Joshua. Nevertheless, much remains that is the same as at the end of Joshua, most obviously the continued presence of Canaanites in the land. Yahweh granted rest to Israel in Joshua (Josh. 21:43–45), but it does not necessarily mean that Israel lives out the reality of that rest. Indeed, a key feature of the introduction is that it draws on the verb translated 'rest' (*nûah*) in Joshua and uses it instead in its related sense of 'leave' to refer to the nations who continued to remain in the land (Judg. 2:23; 3:1). There will be a form of rest in Judges, but not the rest that was achieved earlier. Rather, the threat to rest that Joshua had identified (Josh. 23) is now Israel's experience. It is the problem of the remaining Canaanites and Israel's response to them that is central to the book's introduction. Within this first section the focus is on Israel's increasingly unsuccessful military conquest, whereas the second focuses on their lack of covenant faithfulness.[13] Throughout Judges 1 the tribes are presented more or less as if they are a league table, with Judah topping the league as the most effective, with the others coming further down, and with Dan reported last because they are the least effective, and indeed are pushed back from their allotted territory (Judg. 1:34–35). Because this chapter has so many references to foreigners we will need to pay attention to it.

Read against the background of Joshua, there is an immediate shift in the introduction's first section. Here it is notable that rather than Yahweh's speaking and thus guiding Israel it is Israel who speak to Yahweh (Judg. 1:1). Although Yahweh's response to Israel's question about who should go up[14] first to battle against the Canaanites is brief, it offers the important reassurance to Judah (who are called to go first) that the land has indeed been given to them. The shift between the initial question and Yahweh's answer is important – Israel asks

[13] Olson 1998: 731.
[14] As in Webb (2012: 91–92), the verb *'ālâ* acts as a key structural marker for the first section, introducing the initial question and response (1:1–2) and then Judah and Simeon (Judg. 1:3), Joseph (Judg. 1:22) and finally Yahweh's messenger (Judg. 2:1).

about the Canaanites, but Yahweh speaks of the land. Commentators generally pass over this with little or no comment; but given the background in Joshua the distinction should be noted. Yahweh has given Israel the land, but the status of the peoples who remain in the land remains unresolved. This shift also sheds light on the oft-noted parallel with Judges 20:18, where Israel ask about who should go up first against Benjamin at Gibeah. In that instance there is no initial assurance of victory and it is only at the point of Israel's third enquiry that Yahweh promises to give over Benjamin (Judg. 20:28). Even so, there is a notable difference in that the verb there is future in its focus (yiq.), whereas here Yahweh uses a qatal to indicate that the land has already been given (which is consistent with Josh. 1:3).[15] In Judges 20 it is ultimately a people (Benjamin) Yahweh gives, whereas here it is the land. Nevertheless, although Yahweh has given the land, the balance of this section will show that many peoples remain, while also highlighting a point where Israel (specifically Judah and Simeon) is able to act effectively with some foreigners.

Although Yahweh had indicated that Judah should lead this process, before going up they invited Simeon to join them, something that reflects the tribal allotment for Simeon being within that of Judah because Judah's was too large (Josh. 19:1–9). It is also indicative of the fact that Israel were meant to function as a whole nation, whereas beyond this point the chapter reports on the actions of individual tribes, hinting already at a breakdown in the nation.[16] In the subsequent battle reports it is said that Yahweh gave over the Canaanites and Perizzites[17] to the Israelites (Judg. 1:4). This is consistent with our observations on the chapter's opening verses, because this assumes that these groups fought against the Israelite tribes. That is, where the indigenous people resist, Yahweh gives them and their territory over to Israel. Such a victory is particularly evident in the defeat of Adonibezek, where it is specifically stated 'and they fought against him' (*wayyillāḥămû bô*) as well as defeating those with him before catching him later (Judg. 1:5–6). Throughout the emphasis is on the thoroughgoing nature of the victory that Yahweh gives over peoples who oppose his purposes – in this instance his giving of the land to Israel. This is true even when the numbers opposing Israel are quite

---

[15] Boda (2012: 1070) notes that the verb could still be translated 'I am giving' and so reflect the performative nature of such verbs, but the key point remains.

[16] Cf. Oeste 2011a: 298.

[17] Webb (2012: 98) may well be right that we should read 'the Canaanites, that is, the Perizzites'.

large – and it is notable that the 10,000 Canaanites with Adoni-bezek are the only force mentioned. Even before the rest of the tribes are mentioned it is clear that Yahweh can defeat those ranged against Israel. Moreover, as the first Canaanite mentioned, Adoni-bezek is a clear contrast with Rahab because, rather than seeing what Yahweh is doing and working with Israel, he sets himself against Israel while demonstrating that he is also precisely the sort of Canaanite king that Yahweh showed himself opposed to in Joshua.[18]

Although not mentioned initially, the comments on Judah and Simeon are building towards mention of Jerusalem and its capture. Given that Judges 1:21 also reports on Benjamin's failure to expel the Jebusites from Jerusalem, we are probably not intended to see the capture and burning of the city as total, perhaps referring only to the southern slope that was allotted to Judah (Josh. 15:8). However we resolve this issue, the point is once again that Yahweh overcomes any people who oppose him, something also seen in the defeat of another southern coalition in the Negeb and Hebron (Judg. 1:9–10). Mention of Hebron's previous name (Kiriath-arba) alludes to Joshua 14:14 when the city became part of Caleb's inheritance, though Judges does not report this. The city's allocation to Caleb, as a means of noting the prominent role played by foreigners within Judah and Simeon, will be reported only in Judges 1:20.

In this context Judges 1:11–15 largely repeats the short land acquisition story from Joshua 15:13–19. This may be an independent story that each book incorporates into its narrative, though as noted previously its structure in Joshua suggests that it was originally joined to the Caleb story in Joshua 14:6–15. Here, however, the story is more tightly integrated into its context as Caleb offers his daughter in marriage to whoever captured Debir, though the shift from the plural reference to all Judah in verse 11 to the focus on Caleb alone is awkward. Nevertheless, if we understand him to stand *pars pro toto* for the whole tribe, then he continues to represent Judah, demonstrating the faith the whole tribe was to show in taking the land. Caleb's own background is not emphasized here, but it is immediately noted that Caleb's kinsman Othniel,[19] who does capture the city and

[18] For this reason, Wong's observations (2006: 204–206) on the contrast with Abimelech are also important, showing that Abimelech is in fact operating as a Canaanite king within Israel.

[19] The exact nature of their relationship is not clear and depending on how we read the Hebrew he could be either a younger brother or a nephew. The statement is absent from Joshua. Overall, 'nephew' is more likely.

so marries Achsah, is a 'son of Kenaz'. Unlike the references to Caleb in Joshua 14:6, 14, which used the related gentilic 'Kenizzite', the form in which Othniel is described here follows the normal designation of someone's ancestor. If Caleb was Othniel's uncle, then Kenaz in this instance could be the name of Caleb's younger brother, whereas if he was Caleb's younger brother then Kenaz would refer to a distant ancestor since Jephunneh would then be the father of both. However, whichever option we take, this would still seem to associate Othniel with either the Canaanite people mentioned in Genesis 15:19 or the descendant of Esau (and thus Edomites) mentioned in Genesis 36:11, 15 and 42. Although this family is clearly now a part of Israel, and Judah in particular, Judges seems to hint at Othniel's foreign heritage. This will become more important in Judges 3:7–11, where Othniel is the paradigm judge, much as Caleb was the paradigm figure for the land allocation in Joshua. Here his role is more limited, preparatory for Achsah's request for the springs near Debir, though of course in context she too is associated with a family whose foreign roots were apparently still recognizable.

If Othniel represents a (partially) integrated foreigner, then the report about the involvement of the Kenites in Judges 1:16–19 represents a much clearer statement about those who remained foreign and yet worked with Israel to achieve Yahweh's purposes. Just as Othniel will become a key figure for the stories of the judges themselves, so also mention of the Kenites here prepares for the pivotal role they will play in the story of Deborah and Sisera (Judg. 4 – 5).[20] Although there are uncertainties about aspects of the text here,[21] there is a clear reference to a people who are not themselves Israelite, but have a close relationship with Israel through Moses' father-in-law. Although the exact origins of the Kenites are obscure, they do have a close relationship with Israel, but as far as the text is concerned

[20] In 1 Sam. 15:6 Saul warned the Kenites to leave the region of Amalek because of their previous good relations.

[21] One would normally expect *qênî* to have the article, as is normal with a gentilic (GKC §127d), something that occurs in Judg. 4:11. This absence seems to have triggered a range of emendations in various Greek manuscripts (cf. Butler 2009: 6), but the lack of unanimity among them is an indicator that they are corrections of a difficult text and so should not be used as the basis for emendation. WO §7.2.2a seems to suggest that some gentilics may not have the article. I have not identified any examples apart from this verse, but if correct this would resolve the difficulty. Even if this is not followed, simply adding the missing article (as e.g. Lindars 1995: 35) is not appropriate since one would expect a Qere for this. The difficulty needs to be allowed to stand.

are nonetheless distinct from them.[22] That is why it can be said that they went up 'with' Judah. They are clearly distinct from the Israelites, and Judges makes clear that although they do contribute to Israel's ethnic mix, they are still foreign – that is, they can be traced through Moses' father-in-law, not Israel. The last part of Judges 1:16 is also obscure since the subject of the verb is unstated; but having introduced the Kenites, it seems that they are the ones who have now settled with the people. That is, they are foreigners whose status can be recognized. But most importantly they have not opposed Yahweh, and as a result can live with the people without difficulty.[23]

Within the report associated with Judah and Simeon (Judg. 1:3–20) considerable attention has thus been given to foreigners. In the case of Adoni-bezek readers are introduced to a Canaanite who represents the type of community Yahweh opposes, with later instances thus able to be noted in summary form (Judg. 1:17–18), even if this involved application of the ban. But both Othniel and the Kenites represent groups who, although now largely integrated into Judah, could still be recognized as foreign. Despite this, both are included in positive reports that demonstrate the possibilities that existed for Israel. Caleb's ethnicity is not a feature of Judges, but the book's evocation of the book of Joshua (even while drawing on other source materials) means that his background is not completely forgotten, and his mention in Judges 1:12 and 1:20 also functions to mark off the material that is particularly concerned with more positive presentation of foreigners, even as Judges 1:17–18 demonstrates the continued opposition from others already in the land whom Judah and Simeon needed to defeat.

Although Judah (with Simeon) clearly tops the tribal league table in terms of taking land, something emphasized by the note that Yahweh was with them,[24] they are not wholly successful. After the report of their successes, we are then told that they did not

---

[22] For this reason we do not consider debates about the precise relationship of the Kenites to Israel – from the perspective of the text, and thus Israelite construction of identity, they are non-Israelite, and hence foreign.

[23] As with Caleb, 1 Chr. 2:55 also incorporates the Kenites into Judah, reflecting their integration into Israel; but again it still leaves gaps which show that they are, in effect, adopted into Judah.

[24] The phrase anticipates something that will become a *Leitmotif* in David's story, which frequently notes Yahweh's presence with him (e.g. 1 Sam. 16:18). A member of Judah, this may be a subtle preparation for the question of kingship, which is raised in Judg. 17 – 21 and finds its focus in David.

dispossess[25] the inhabitants of the lowland because of the latter's iron chariots (Judg. 1:19),[26] something that is immediately contrasted with Caleb's success in driving out the Anakites. This initial statement of failure is striking, because to this point everything has pointed to Israel's success, even if a rereading of this chapter might note that the division of the nation into largely independent tribes is potentially problematic. Given Joshua's earlier success against chariots (Josh. 11:1–9), this note is even more striking. Indeed, readers are almost certainly meant to be taken by surprise, because even the short note about continuing Jebusites (Josh. 15:63) has not prepared us for this.

I would suggest that this is an intentionally jarring experience for readers, but not indicative of variant sources. Rather, the narrator reports this from Judah's perspective, but this is not yet the narrator's perspective, something that is disclosed only in Judges 2:1–5 when Yahweh's messenger speaks.[27] The exceptive statement surprises because nothing has prepared for it, but it in turn leads into an expanding list of statements about peoples who are not expelled. A key feature of this is the absence of any theological evaluation of the success or otherwise of the tribes save for the statement of Yahweh's presence with Judah and subsequently Joseph (Judg. 1:22). But this simply makes the contrast more striking: How can Israel fail if Yahweh is with them? The note in Judges 1:19 raises the important question of how this failure can happen, something pushed further as the other tribal reports are given. This is resolved only once the narrator's perspective is disclosed in Judges 2:1–5 through the speech by Yahweh's messenger; it is not that Yahweh has failed, but rather Israel has failed and the 'exceptions' turn out to be part of a wider pattern of failure.

The wider pattern of failure is then introduced in the report card for the balance of the tribal league, with successively reported tribes gradually less successful than the earlier ones. Judah and Simeon top

[25] The text is commonly emended to add the verb *yākĕlû*, following the LXX, thus making this a statement about what Israel could not do (e.g. Chisholm 2013: 129); but the text can be understood without this as a simple statement of exception by negating a gerundive (Butler 2009: 7).

[26] In Josh. 17:18 Joshua had told the Joseph tribes they could take additional land even though the residents had iron chariots; so this is another intentional contrast. Given that this passage is set in the late Bronze Age or early Iron Age, it is unlikely that the chariots would be made of iron (which would be too heavy anyway), and neither should we follow Drews (1989) in seeing this as a retrojection of Assyrian practice. More likely, some iron-tipped weaponry was carried. These chariots are a particular, but not undefeatable, problem in Judg. 4.

[27] Hamilton 2001: 106.

the league, but Benjamin are the runners up. As with Judah, no comment is made on the fact that they have not driven out the Jebusites, with the result that the Jebusites continue to live with Benjamin (Judg. 1:21). This statement is consistent with Joshua 15:63, except there it was Judah who had not driven out the Jebusites, but it does not indicate whether this was because the Jebusites were prepared to work with Israel or not.

The balance of the tribal league table continues to move north. As with Joshua 16 – 17, Joseph is initially presented as a single tribe, though reference to them in verse 35 also provides a boundary marker for the tribal league table. Like Judah, Joseph has an embedded narrative, this time dealing with some scouts the latter sent to Bethel, though only after the note that Yahweh was with them. As with Joshua 2, the sending of scouts is not necessarily problematic, and their offer to 'deal kindly' with the man they met there clearly echoes Rahab's statement to the scouts (Josh. 2:12). But whereas Rahab raises the issue because she has already acted for the scouts, here Joseph's scouts make this offer to the man to entice him to act for them. Although there is a clear parallel between Bethel's capture and that of Jericho, including the survival of a whole family, there is enough that is different here to raise questions. Further questions arise when we note that the replacement Luz he builds is in the land of the Hittites. Is this Anatolia, and thus well away from Israel? Or is it among the 'sons of Heth', the Hittites who apparently continued to live towards the coastal plain? By Judges 3:5 we know that Hittites were among the peoples who continued to live in the land. This embedded narrative does not resolve these questions, but the contrasts with Rahab may be troubling – and in any case we now know that a Canaanite family continues to live as Canaanites rather than integrating into Israel, and this is a problem.

Having first treated Joseph as a whole, its constituent tribes (Manasseh and Ephraim) then receive independent reports (Judg. 1:27–28). Although the order of these reports is the reverse of the equivalent passages in Joshua (Josh. 16:10; 17:12–13), they are clearly based on the earlier passages, though drawing in some wider allusions from their context. The more important change is that whereas Joshua reports that Manasseh 'could not' (*lō' yākēlû*) drive out the Canaanites, here it is simply said that they 'did not' drive them out, consistent with the approach of this chapter, where evaluative comments are held back until Judges 2:1–5. Exactly when these Canaanites were put to 'forced labour' (*mas*) is not said, though we are probably to imagine the period of the monarchy. Here Canaanites continue to survive, and this is potentially, but not necessarily, negative. The report for Zebulun (Judg. 1:30) is similar.

Asher (Judg. 1:31–32) were slightly less successful. Not only did they not drive out various Canaanites; it is now said that Asher lived among them. That is, where the report for Joseph and Zebulun indicates that Israel had the upper hand, the report for Asher suggests that the Canaanites were more powerful. The same is true for Naphtali (Judg. 1:33–34), so although they ultimately put the Canaanites from their area to forced labour, this was apparently not true in the period of Judges.

The bottom of the league is given to Dan (Judg. 1:34–35). Joshua 19:47 had indicated that Dan had not kept their allotted territory on the coastal plain but did not explain how this happened as the Amorites pressed them back to the hill country (from which Judges 17 – 18 will recount Dan's move to the far north). The Canaanites are here referred to by the more specific term 'Amorites', reflecting an interest in particular groups where necessary, though they were displaced from the coastal plain quite early by the Philistines. Dan's place at the end of the tribal league table shows them as the tribe that represents Israel's low point, and this matches the placement of the Samson story at the end of the gradual deterioration among the judges themselves (Judg. 13 – 16).[28] Rather than Israel's displacing Canaanites, or at least offering a new alternative to them, it was the Amorites who took control and lived in towns allotted to Dan (Josh. 19:40–48). Only the house of Joseph prevented the Amorites from expanding – a statement that may allude back to the reference to Yahweh's presence with them (Judg. 1:22).

Although Judges 1:35 might have provided a (narratively) satisfying conclusion to this chapter, one final note is appended, reporting the existence of a continued Amorite border. Although one might have expected this to cover the coastal plain, this note places them south of the Dead Sea, perhaps anticipating the emergence of the Philistines while also flagging a continued threat to Israel in the south, even as the reports on the northern tribes have shown the threat to both the north and the coastal plain. It is this threat that the balance of the book will resolve, with the reason made clear only in the speech of Yahweh's messenger at Bochim (Judg. 2:1–5). Here, in the brief report of the exodus and entry into the land, it is made clear that Yahweh

---

[28] Cf. Webb 2012: 126.

has been faithful.[29] But whereas Yahweh kept his covenant, Israel has not – they have made covenants with the inhabitants of the land and failed to tear down their worship centres. The continued existence of Canaanites was a potential problem, but the worship centres was a real problem. This makes clear that it is not the continued existence of the previous population that was the problem but rather the religious threat they posed. These peoples would be Yahweh's means of disciplining Israel, though the snare to Israel was their gods. The expulsion of the Canaanites could have happened, but it did not happen because of Israel's unfaithfulness. Nevertheless, by including positive notes on both Othniel and the Kenites, this opening section makes clear that foreigners themselves are not the issue. What matters is worship that draws Israel away from Yahweh, and it is the foreigners who do this who are the threat.

After the dismissal: Judges 2:6 – 3:6

After the more matter-of-fact reporting of the introduction's first section, this second section offers a more programmatic interpretation of Israel's circumstances.[30] Once again this section links itself to Joshua, this time to the dismissal of the tribes in Joshua 24:28, though Judges 2:6–10 also offers an abridgement of Joshua 24:29–33. Apart from this, the whole of this second section is marked by more directly evaluative comments rather than reports of specific actions. Hence Judges 2:11–15 outlines the pattern of behaviour that will be explored in the accounts of the judges themselves, though it is particularly noted that the problem is not so much the continued existence of the Canaanite groups but rather Israel's giving themselves over to the worship of other gods – in effect a reversal of the commitment made in Joshua 24:21 and thus demonstrating that Joshua's claim that they could not serve Yahweh was correct. Because of this worship of other gods Yahweh gave Israel into the power of enemies so that Israel could not succeed in battle. But it is also recognized that in their distress Yahweh would raise up judges who would save Israel from their plunderers. The longer reflection on the judges (Judg. 2:16–23) also notes that Israel's loyalty at any given point would only be transitory, leading to Yahweh's anger being kindled because of their breach of covenant, precisely the sort of thing Yahweh's messenger had implied (Judg. 2:1–2). The book of Joshua had ended with Joshua's death and

---

[29] Reference to 'the Gilgal' ties this passage to Josh. 4:19–24, and there are also significant references to Exod. 23:20–33 and 34:11–15 (cf. Block 1999: 110).

[30] Webb (2008: 119–120) points to an important shift in the mode of narration here.

many nations still in the land, and Yahweh would not continue to drive them out to test Israel. Note, however, that the problem is not the nations themselves. Rather, these foreign nations are to 'test' (*nsh*) Israel, to see if the latter will follow their ancestors (presumably Joshua's generation) and be faithful to Yahweh. Those nations are listed in Judges 3:1–6, a drawing together of those noted in Judges 1 as having continued, plus the Hivites and Philistines. Mention of the Hivites presumes Joshua 11:19, which had noted their continuation in the land, while the border report for the Amorites (Judg. 1:36) had prepared for mention of the Philistines. These foreigners are Yahweh's means for testing Israel and for educating the latter about war. However, the concluding note (Judg. 3:6) prepares us for a less than positive experience as it notes that Israel intermarried with these peoples, something Joshua had warned against (Josh. 23:12–13). His concern there was that this practice would lead to the worship of other gods, and it is indeed this that Israel did.

The stories of the judges: Judges 3:7 – 16:31

Many of the book's main themes have already been hinted at in the introduction, but it falls to the stories of the various judges to develop them. There is a close parallel between the presentation of the tribal league in Judges 1 and of the judges themselves in that the gradual deterioration of the tribes is matched by the deterioration of Israel's success in the stories of the judges. The first section of the introduction thus establishes key themes, including noting the foreigners who will be significant for the judges themselves, particularly Othniel and the Kenites. The second section of the introduction has also presented the theological framework through which to read these events, demonstrating that the hostile nations Israel encounters act because of Israel's sin, particularly the gradual breakdown of the kinship structures that exist within the nation.[31] Through this these deliverer stories also exemplify another key theme from Joshua, where an Israel that becomes indistinguishable from Canaanites and their social and religious structures ceases to be the people of God in any meaningful way. Although not as pronounced as in Joshua, there is still a counternarrative to this, whereby foreigners who may have no historical claim to being part of Israel can do so because of their commitment to Yahweh. The stories of the judges also demonstrate

---

[31] Oeste 2011a: 300–309.

that the delivers do not have to be ethnically Israelite, and that Yahweh can and will work through foreigners.

Othniel: Judges 3:7–11

In many ways Othniel functions both to conclude the theological reflection in the introduction (Judg. 2:6 – 3:6) and introduce the rest of the stories of the judges. The reason for this can be noted when we note the unique aspects of his presentation, the most obvious of which is that his passage may be more accurately described as a report than as a story.[32] This is because his account simply states the key facts about his work as a judge, establishing what will be a key structure for the remaining major judges,[33] even if each of them deviates from it to some extent. In this case it is the absence of the features typically associated with storytelling that is important, because this enables Othniel's report to focus on the key themes established by the introduction while also bringing the relationship between the judges and the Spirit of God into focus. Indeed, mention of the Spirit is particularly important for understanding Othniel. In so doing, it also distinguishes him from the judges who follow who are not as successful as him, and whose experience of the Spirit will be comparatively problematic.[34] Within such a compressed report focus on the Spirit and continued allusion to Othniel's foreign heritage are key elements.

Othniel's account thus functions in two almost paradoxical ways. First, it is a paradigm for the judges who follow, even as they gradually deviate from him and so are less successful. But second, whereas the stories of the other major judges are also intended to entertain to some extent,[35] Othniel's does not. He is thus precisely what a judge

[32] Cf. Webb 2008: 127. Frolov (2013: 102) thinks it is inconceivable that it ever existed apart from its literary context. As an observation on written form this is probably correct, but it does not mean that there was no previous tradition about Othniel.

[33] Traditionally, the label 'major judge' is given to a judge for whom some account of delivery is provided, whereas a 'minor judge' is someone for whom this is not provided. Othniel's account is so brief that he stands in between these divisions. It should be stressed that these labels are about the literary presentation of these figures and involve no historical assessment (see Hauser 1975). Nelson (2007) believes that the formulaic language in their presentation means there is no necessary historical reality behind them, but this seems to presume that one rules out the other, though, as noted above for Othniel, this is not necessarily the case. Nevertheless, with Nelson (2007) and Finkelstein (2017), and apart from Shamgar, the evidence suggests that these reports originated in the north.

[34] McCann 2002: 43.

[35] Olson 1998: 763.

should be, but also what no other judge is. That he fulfils the key requirements for a judge is apparent from the fact that all the key terms from Judges 2:11–23 recur in his report, both in terms of Israel's actions and what Yahweh does through Othniel. As Webb comments, he is the 'embodiment of an institution'.[36]

The elements of the report can be seen as a drawing together of the previous statements, and indeed it follows the structure of the previous passage. These can be seen easily in tabular form (see Table 1).[37]

Table 1: Othniel as the paradigm judge

Judges 2:11–23	Judges 3:7–11
The people of Israel did evil in the eyes of Yahweh (2:11)	The people of Israel did evil in the eyes of Yahweh (3:7)
They served the Baals and Ashtaroth (2:13)	They served the Baals and Ashtaroth (3:7)
Yahweh's anger was kindled . . . and he sold them into the hand of . . . (2:14)	Yahweh's anger was kindled, and he sold them into the hand of . . . (3:8)
Then Yahweh raised up judges who saved them (2:16)	Yahweh raised up a deliverer for the Israelites and he saved them (3:9)
Yahweh was with the judge . . . (2:18)	The Spirit of Yahweh was upon him . . . (3:10)

Othniel's report is thus full of formulaic elements, but although these have often been the focus of previous studies, the differences should also be noted, because in a text that adheres so closely to a template, the variations stand out with particular clarity.[38] Two are of especial importance (that Israel 'forgot' [škḥ] Yahweh [Judg. 3:7] adds an element not previously noted), one unique to Othniel. Although the worship of other gods will be a key element in all that follows, forgetting Yahweh is not. The problem for much of the book is thus syncretism: the attempt to fuse the worship of Yahweh with that of other deities. This is made explicit in the Jephthah story (Judg. 10:6) but is evident in the stories of the other judges. But here forgetting Yahweh goes beyond what happens elsewhere in Judges.[39] There is a

---

[36] Webb 2008: 127.

[37] Adapted from Butler 2009: 69.

[38] On this as an important pattern in Judges, see Chisholm 2009.

[39] A similar statement occurs in 1 Sam. 12:9 as Samuel reflects on the period of the judges, though without mentioning Othniel, but in that case it is probably a telescoping of the whole period.

degree of severity in Israel's evil here that exceeds what happens elsewhere.

The other important variation is the statement that the Spirit came upon Othniel (Judg. 3:10). This is clearly related to the note about Yahweh's presence with the judges (Judg. 2:18), but is also a variation on it. Yahweh's presence has been noted previously (Judg. 1:19, 22), but no form has been given to it. Here, however, that presence is expressed through the coming of the 'Spirit' (*rûaḥ*). As Martin has argued,[40] the presence of the Spirit is a sign of Yahweh's dynamic presence with the judge, though the form of that presence certainly varies, and in any case not all judges are marked by a special endowment of the Spirit (neither Ehud nor Deborah is noted as having any experience of the Spirit). In Othniel's case it is notable that, consistent with his whole report, this statement is as colourless as possible, simply stating that the Spirit 'came upon him' (*wattĕhî 'ālāyw*), something that contrasts with the other judges who were 'clothed' with[41] or 'rushed' upon by the Spirit.[42] Samson also seems to have been 'troubled' by the Spirit (Judg. 13:25).[43] Only Jephthah's experience of the Spirit seems to match that of Othniel (Judg. 11:29), and there may well be reasons within Jephthah's narrative why this more limited expression is used.

But why introduce such a dynamic element (albeit in a restricted way) in a report that otherwise goes out of its way to offer a statement on Othniel that says as little as possible? The answer seems to be that marking a leader with the Spirit is a means of testifying to people who will not otherwise recognize that person as a leader through whom Yahweh intends to work. This feature is clear in the cases of Gideon, Jephthah and Samson, as each would otherwise seem an odd choice to lead Israel. Ehud (Judg. 3:12–30) has no experience of the Spirit, but his leadership is recognized after he assassinates Eglon; while Deborah (Judg. 4 – 5) is established as a prophetess (Judg. 4:4) before being noted as a judge. In their cases, therefore, there was already evidence that the people could see of Yahweh's presence before they became military deliverers.[44] But according to Judges 1:13, Othniel was already known as a military leader, having captured

---

[40] Martin 2008a.
[41] Gideon, Judg. 6:34.
[42] Samson, Judg. 14:6, 19; 15:14.
[43] Cf. Firth 2011: 275; 2014: 17.
[44] Though, as we will see, Deborah's case is more complex because she directs others rather than being directly the one through whom deliverance comes.

Kiriath-sepher. Why would he be the only judge with previous evidence of leadership to be noted as having an endowment of the Spirit?[45]

It is not possible to answer this question absolutely, but within the narrative framework two possibilities suggest themselves, neither of which rules out the other. First, his exploits in Judges 1:13 were in the far south of Judah, but for him to engage in battle with Cushan-Rishathaim in Aram would mean he would need to have led the nation in the far north. Given that one of Judges' key themes is the gradual breakdown of Israel's kinship structures, such a movement to the north is certainly possible. Othniel was previously known in the south, but the people of the north would not have known about him. In this case Spirit endowment becomes a mechanism for demonstrating to the northern tribes that Othniel was someone through whom Yahweh would work, a testimony that was needed because they had no experience of their own of him as a military leader. The other is that Othniel's foreign descent, again noted by calling him 'son of Kenaz' (Judg. 3:9, 11), could mean that Israel would not have regarded him as a potential national leader – he might well have captured a city in the far south, but this did not mean he would be recognized as one through whom Yahweh would bring deliverance. It is perhaps unnecessary to choose between these elements as they both draw on elements highlighted in the book's introduction. If so, then the judge through whom Yahweh brings deliverance from the most marked failure on Israel's part is a foreigner. Israel might not have recognized him as a potential deliverer, but Yahweh did.

Shamgar and Abdon: Judges 3:31; 12:13–15

Interspersed with the stories of the major judges are brief reports of the minor judges,[46] figures who can be said either to have 'delivered' or

---

[45] It is, of course, possible that the events in Judg. 1:12–15 are chronologically later than those of 3:7–11. As we have noted, the book is not presented within a strict chronological form. But within the narrative form of the book, introducing readers to the events at Kiriath-sepher before Othniel acts as a judge means that they would not need to know about his Spirit endowment. Moreover, because the events at Kiriath-sepher are very early in Israel's emergence in the land, perhaps only five years after Joshua crossed the Jordan (cf. Josh. 14:10), it is much more likely that events here are much later.

[46] Klein (1989: 103) notes that Yahweh's activity is never mentioned for the minor judges, and that this points to a weakening of the bond between Yahweh and the people. Although not impossible, these reports are so brief and matter of fact that it is difficult to make a case for what is missing save for those points where the minor judges' reports vary among themselves.

'judged' Israel. Although six minor judges are noted, Shamgar (Judg. 3:31), Tola and Jair (Judg. 10:1–4), Ibzan, Elon and Abdon (Judg. 12:8–13),[47] our concern is only with Shamgar and Abdon since they both seem to have some association with foreigners; though the limited information provided about the minor judges means that there is uncertainty here.

Shamgar is important as the first of the minor judges,[48] though his report is even briefer than those of the other minor judges, confined to a single verse which notes that he killed 600[49] Philistines with an ox goad and saved Israel.[50] This account is so compressed that it omits even stating that he was a judge, though his placement at this point in the book indicates that we are to read him that way. That his actions were against the Philistines would place his work towards the south and the coastal plain, though of course the Philistines do also enter the hills. The note, however, stands out against the report of Dan's inability to take that territory (Judg. 1:34–35) since the Philistines rather than the Amorites are the adversaries here; Shamgar is presumably from later in this period, though not terribly late since Deborah's song (Judg. 5:6) looks back on him.

In such a compressed report the presence of key details stands out, and the most obvious here is that the name Shamgar is not Israelite, being based on four root letters, not three as would be typical for an Israelite name.[51] Block[52] believes that the name is probably Hurrian. Perhaps more surprising is that he is called 'son of Anath'. Although the 'son of' form often indicates someone's patronym, that is not the case here since this is most likely a feminine term. The name 'Anath' refers to a Canaanite goddess associated with Baal, meaning that in

---

[47] According to Noth (1981: 70–71), Jephthah was a minor judge brought into the major judges. Although the traditions on which Judges draws are not themselves consistent, probably representing a range of sources, this conclusion reads more into the minor–major division than seems warranted.

[48] Lindars (1995: 156), drawing on G. F. Moore (1903: 104–106), believes this note may originally have belonged after 16:31. Even if this were so, and the evidence is not strong, the final shape of the book has incorporated Shamgar into Ehud's story (which technically ends only at 4:1).

[49] As with Joshua, there may be some hyperbole here, and such a brief note would not rule out Shamgar's commanding a group, but certainty here is not possible.

[50] Lindars (1995: 162–163) notes several textual issues here, but as none of these bear on our theme they are not considered here.

[51] Soggin (1987: 57–58) however proposes that it could be derived from a shaphel of the root *mgr*, which is known in at least one Canaanite name, but this view has not found widespread support. Even if correct, it would still mean Shamgar was a foreigner.

[52] Block 1999: 173.

this case Shamgar is someone devoted to Anath.[53] By the period of the judges Anath's fame had also reached Egypt, so it is not possible to be certain about Shamgar's ethnicity save for the fact that he was almost certainly not Israelite. But the more remarkable thing here is that he was apparently not even a Yahwist, and one of the main concerns of the book of Judges is to show the dangers Israel faces when they are associated with other gods. This may also explain the fact that Shamgar is said to have saved Israel, but unlike the other minor judges no statement is made about his judging Israel. Yahweh, it seems, has no problem in using a foreigner to deliver Israel even as he has also used foreigners to punish Israel, but he does not grant them positions of leadership.

Like Shamgar, the last of the minor judges, Abdon[54] the son of Hillel, also has some association with foreigners, though to a lesser extent. Abdon himself is an Israelite, which is why it can be said that he 'judged' Israel, though (as with many of the minor judges) he seems to have had some royal pretension if the note about his forty sons and thirty grandsons and their seventy donkeys is anything to go by – in this he continues a pattern that emerges in the minor judges in the note about Jair the Gileadite (Judg. 10:4) and Ibzan of Bethlehem[55] and that echoes part of the closing note about Gideon (Judg. 8:29–32). Especially in the light of Abimelech's story, notes about so many sons, who require multiple wives, most probably implies some degree of criticism.[56] Otherwise, attention is given to his own descent from the otherwise unknown Hillel, and that he was a Pirathonite, something usually understood to mean that he came from the town of Pirathon, near to Shechem, since this is said to be where he was buried.[57] This is broadly consistent with the statement that it was in the land of Ephraim, because although its most probable site (modern Farata) about 6 miles (9.6 km) south-west of Shechem would more probably seem to be part of Manasseh, Joshua 16:9 already attests to some flexibility about the exact border points.

---

[53] M. J. Evans (2017: 72) wants to locate him at Beth Anath in Naphtali, but this would be an awkward way of expressing this and would also leave him in the wrong area for the work attributed to him.

[54] Jacobson (1992; 1994) has wanted to equate Abdon with the otherwise unknown judge Bedan (1 Sam. 12:11), but Day's (1993) criticism of the case is impressive.

[55] If the minor judges in Judg. 10:1–5 and 12:8–15 are northern figures, this would be the town in Zebulun (Josh. 19:15), not the well-known town in Judah.

[56] Cf. Webb 2012: 345.

[57] Also the home of one of David's elite warriors (2 Sam. 23:30).

The more curious note is the statement that Pirathon was also in the 'hill country of the Amalekites' (Judg. 12:15). In that Amalekites are more typically associated with the south, in the region of the Negeb, mention of them this far north is unusual. It could mean that they had at some point exerted influence further north than normal, perhaps during the time of Gideon,[58] but the note is not interested in providing this information. What it does indicate, however, is that Israel continued to live with foreigners, and that even though this area was apparently influenced (and perhaps controlled) by foreigners, Abdon was still able to act as judge here.

Deborah and Barak, Jael and Sisera: Judges 4 – 5

Foreigners tend to play increasingly stereotyped roles in the remaining stories of the major judges – they are the people through whom Yahweh brings about Israel's punishment because of their unfaithfulness to Yahweh, just as Judges 2:14 indicated. Nevertheless, Judges 1:11–16 reported successful interaction with foreigners – the Kenizzite family of Caleb and the Kenites. Othniel's presentation as the paradigm for the major judges explored this further within the stories of the major judges, while the relationship with the Kenites is an important motif in the story of Deborah's time as judge (Judg. 4 – 5). Hence the two positive references to interaction with foreigners in Judges 1 are taken up in the first two stories of the major judges. Although this account poses some complex issues for interpretation, not least the relationship between its prose (Judg. 4) and poetic (Judg. 5) forms, only those that bear directly on the issue of foreigners are attended to here.[59]

The story begins with the standard formula in the narrative frame that sets the scene. Once again Israel has done what was evil, though in this case it is specifically after Ehud's death (Judg. 4:1).[60] Apart from the integration of Abimelech's story into that of Gideon, this is the only instance of a story opening with reference to the death of the previously narrated judge. In this case it may explain the presence

[58] Block 1999: 390.

[59] For a helpful summary of approaches to Judg. 4, see Neef 1989: 28–31.

[60] Structurally, I follow Neef's divisions for Judg. 4 (1989: 48), where vv. 1–3 and 23–24 form the narrative frame around three main sections – the war between Israel and Canaanites (vv. 4–9), Deborah and Barak (vv. 10–16) and Jael and Sisera (vv. 17–22). This is more helpful than that of Amit (1987: 90) since her opening frame does not allow for the spatial shift in v. 4. However, this still needs to be integrated into the parallel form in Judg. 5, for which Brenner's literary model (1990) is the most helpful.

of Kenites further to the north than we have previously encountered them (Judg. 1:16). As is usual in the introduction, the oppressor into whose power Yahweh has sold Israel is introduced, in this case Jabin.[61] Notably, in the narrative frame (Judg. 4:1–3, 23–24) he is called 'king of Canaan' four times, whereas in the body of the story he is 'king of Hazor' (Judg. 4:17). Given the power of Hazor noted in Joshua 11:1–9, a king there would have been particularly powerful; though given that Joshua had destroyed Hazor, mention of the city here serves to highlight the area of his reign within Canaan rather than tie him to a particular city. Nevertheless, use of the label 'Canaan' is important because it suggests that there is more than just one group opposing Israel – this is pressure placed upon the whole of the north of the country (note that the tribes of Zebulun and Naphtali are particularly involved in this narrative). That Jabin has a functional role is indicated by the fact that within the battle he largely falls into the background, with the focus instead being on his general, Sisera, who is thus also introduced here.[62]

Although often referred to as the Deborah story, the narrative structure makes clear that she is introduced as part of the background to the story.[63] As with the introductory statements in the narrative frame, the focus is on Israel since they are the subject of the verb (Judg. 4:5). That they came up to Deborah for judgment may therefore refer not so much to judicial concerns but rather that she should lead the nation in its military need against Jabin and his iron chariots.[64] This would be consistent with the other judges, though given that within the narrative it is not Deborah who does this, it would also explain why it is never said that 'she judged' Israel. Rather than leading Israel directly into battle, Deborah instead summons Barak to gather 10,000 men from Zebulun and Naphtali to nearby Mount Tabor with the promise that Yahweh will draw Jabin's army, and specifically his chariots, to the river Kishon, where he will hand them

---

[61] Another Jabin was king of Hazor in the time of Joshua (Josh. 11:1–9). Since the name means 'insightful' it is plausible that this was a dynastic name.

[62] Webb 2008: 133.

[63] Van Wolde 1995: 240–241.

[64] Yee (1993: 111) argues that because military structures in pre-state Israel were largely domestic, this gave more space for women to serve as military leaders. Järlemyr (2016: 50–51) is more cautious about determining potential roles for women in this time. Bal (1992: 52) suggests that she is the only judge known for doing more than killing enemies, though this assumes that Deborah's actions to this point do not include military action, and overlooks many of the other actions of the various judges.

over to Barak.[65] Where Ehud largely determined his own strategy against Eglon, this time Yahweh (through Deborah) outlines the arrangements for battle while also promising victory. Despite this (and introducing a fear motif that will become more pronounced in the Gideon story), Barak asserts that he will go only if Deborah comes with him. In response, Deborah declares that although she will go with him, the victory over Jabin will be achieved by a woman. Deborah promised Barak that he, like Othniel, would win a victory, but instead Barak pulls back from this. Considering the story to this point, we might expect that Deborah will win the battle, but if so this is an expectation that the story is about to subvert.[66]

Within the central section of the narrative (Judg. 4:10–16) there are in fact several points of narrative subversion. At first, it seems to be straightforward as Barak summons his men, though only to Kedesh,[67] his home town, rather than to Mount Tabor. But Deborah is with him, so the story can proceed according to expectation. But in Judges 4:11 we are suddenly introduced to Heber the Kenite, though quite what a Kenite is doing in Naphtali rather than the southern wilderness is never made clear. In more standard Old Testament narrative patterns, the introduction of a character like this would signal his importance for what follows,[68] but this in turn only makes his absence from the ensuing battle more surprising. We are, however, told that he has separated himself from the other Kenites, even if no reason for this is provided. Only after this surprising introduction of an unexpected foreigner does the narrative return to Deborah and Barak, who now move to Tabor, with Sisera taking his troops to Kishon. As is common with battle accounts, the story around the battle is more complex than the battle report itself; so Barak's victory over Sisera's powerful forces (including chariotry) following Deborah's encouragement can be reported briefly. Yahweh does indeed give Sisera over to Barak, though the text is clear that it was Yahweh who routed Sisera and all his chariots and army before Barak. Barak pursued the army to Harosheth-hagoyim, with no one surviving – except for Sisera, who seems to have gone away from the rest of his forces. At one level we might believe this is the

[65] Given that Deborah herself was active in the central highlands (Judg. 4:4–5) rather than the far north could suggest that she believed it was a matter for local tribes, and this could provide a subtle reference to the tribal breakdown in Judges.

[66] McCann 2002: 53.

[67] Presumably a short form for 'Kedesh-Naphtali'.

[68] Chisholm 2009: 175–176.

comprehensive victory that was promised, but knowing that Sisera has escaped undermines this possibility.

With his army destroyed, the narrative follows Sisera, and in so doing introduces a new character – Heber's wife, Jael. A further piece of additional information is now provided – there was 'peace' (*šālôm*) between the houses of Heber and Jabin. Jael's own ethnicity is never indicated, but she was clearly integrated within a Kenite family and so would have been regarded as a Kenite. Sisera would therefore approach her as a potential ally, though if so he goes about it in a strange way, subverting the expectations of hospitality since the normal protocol would be to go to the man (Heber) first.[69] Rather, in a camp that would have included some warriors, Sisera goes to Jael's tent 'on foot' – a phrase that can also mean 'secretly' and is often associated with spies. Given that he reaches Jael's tent, we have to assume a degree of secrecy because the normal expectation was not that he would go to a woman's tent – though at the same time the rather ribald reflection of his mother in the Song of Deborah (Judg. 5:30) suggests that she expected him to rape several women as a spoil of victory; so in another way perhaps this is what one might expect of Sisera.[70] But it is not customary behaviour.

The balance of the interaction between Jael and Sisera continues to subvert expectations – Jael's initial invitation could be a double entendre, but if so it is a strategy to draw in Sisera. Certainly, he exceeds the expectations of hospitality by asking both for provisions and that she should lie on his behalf. Throughout, Jael is shown to be a shrewd woman who understands how to manage Sisera from a position of physical weakness, ultimately ensuring that he sleeps, but not with her, before driving a tent peg through his head and killing him.[71] Like Rahab, Jael makes a decision to work with Israel, not their enemies,[72] and it is through her that the victory is ultimately won. Only after Sisera's death does Barak reappear in the story, and then only to see Sisera's corpse. Barak has not gained the glory of the victory that God has won, a victory that according to the closing frame of the prose narrative ultimately leads to Israel's destroying

---

[69] On this and other social values in this story, see Matthews and Benjamin 1993: 87–95.

[70] Of course, the mother in the song is a literary creation of Deborah and Barak, but the implication of this verse is that they believe he was a potential rapist, something consistent with his coming to Heber's camp secretly.

[71] The verb *tq'* (Judg. 4:21) here echoes the use of the same verb when Ehud murdered Eglon (Judg. 3:20–22). On parallels between these accounts, see Webb 2012: 185–186.

[72] See ibid. 193.

Jabin. That glory has gone to a foreign woman who has thrown her lot in with Israel against her husband's allies.

That Yahweh wins battles for Israel through foreigners and not merely through Israelites is of pivotal importance in the opening accounts of the judges, and this feature comes to focus in the Song of Deborah (and Barak, though I will use the song's traditional title) of Judges 5. The song is justly famous, though textually very difficult at several points. It also raises issues not addressed in the prose account, though since they do not affect our main issue they are not addressed here. However, what can be noted is that the song makes a point of celebrating foreigners as figures through whom Yahweh brings victory for his people through its linking of Shamgar and Jael. The two initially appear together (Judg. 5:6), and since Shamgar appears nowhere else in the song that is otherwise concerned with the events just examined this is most likely a key to the song's interpretation. Admittedly, in this initial reference the concern is with the unsettled conditions of their times but, given that victory ultimately came through both, this is simply setting the scene. Although Deborah speaks of the 'people of Yahweh' (Judg. 5:13) as engaging with Sisera, the song comes to a focus in verses 24–27 when Jael comes to the fore. Here Deborah recounts the events of Judges 4:17–22, but with the opening declaration that Jael should be 'the most blessed of women' (Judg. 5:24), while still noting that she is the wife of Heber the Kenite. Her foreignness is thus crucial, and this and her blessedness are given as the key elements through which to interpret her actions. And although the observations of Sisera's mother are then reported (Judg. 5:29–30), the concluding observation of the song (Judg. 5:31) surely looks back to the section on Jael and Sisera as it expresses the wish that Yahweh's enemies perish like him, while his friends (who now include Jael) may be like the sun as it rises in its might. Just as Deborah indicated, the glory of the victory over Sisera does go to a woman, but it is not to an Israelite woman. Jael, a foreign woman, has abandoned the political commitments of her husband to fight for Israel, and in so doing has become the most blessed of women.

Gideon, Abimelech, Jephthah and Samson: Judges 6 – 16

The stories of the remaining major judges, and the minor ones woven into this section of the book, focus much less on stories of foreigners apart from two key repeating motifs. First, there are foreign nations into whose power Yahweh sells Israel because of their sin, thus continuing the pattern announced earlier (Judg. 2:14). Second, individual foreigners are encountered (particularly in the Samson story) who, because their commitment is not to Yahweh or Israel, are part of the process of Israel's falling into sin. Nevertheless, within both the Gideon and Samson stories these foreigners can also be Yahweh's means for achieving his purposes for Israel. Although it is not made explicit, there is also an emerging pattern in which Israel's life comes to mimic Canaanite patterns, and hence echoes the earlier story of Achan (Josh. 7), and in so doing prepares for this to be a more explicit motif in Judges 17 – 21. This latter element begins to emerge in the Gideon story and becomes clearer in the Abimelech and Jephthah stories. It is less evident in the Samson story, though this is perhaps because of the greater focus on Samson's interaction with the Philistines, who were not regarded as Canaanites.

Foreign powers and Israel
Throughout this section of the book the pattern announced in Judges 2:14 is worked out consistently, though not without variations that are important. The Gideon story is closest to the pattern, opening with the statement that Israel has done evil so that Yahweh gave them into the power of Midian, who then oppressed Israel for seven years (Judg. 6:1). In the balance of the Gideon story, the Midianites are linked with other wilderness groups (Judg. 6:33), meaning that subsequent references to Midian (e.g. Judg. 7:1, 23) are probably meant to be a shorthand for all the foreign groups. Israel's own emerging disunity is worked into this in the presentation of Ephraim (Judg. 7:24 – 8:3), and the unwillingness of some to support Gideon in his pursuit of Midian (Judg. 8:4–21).

By contrast the Abimelech story (Judg. 9) is notable for the lack of foreign enemies, since in this case parts of Israel become enemies to each other. This is partly because the Abimelech story follows directly from the Gideon story, and the absence of foreign powers could be the 'rest' of which Judges 8:28 speaks. Nevertheless, although an epilogue to the Gideon story, the Abimelech story also needs to be understood as a story of its own,[73] a continuation of the downward spiral already noted in the end of the Gideon story (Judg. 8:29–33).[74] In this story when Israel acts like Canaanites, there is no need for an external adversary.

[73] Oeste 2011b: 55–57.
[74] Hence Endris (2008) can also offer a narrative-critical reading of the whole Gideon–Abimelech complex.

Before the Jephthah story two minor judges (Tola and Jair) are noted (Judg. 10:1–5). There are no references to foreigners in these reports. However, in the Jephthah story the pattern announced in Judges 2:14 is reintroduced (Judg. 10:6), though with some important variations that are included in the longer introduction to this story.[75] These focus more on Israel's internal problems and Yahweh's resultant unwillingness to raise up a deliverer, and thus show an important link to the Abimelech story. Within this story there is the unusual combination of Ammonite and Philistine oppression (Judg. 10:7), a combination that is unexpected in that the Ammonites were east of Israel whereas the Philistines were to the west, on the coastal plain. These two oppressors were already named in the previous verse in the list of the foreign gods Israel served. The Philistines, however, play no further role in this story, but are the main foreign nation in the Samson story instead, so that Judges 13:1 essentially picks up on the note here. The note about the nations here serves as an introduction to both the Jephthah and Samson stories.[76] In both, the internal conflicts within Israel also continue to develop (Judg. 12:1–6; 15:9–13), demonstrating an inappropriate ability to treat one another as foreigners.

Foreigners and Yahweh's purposes
Along with the more stereotypical references to foreigners, both the Gideon and Samson stories also continue to develop the motif of foreigners as figures through whom Yahweh works. Although Jephthah also interacts with the Ammonite leadership as he attempts to negotiate with them, they remain within the standard presentation of foreign oppressors; the surprise in this case is that Jephthah attempts to negotiate rather than lead Israel in a military campaign. But for Gideon and Samson key foreigners become a mechanism for evaluating Israelites, anticipating a technique that is developed more thoroughly in Samuel.

A key feature of the Gideon story is his initial unwillingness to take on a leadership role, something that already seems implied by his encounter with Yahweh's messenger, a story that seems deeply ironic in its presentation of Gideon as a 'mighty warrior' (*gibbôr ḥayil*, Judg. 6:12) while he threshed wheat in a wine press and hid from the Midianites. This motif runs through his initial attempt to avoid taking

---

[75] Cf. Webb 2008: 41–43.
[76] Webb 2012: 302.

up the role in his discussion with the messenger (Judg. 6:13–24), and is then developed in his taking some of his servants when he pulled down his father's Baal altar, along with the Asherah beside it, at night because of his fear of his family and the residents of the town. Even after he was clothed with the Spirit of Yahweh (Judg. 6:34) and had summoned his clan to join him, the incident of the fleece is reported as his means of seeking proof that Yahweh intended to save Israel through him (Judg. 6:36–40), thus demonstrating Gideon's fear.[77] In the light of this, Yahweh's declaration that Gideon has too many men with him because of the risk of Israel's believing that they will win the victory through their own power comes as a surprise. Nevertheless, Yahweh establishes a process by which Gideon's forces are hacked back to only 300 men (Judg. 7:1–8). Yahweh then directs Gideon to go down to the Midianite camp, with the proviso that he can take his servant Purah if he is afraid, but with the additional note that Gideon will 'hear what they say, and afterwards strengthen your hand and go down against the camp' (Judg. 7:11). Despite the massive Midianite camp (Judg. 7:12), Gideon hears a Midianite man recounting a dream that his companion interprets as evidence that God has given Midian over to Gideon's power. It is this that convinces Gideon that Yahweh has indeed given the Midianites over to him – rather than the earlier signs that Yahweh performed, it is ultimately some Midianites who unwittingly convince Gideon of his task. Of course, in doing so they simply do as Yahweh indicated, but here again in Judges Yahweh works through foreigners, even if only to convince Israelites of their role.

This surprising development is taken further in the Samson story in his various encounters with Philistines. As with Gideon, his story also has an encounter with Yahweh's messenger at the start and offerings involving the messenger (Judg. 13). There is also the intriguing relationship he has with the Spirit, a motif that becomes more pronounced in Samson's story.[78] Samson's relationships with foreigners are, however, strikingly different from those of Gideon in that he never seems to lack a reason to enter a fight, irrespective of the odds. But in each of Judges 14, 15 and 16 there is an encounter with the Philistines that provides some evaluation of Samson, each of which in its own way is unexpected.

---

[77] Scherer (2005) argues that because this was a genuine act by Gideon, we should not interpret him as a flawed hero. But this seems to confuse sincerity with legitimacy.
[78] See Merrill 2011.

In the first of these Samson is said to have gone to Timnah, a town on the coastal plain originally allotted to Dan (Josh. 19:43). Although it would ultimately belong to Judah,[79] at this point it was controlled by the Philistines. It was there he saw a Philistine woman he wished to marry, something he asked his parents to arrange. Although they clearly did not support this, being concerned that he wanted to marry into the 'uncircumcised Philistines' (Judg. 14:3), the narrator overrides any reader's concerns by noting that it 'was from Yahweh', who was seeking a means of working against the Philistines.[80] Although the subsequent wedding goes badly wrong from Samson's perspective after the exchange of riddles following Samson's slaying of the lion, the point where the Spirit rushes upon Samson (Judg. 14:19) becomes the point where he acts against the Philistines. The story also introduces the motif of Samson's inability to resist the pleas from women with whom he is involved (Judg. 14:15–18), but this too is a mechanism by which Yahweh acts against the Philistines. In that the events of Judges 15 follow directly on from this, here too the various elements contribute to Yahweh's actions against the Philistines. However, there is also a degree to which this chapter has its own events in which the Philistines' choices continue to be Yahweh's means of acting against them, though Samson's setting fire to the standing grain and olive orchards (Judg. 15:5) certainly counts as provocation. But this time there is the additional element of the men of Judah's fear of resisting the Philistines. Curiously enough, it is their willingness to submit to the Philistines that provided Samson with his famous opportunity to kill 1,000 Philistines with an ass's jawbone as the Philistines' desire to capture Samson led to their own destruction.

The motifs developed in Judges 14 – 15 come to their climax in Judges 16. Here we again see Samson's inability to resist a woman's pleas, but where the account of his wife mentioned three days of failure to discover his riddle before succeeding on the fourth while only recounting the final plea, this time there are three unsuccessful pleas from Delilah (Judg. 16:1–14) before a successful fourth plea leads to Samson's capture and shave (Judg. 16:15–22). From a Philistine perspective, this seems like a great success, and it is notable that there is no repeat of the statement of Judges 14:4. Only the short statement of Judges 16:22 (that his hair begins to grow again) leads to any expectation of hope. This hope emerges in an unexpected

---

[79] Josh. 15:10 puts it on their border.
[80] This is a common way of integrating human decisions with Yahweh's purposes; see Carson 1981: 11.

setting when the Philistines hold a feast to Dagon to celebrate Samson's capture, where, in response to Samson's prayer[81] to avenge himself on his enemies,[82] he is enabled to bring Dagon's house down, killing more in his death than in his life. The Philistines have made numerous decisions, as did the Midianites with Gideon, but those decisions all ultimately lead to Yahweh's purposes for Israel being fulfilled. None of these stories show Israelites in a good light, but Yahweh achieves his purposes even among a deeply flawed people.

Israelites becoming Canaanites

A third motif running through these chapters is the way in which Israelites act as Canaanites, and thus move away from Yahweh's purposes for his people. This motif is present in both the Gideon and Samson stories, but comes to a point of focus in the Abimelech and Jephthah stories.[83] Even in redemption these stories show that Canaanite life, and in particular their worship and social structures, continued to hamper Israel. Although Judges 1 – 5 has shown that Yahweh could work for Israel through foreigners, it does not mean that Israel was to lose their distinctiveness. Because the act of turning away from Yahweh that leads to Israel's domination by a foreign power has been treated above, it will not be considered again here.

In the Gideon story there is the interesting variation in his name – until Judges 6:32, he is always 'Gideon', and with thirty-nine occurrences this remains the dominant way of naming him. But after Judges 6:32 the alternative name Jerubbaal (let Baal contend) is introduced, occurring a further four times in the balance of the Gideon story proper, before becoming standard in the Abimelech story. Within Gideon's story the name is explained by the response of Gideon's father, Joash, to his townsfolk after Gideon has torn down the Baal altar. The story at this point is something of a surprise, because although the story has already established the reality of the worship of other gods in Israel at this point (Judg. 6:10), prior to the first mention of the altar (Judg. 6:25) there has been no mention

---

[81] This is the first point in the story where he addresses God as 'Yahweh'.

[82] Paynter (2018) reads this act in Girardian terms, but despite her many insights it is not clear that Samson brings an end to violence through his act, since in his case, as with Jephthah, there is no statement of rest for the land.

[83] It is possible that reference to Ibzan's (Judg. 12:8–10) giving his daughters in marriage 'outside' and likewise bringing in wives for his sons from 'outside' (*haḥûṣ*) could refer to non-Israelite marriage and thus contribute to this theme (so Way 2018: 281), but the term is not specific and so could refer to actions outside the clan rather than Israel as a whole.

of Baal. Now, however, we discover that Gideon's own family are active in Baal worship. Hence at the heart of the Gideon–Abimelech complex is the larger conflict between Yahweh and Baal.[84] With the destruction of the altar (and the Asherah beside it), and the subsequent defeat of the Midianites (Judg. 7), it could seem this issue was resolved. However, internal conflicts within Israel are flagged up in the account about Oreb and Zeeb (Judg. 8:1–21) before they are killed by Gideon. Although their deaths seem to conclude the account, the brief note about Gideon's taking spoil from Oreb and Zeeb (Judg. 8:21) prepares for the note that everyone has taken spoil from the Ishmaelites (who are here identified with the Midianites) that Gideon used as the basis for his construction of an 'ephod' after which Israel whored.[85] Exactly what this ephod was is unknown; though since an ephod was usually a priestly vestment associated with seeking the will of God, this was presumably its intended function even if it quickly became an object of worship in its own right, a distortion of worship that associated priestly access to God with a ruler.[86] Making this ephod also anticipates Micah's ephod (Judg. 17:5), creating a link between these stories.[87] Gideon's first positive act was to destroy a Baal altar, but his final act created a pattern of worship that was equally flawed, and on his death it can be said that Israel 'whored' (*znh*) after the Baals (Judg. 8:33). Israel in the Gideon story have an ability to turn to Baal that judges on their own cannot overcome.

Linked to this pattern of worship was a desire for a royal structure, a pattern apparently modelled on the Canaanites. This was already hinted at in the Gideon story as the Israelites asked him to rule over them, establishing a dynasty, based on his victory over Midian (Judg. 8:22). Although the pattern requested here is dynastic, it is not necessarily royal since the verb used, 'rule' (*mšl*), does not have royal associations. Within the Abimelech story, though, the royal elements that were implicit in the request to Gideon are developed into royalty.[88] So, although he starts with the language of 'rule' (*mšl*) rather than 'reign' (*mlk*), he very quickly becomes king at Shechem (Judg. 9:6). Language of kingship then runs through Jotham's fable, even as he mocks Abimelech's pretensions. Moreover, the conflict with

[84] Endris 2008: 175.

[85] *znh*, Judg. 8:27.

[86] Cf. Ortlund 1996: 42–45. However, a ruler could be associated with an ephod (2 Sam. 6:14), so care must be taken not to overinterpret the details here.

[87] Wong 2006: 83–89; Boda 2012: 1166.

[88] See Heffelfinger 2009 for why the expectation of dynasty continued after Gideon refused it.

Baal is evident in wordplays that run through the narrative as his approach to the 'lords' of Shechem refers to them by the title *ba'al* (Judg. 9:2). We cannot trace the whole of this story here, but it is clear that the model of kingship that Abimelech sought was precisely the sort of stratified model that Deuteronomy 17:14–20 had resisted and that Joshua 10:1 – 11:9 had shown Yahweh particularly opposed. Kingship will recur as a theme in 1 Samuel 1 – 12, but the model there needs to be distinctively Yahwistic. In the Abimelech story, Canaanite worship and social practice come together to demonstrate what happens to an Israel that loses its distinctiveness, both religiously and socially. This in turn anticipates the reasons for Yahweh's rejection of Israel in Judges 10:13, 16 while preparing for the same problems on a larger scale in Judges 17 – 21.[89]

The Jephthah story demonstrates a range of variations from the other accounts of the major judges, but the most distinctive of these is clearly the report of the sacrifice of his daughter (Judg. 11:29–40), though arguably from the perspective of the narrative this is only a step towards the death of 42,000 Ephraimites because of their inability to pronounce 'Shibboleth' in the Gileadite way (Judg. 12:1–6). Jephthah might have granted rest to the land for six years (Judg. 12:7), but it required an inordinate amount of unnecessary bloodshed.[90] Much of this can, in fact, be traced to the pattern of negotiation and manipulation that runs through the earlier part of the story, including discussion of rulership (Judg. 10:17 – 11:7). As Webb argues, this is a story about accommodating religion to political norms, and as a result Israel's faith is debased.[91] The internecine conflict with which the story ends (Judg. 12:1–6) is thus the result of this, and there is no clearer example of it than the sacrifice of his daughter. This is particularly so if Jephthah's vow (Judg. 11:31) intended the sacrifice of a human and not an animal. In that animals are never said to go out to greet a human in the Bible, it seems most likely that he did indeed intend to sacrifice a human,[92] even if the text leaves enough initial ambiguity that readers might hope that an animal was intended. Jephthah's attempt to dictate Yahweh's actions,[93] something that might have been acceptable in Canaanite worship, has

---

[89] Endris 2008: 189. Way (2018: 276) also notes that the reports of Tola and Jair (Judg. 10:1–5) extend these themes through their emphasis on dynasty.

[90] Similarly, Baker 2018: 50.

[91] Webb 2008: 74.

[92] See Marcus 1986: 13–18. Gunn (2005: 134) notes that Hebrew does not distinguish between 'whoever' and 'whatever', but this does not attend to the whole construction.

[93] So Sjöberg 2006: 61.

brought him nothing but sorrow. His sorrow after this is not reported; only that he did indeed sacrifice his daughter, demonstrating his own conformity to Canaanite practice.[94]

The association with Canaanite practice and religion can also be seen in the Samson story, and not only because Samson seems almost to go out of his way to break the perpetual Nazirite status announced by Yahweh's messenger (Judg. 13:5). Even his moments of delivering Israel demonstrate this, as for example his eating of the honey from the corpse of the lion he has killed (Judg. 14:8–9) means taking the honey from something unclean. The same is true with his famous use of the donkey's jawbone (Judg. 15:15–17). Although not a breach of his Nazirite status (Num. 6:1–21), he is also noted as having gone to a prostitute in Gaza (Judg. 16:1), something clearly contrary to Israelite law. Although this creates an echo of the Rahab story (Josh. 2), this time there is no help from the prostitute when the locals come for him (Judg. 16:1–3). His Nazirite vow also comes into focus in his encounter with Delilah (Judg. 16:4–22), ending with his disclosure that his strength came from his uncut hair and then subsequent capture by the Philistines after Yahweh left him without his being aware of this.[95] Even his approach to God in calling on him to meet his desires, rather than honouring him, seems closer to Canaanite models (Judg. 15:18–20; 16:28).

In all, each of the major judge stories in this part of Judges demonstrates some degree of conforming to Canaanite life and practice. Although this is clearest in the Abimelech and Jephthah stories, it is also present in the stories of Gideon and Samson. Despite this tendency towards conformity with Canaanites, Yahweh continued to work through these figures, bringing deliverance for Israel through them. This motif emerges most clearly after stories where Yahweh brought deliverance through foreigners. None of these judges matches Othniel, an Israelite with foreign heritage, whose success and experience of the Spirit is unblemished. Although these judges show a pattern of moving towards being Canaanite, they have not fully crossed that line. But that line will be crossed in the conclusion to

---

[94] There is an interpretative tradition which suggests that his daughter was not sacrificed but rather dedicated to virginity. But this is difficult to reconcile with the statement that he 'did as he had vowed' (Judg. 11:39), given that the only vow was to sacrifice someone.

[95] Admittedly, the text never reports his drinking alcohol, though his presence at feasts (Judg. 14:10–20) strongly suggests that he broke this element of his Nazirite status too.

Judges, where the shadow of Achan is most notable, and Israel treats its own people as foreigners with all the grief that this brings.

When there was no king: Judges 17 – 21

Although Judges 17 – 21 has long been treated as an appendix to the book with little real connection to the rest, it is increasingly being recognized that these chapters form an intentional conclusion to the book, with links both to the introduction (Judg. 1:1 – 3:6) and to the stories of the judges themselves (Judg. 3:7 – 16:31).[96] As should be apparent from the discussion to this point, these chapters are here read as an intentional conclusion to the book, with elements that particularly address the issue of foreigners who were noted in Judges 1, and the pattern of Israel's gradually adopting Canaanite life is particularly important for our purposes. Through this it will be seen that the figure of Achan lies in the background. In forming a conclusion to the book, these chapters also introduce the theme of 'no king in Israel' as their *Leitmotif* (Judg. 17:6; 18:1; 19:1; 21:25). The dangers of the wrong sort of king have already been noted (Judg. 9). Now the dangers of no king, best understood through the frame of the kingship of Yahweh, come to the fore in the two stories that make up this conclusion in a carefully integrated manner.[97]

Micah and his idol: Judges 17 – 18

This story has many links to earlier parts of the book and continues to develop the motif of the breakdown of the family unit within Israel.[98] More particularly for our purposes it also develops issues concerned with foreigners, where Israelites gradually become Canaanites through idolatry, matching the earlier statement in Judges 2:6 – 3:6.[99] There are also clear links to the Samson story through the relationship to the tribe of Dan and their ultimate migration to the north (cf. Judg. 1:34), but also through the catchphrase of 1,100 pieces of silver as the reward offered to Delilah (Judg. 16:5) and the same sum stolen by Micah and that he eventually made into an idol (Judg. 17:1–5), preparing for the first occurrence of the theme statement

---

[96] On the move to this approach to reading the book, see Beldman 2017: 10–51; Hamley 2019: 90–101. This can be contrasted with the older approach, exemplified by Soggin (1987: 261), who describes these chapters as an 'appendix on various themes'.
[97] On the narrative relationships in these stories, see Satterthwaite 1994.
[98] N. Hays 2018.
[99] Martin 2008b: 90.

about the absence of a king (Judg. 17:6). This link seems to have been important since he used only 200 pieces to make his idol.

This story starts in the middle, as it were, of the account of Micah's theft from his mother (Judg. 17:1–3), the theft itself being of no interest. Rather, what matters is that Micah's mother declared on the return of the money that it was consecrated to Yahweh to make an image. This language is immediately troubling since Israel were prohibited from doing this (Exod. 20:4), though Micah goes on to make an ephod and teraphim[100] as well as ordaining one of his sons. None of this is consistent with how Israel are meant to live and becomes the first example of everyone doing what is right in their own eyes (Judg. 17:5–6). That this is an Israel living contrary to the purposes of Yahweh becomes clear as a Levite from Bethlehem is introduced. Journeying through the hill country of Ephraim, he stays with Micah and is invited to become his priest in return for clothing, lodging and ten pieces of silver a year. The Levite becomes like one of his sons, and not only because Micah also ordained him (Judg. 17:11–12). Micah's self-assured comment that he has a guaranteed blessing from Yahweh (and thus not the curse his mother announced) is thus presented as pure irony in Judges 17:13, because the one thing that is clear from this is that this is an Israel who are living out of the context Yahweh established.

Although Judges 17 has its own narrative form, in reality it sets the scene for the migration of Dan to the north that is reported in Judges 18, a story that points to Israel's fragmentation as civil war is narrowly avoided when Micah realizes he cannot overcome a whole tribe. That we move into the main part of the story here is perhaps why the theme statement is mentioned again in Judges 18:1. The chapter links itself back to Judges 1:34 because that verse has said only that Dan was driven back from their allotted territory but does not report what else took place. It is that which is recounted here as they spy out the land – though this is the land Yahweh has already allocated to other tribes. The spies in Joshua 2 were incompetent, but at least they went to a valid location. The spies in Joshua 7 are competent but fail to include Yahweh. These spies, however, do not spy out territory to which Dan can have any claim, having left the coastal plain (where Zorah and Eshtaol are) and reached Ephraim. There they encounter the Levite in Micah's house, where they ask for an oracle from God

---

[100] Often rendered 'household gods', but the term can also be emblematic for rejection of Yahweh (1 Sam. 15:23).

and receive the assurance that their journey is before Yahweh (Judg. 18:1–6). However, the value of this oracle is dubious – not only because this is not a valid priest[101] but also because the oracle itself is fundamentally ambiguous. Although the Levite sends them on in peace, to say that their journey is before Yahweh does not necessarily mean that it is approved – it can equally be in judgment. Moreover, the territory they reach at Laish lies outside the boundaries of the land as allotted. Although the spies therefore report that God has given it into Dan's hand (Judg. 18:10), nothing in the text suggests that this is God's perspective.

That this is a tribe living outside the patterns Israel are to follow is made clear in Dan's subsequent dealings with Micah: taking by force his ephod, teraphim and cast image along with his Levite (Judg. 18:11–26). Violence is threatened, and Israel disintegrates as Dan claims the very things Micah was previously sure would ensure blessing from Yahweh. This violence escalates when Dan captures Laish, which they rename 'Dan', even though this is a quiet and unsuspecting people. Unlike Israel earlier in the book, the people of Laish have no deliverer. The tribe of Dan has become like Canaanites, exercising violence, and establishing a pattern of worship that sustains this (Judg. 18:27–31).

The rape of the concubine and Benjaminite war: Judges 19 – 21

The pattern of Israel's becoming Canaanite in Judges 17 – 18 is developed further in Judges 19 – 21. Whereas this transformation is only alluded to in Judges 17 – 18, these chapters still move in this direction while continuing to interact with the previous narrative. That this story is linked to the previous one is clear from the repeat of the theme statement (Judg. 19:1) as well as the motif of an anonymous Levite,[102] though this time the Levite has travelled from the hill country of Ephraim to Bethlehem rather than the other way around as in the previous story. However, from the outset it is also clear that this story has its own allusions as well as unique elements, most notably the importance of his concubine. Apart from Judges 8:31, which mentioned that a concubine was Abimelech's mother, no other concubine is mentioned in Judges, though perhaps that one other mention should warn readers to link these stories because of their shared

---

[101] Bauer 2000: 39.

[102] In much of the story he is just 'the man', but for consistency here will always be called 'the Levite'.

interest in kingship and concubines. In this case the Levite has travelled to bring his concubine back after she has in some way been unfaithful to him.[103] There he stays with his father-in-law, someone who offers him seemingly excessive hospitality while he attempts to convince the woman to return with him. This, however, establishes a contrast with later events in the story.

Having eventually left his father-in-law late in the day, he travels with his concubine, a servant and some donkeys, arriving at nearby Jebus. The use of the previous name ties this story back to Judges 1:21, which noted the continued residence of the Jebusites in Benjamin. Although his servant encourages him to stay with the Jebusites, the Levite refuses, stating that he will not stay in a 'foreign' (*nokrî*) city, with people who are not Israelite. Instead, he proposes going on to Gibeah. The Levite thus represents those who identify Israel only in terms of blood kinship, not even granting the Jebusites the status of resident aliens. But his rejection of Jebus will turn out to be deeply ironic, because his experience in Gibeah is told in a way that is deliberately evocative of Genesis 19.[104] Just as with the Sodom story, this chapter presents an inverted world in which hospitality is tied to sexual abuse through the threat of homosexual rape. Nothing could show more clearly that this is an Israel that is living out the Canaanite patterns Israel was meant to reject. The Levite's rejection of Jebus as a possible place to stay looks from this point like a poor decision, because they could hardly have done worse than Gibeah. But neither are the Levite's choices in Gibeah defensible since he seized his concubine and gave her to the mob who raped her all night (Judg. 19:22–26). In the morning the Levite found her at the door, with her hands at the threshold. It is not clear if she was dead at this point, but having taken her home on his donkey, he then divided her into twelve pieces with a knife and sent her to each tribe, summoning them to respond (Judg. 19:27–30).

The result of this is reported in Judges 20 as all Israel gather 'as one' before Yahweh in Mizpah, where the Levite responds to a request to explain how this evil happened with an attenuated report, one that carefully avoids any mention of his own role in events while stressing

---

[103] There is a textual tradition, represented in the LXX and some Hebrew MSS, that she was angry rather than unfaithful in some way, requiring only a change of the verb from *znh* to *znḥ*. But Hamley (2015) has demonstrated the superiority of the MT at this point on both internal and external grounds. The concubine is dreadfully wronged within the narrative, but this does not require her to be innocent.

[104] Klein (1989: 165) regards Gibeah as a Levitical city, and thus a place where he would expect hospitality, but in this she seems to confuse Gibeah with Gibeon.

the infamous behaviour of Gibeah, before asking for the nation to give an opinion (Judg. 20:1–7). They respond by agreeing to go up against it by lot with an army made up of one Israelite in ten to repay Benjamin for the 'outrage' (*nĕbālâ*) they have committed (Judg. 20:10). In their response the Israelites echo the Levite's own words, convicting Gibeah without hearing an alternative account. But although 'all Israel' is said to have come to Mizpah (Judg. 20:1), it becomes clear that this is hyperbole. Benjamin is apparently not represented since messengers need to be sent to them, asking for Gibeah to be handed over, something the Benjaminites refuse. Immediately, therefore, a schism has opened up within Israel, within which it is possible to speak of 'all Israel' while excluding Benjamin. There are clear echoes here of Joshua 22, where a similar strategy was employed through the use of geographic boundaries; but where warfare there was prevented, this time civil war results. The echoes of Joshua 22 at this point are important because of the links that story makes to the earlier story of Achan, and those links are also developed in the subsequent story of the battle here.[105] These are most obvious in the clear parallels that exist between the battle for Gibeah and the earlier battle for Ai (Josh. 8:1–29), with this story seeming to echo elements there, most obviously the initial failures in battle, the use of an ambush when the defenders are drawn out of the city and the signal given to the ambushers. But there is also the additional note about the ministry of Phinehas (Judg. 20:28), a note that is otherwise unnecessary save for the fact that it creates a link back to the last time he was mentioned in the Bible in Joshua 22. All of these intertextual elements are important for the interpretation of the story in which Benjamin is treated like Achan and denied the status of being part of Israel. In effect, they have become an expression of Canaan, just as Achan was.

Unlike Achan's family there were 600 survivors from Benjamin, and Judges 21 then focuses on how Israel sought to get around another vow made at Mizpah, that no one would give their daughter in marriage to Benjamin, as they lament the absence of one tribe in the nation, conveniently setting aside their own role in bringing this about. Clearly, if the Benjaminites could not marry, then the rest of the tribe would die out completely. The resolution is twofold – first, they must identify a town that did not come up to Mizpah, agreeing they will be put to death, even though there is no reason for this.

---

[105] This use of irony makes the diachronic analysis of Hentschel and Nießen (2008: 29) unnecessary. For a careful reading of the passage as a whole, see Satterthwaite 1992.

When the town of Jabesh-gilead is revealed to have been absent, a force of 12,000 is sent to kill everyone other than female virgins. But in doing so, the command to them extends beyond even the original plan, as these people are placed under the ban – something that only Yahweh can initiate, and that was restricted in Deuteronomy 7 and 20 to the Canaanites.[106] But now, at Israel's own initiative, a town that has done nothing wrong is treated not only as foreign, but as Canaanite. Even this appalling process did not yield enough brides and led to a second process whereby virgins dancing at a festival in Shiloh[107] would be kidnapped and forced into marriage. The possibility of taking a wife by capture is noted in Deuteronomy 22:28–29, though it is hardly regarded as a positive outcome, and may not be the best background here. Rather, because the verb *ḥtp* means 'to capture',[108] and this practice emerges from the laying of an ambush, a more likely background is to be found in Deuteronomy 21:10–14, which allows for a woman captured in war to become the wife of an Israelite man. In Deuteronomy the enemies involved are clearly foreign, and as such the women in Shiloh (though innocent of the events around them) are effectively treated as if they are foreign so that Israel may find a way around its vow. The closing note of the book, which repeats the full form of the theme statement, thus draws this episode to a close along with the book as a whole. There was no king in Israel, in part because Israel could not determine who or what Israel was.

Conclusions on Judges: the people through whom Yahweh works

Reading Judges as a whole shows that the theme of foreigners is important. In doing so, it becomes clear that Judges is extending the issues developed in Joshua, where the leading question was about the identity of Israel as the people of God. Judges reports on a period in Israel where Israel's relationship with foreigners, especially those still

---

[106] Deut. 13:12–18 does allow for this possibility for an Israelite city, but only when that town has encouraged the worship of other gods (and thus denied their status as Israelites). But that condition does not apply here.

[107] The nature of this festival is unclear, though reference to vineyards (Judg. 21:20–21) may suggest Tabernacles. However, 1 Sam. 1 indicates that there might have been other festivals celebrated at Shiloh, and this one does not have to be one of those required by the Torah.

[108] Judg. 21:21. This is the only time the verb occurs, but the cognate noun in Prov. 23:28 (also its only use) refers to the strange woman treating her victims as prey.

in the land, was complex because of their continued existence and the fact that Israel had not yet reached a point of total control. Foreigners could be those through whom Yahweh disciplined Israel, but foreigners (or at least those with a recognizable foreign heritage) could also be the ones through whom Yahweh wrought deliverance for the people. But beyond this Judges also raises more profound questions about the identity of Israel as the people of God. This is done by progressively showing Israel's becoming more like Canaanites as the book proceeds, so that by the time we reach chapters 17–21 Israel cannot even understand their own identity. Where Joshua 22 showed resistance to the division of the nation, Judges 17 – 21 shows Israel's dividing itself, treating each other as foreign, even as foreigners who lived among them showed a better alternative than did Israel themselves. This poses questions about how Israel can function as the people of God, and how they can be recognized. It is this that is taken up in the books of Samuel.

Chapter Four

The books of Samuel: foreigners as the means of assessing Israel

Initial orientation

Although Samuel in the English Bible immediately follows Ruth, in the Hebrew Bible it follows Judges. Because Ruth explores the inclusion of one foreigner (Ruth herself, becoming an ancestress for David), it demonstrates an interest in our larger theme.[1] Nevertheless, for two closely related reasons, it is not treated here. First, it is not technically part of the Former Prophets, and therefore falls outside the boundaries set for this study. Second, and perhaps more importantly, it is better interpreted as an early canonical reflection on the very issues with which we are concerned in this study as a whole.[2] That is, Ruth is best understood as an early witness to the interest in the place of foreigners that is explored across at least Judges and Samuel (links to Joshua and Kings are less pronounced) rather than as a key link between Judges and Samuel. This does not make its placement in our English Bibles inappropriate; after all, the book consciously places itself in the days of the judges (Ruth 1:1); but it does result in the book being read as a part of that body of text rather than as an early reception of it. When Ruth is read as an early reception of Judges–Samuel we see that it serves to confirm the main line of the reading developed here.

Samuel should therefore be read in the light of Judges, though there are important elements that also refer back to Joshua. This is because Samuel extends issues already established in Joshua and Judges – that

---

[1] It is notable that Mann (2011: 94–106) chooses to include Ruth even though he is discussing the Former Prophets. As well as Ruth herself, attention is also given to another prominent foreigner, Tamar (from Gen. 38), in the blessing the women of Bethlehem place upon Ruth (Ruth 4:12).

[2] See McKeown (2015: 79–85) on reading Ruth within the theological horizons of Judges and Samuel.

foreigners can become part of Israel (with Israelites excluded) and that they can be important figures through whom Yahweh works. Samuel does not need to establish these points, and so its presentation of foreigners is largely concerned with those who are now in Israel. Where Joshua established the possibility of foreigners forming part of Israel, and Judges demonstrated Yahweh could work deliverance for Israel through them, Samuel uses foreigners as a means of evaluating Israelites. That is, foreigners are present throughout Samuel, but their primary function is to help readers evaluate Israelites. So one mechanism by which Saul and David (the main human characters in Samuel) are assessed is through the foreigners with whom they interact. Given the book's overall focus on David as Yahweh's chosen king, it is not surprising that the company Saul keeps reflects badly on him. That is, the foreigners with whom Saul associates (such as Doeg the Edomite) reflect negatively on him. What is perhaps surprising is that David is frequently contrasted with foreigners (such as Uriah the Hittite), so that we see his flaws more clearly through them. David may well be the chosen king, but he is deeply flawed, and the comparative faithfulness of the foreigners around David often makes this clear.

The focus on Saul and David, Israel's first two kings, holds Samuel together.[3] The focus on kingship provides a natural link to the closing chapters of Judges. The meaning of that refrain is debated, but we need not be detained by that here because whether this was an argument for kingship or an expression of exasperation that Yahweh's kingship was not properly recognized, it is clear that Samuel recounts the rise of kingship in Israel. In these books we reach the point where it can no longer be said that there was no king in Israel. The existence of that kingship will prove to be something of a mixed blessing, but as becomes particularly clear in the covenant made with David (2 Sam. 7),[4] kingship is something with which Yahweh is prepared to work, though it is also the case that much of Samuel is given over to the process of reframing what kingship is to be within Israel.[5]

The importance of kingship as a key theme for the book is perhaps not entirely obvious at its beginning. Here it directs readers' attention

---

[3] Although English Bibles follow the tradition of dividing Samuel into two books, this represents a matter of convenience for scroll length rather than an essential division of the material. It is notable that the Masoretes provide their summary notes for these books as a single entity rather than as two distinct works.

[4] For why this chapter needs to be seen as a covenant, see Firth 2005b. For a helpful discussion of this covenant overall, see P. R. Williamson 2007: 120–145.

[5] See Firth 2017a: 58–60.

to a man named Elkanah and the family problems he faces as he journeys each year to the sanctuary at Shiloh along with his two wives, Hannah and Peninnah (1 Sam. 1). Elkanah will be a fairly minor character even in this story, with more attention given to his wife Hannah and the high priest, Eli. That the sanctuary is at Shiloh provides an important link back to Joshua, since it was there that Joshua set up the tent of meeting (Josh. 18:1). But now the sanctuary at Shiloh has taken on a more permanent feel, and is referred to as a temple (1 Sam. 1:9). It even has doorposts where Eli can sit, and one of Samuel's tasks will be to open the doors (1 Sam. 3:15). But it quickly becomes apparent that the sanctuary was not functioning as it should have done. Judges had begun to report ways in which Israel had been unravelling much of what had been achieved under Joshua, but the importance of the Shiloh sanctuary did not feature as part of this. There are certainly hints in Judges of this, especially in the closing chapters that report various irregular practices in order to provide wives for the survivors in Benjamin (Judg. 21:8–24) along with an initial hint (Judg. 18:31) that Shiloh was not to endure as the central sanctuary,[6] but it is only in Samuel that the problems in the sanctuary itself come to prominence. Those problems are quickly evident as we are introduced to the high priest, Eli, and discover that he is unable to distinguish between Hannah's passionate prayer and the speech of a drunk woman (1 Sam. 1:9–18). Although there is an initial resolution when Eli pronounces a blessing on Hannah prior to Samuel's birth (1 Sam. 1:19–20), this is a sign of wider problems. These are particularly clear in the actions of Eli's sons in abusing both the sacrificial system (1 Sam. 2:12–17) and the young women who were there (1 Sam. 2:22–25), leading to judgment being announced on Eli's household by an unnamed man of God (1 Sam. 2:27–36). This message was confirmed in Samuel's initial call (1 Sam. 3:10–14), a call that also began the process of reversing the situation in which there was a scarcity of Yahweh's word (1 Sam. 3:1; 3:21 – 4:1a).

Although these chapters thus discuss a range of matters, they are focused on the rise of kingship. This becomes explicit in two direct mentions of the king (1 Sam. 2:10, 35). Neither, in fact, predicts a king. Rather, both texts speak about the king as an existing reality, even though at that point there was no king (1 Sam. 2:10, 35). More subtly, the first chapter plays on the Hebrew form of the name 'Saul', though without mentioning him because of the focus on

---

[6] On Shiloh's function in the conclusion to Judges, see Beldman 2017: 109–110.

Samuel.[7] This seems to be part of a strategy that runs through the opening chapters of introducing the theme of kingship indirectly. Kingship is coming, and the opening chapters of Samuel prepare us for it, but in a way that downplays the sorts of narratives that might be expected. Rather than immediately introducing readers to the deeds of a mighty warrior who becomes king by dint of his might, Samuel prepares us for kingship by focusing on a relatively normal family and the challenges they faced.[8] Emerging from this is a focus on three central characters – Samuel, Saul and David. In each case their interaction with foreigners provides a key lens through which we understand them within the account of the rise of kingship.

Samuel: 1 Samuel 1 – 12

Although Samuel himself is a major figure, his principal role is to initiate kingship through Saul and then subsequently begin the process of David's becoming king, though Samuel died (1 Sam. 25:1) before David became king. Of the three pivotal figures, Samuel has the least interaction with foreigners, reflecting the fact that his role was primarily about bringing about change within Israel. There is, however, a progression running through Samuel, where each of Samuel, Saul and David gradually have more involvement with foreigners.

Samuel's interaction with foreigners is largely at the level of engagement with foreign powers who engage in warfare with Israel. There are no narratives that report his interacting with individual foreigners. However, there is an intriguing development of the themes developed in Judges (where Yahweh acts through foreigners) in the story of the capture and return of the ark (1 Sam. 4:1b – 7:1).[9] Judges has demonstrated that Yahweh could work through foreigners, particularly Othniel (Judg. 3:7–11) and Shamgar (Judg. 3:31), and even bring deliverance through them. Of course, a repeating feature of Judges is

---

[7] See Firth 2009: 58–59.

[8] Cf. Brueggemann 1990a.

[9] These chapters, along with 2 Sam. 6, are often assigned to a putative source known as 'The Ark Narrative'. This concept can be traced back to the work of Rost (1982; German 1926), and was developed in subsequent studies (e.g. A. F. Campbell 1975; Miller and Roberts 1977, and with a more theological twist, Brueggemann 2002). But whether we can access such a source is by no means clear, not least because its boundaries are disputed, while the material is closely integrated into the larger section in which we find it (Willis 1971: 297–301; Gitay 1992: 222–224; Firth 2017a: 42–46). As such, we consider this material here only within the context of the book of Samuel rather than as a discrete source.

that Yahweh would raise up foreign nations to discipline Israel because of their sin (Judg. 2:11–23), so his control over all nations is acknowledged. Nevertheless, the story of the ark's capture and return introduces an intriguing nuance to this. Samuel's initiation narrative (1 Sam. 3:1 – 4:1a) sees Israel move from a situation where Yahweh's word is scarce to one in which it is abundant. Like the allusions to Saul in 1 Samuel 1, this is done indirectly through a gradual increase in uses of the word *dābār* (commonly translated as 'word') through the chapter, so that the account ends with the declaration that 'Samuel's word came to all Israel' (1 Sam. 4:1a). However, by the end of the chapter only one word from Samuel has been reported – the message he received from Yahweh about the downfall of Eli's house (1 Sam. 3:11–14), a message that can be traced back to the earlier message from the man of God (1 Sam. 2:27–36). Samuel himself is seemingly absent from the narrative that follows, but this is because one of the key functions of this account is to demonstrate the reliability of Yahweh's word through Samuel (and the man of God) in Israel's defeat at the hands of the Philistines,[10] in spite of Israel's deploying the ark in the battle (1 Sam. 4:4), something that provides a further link to the Shiloh motif running through 1 Samuel 1 – 7. Unlike Judges, which consistently reported how Israel did evil before Yahweh sold them into the hand of the enemy power in order to demonstrate the link between the nation's sin and being afflicted by a foreign power, Samuel makes no mention of Israel's sin. That sin was a very real problem is certainly implied through these chapters (not least through their attempt to manipulate God through the ark), and of course the sin of Eli's family follows a pattern seen elsewhere when the sin of the leaders affects the nation, but this is not the primary concern here. Rather, the focus is on how Yahweh's word, spoken through his prophetic figures, was coming true. But what neither of these prophetic figures mentioned was that Yahweh would act against the sanctuary through a foreign power. That might be implied (and it would make sense of features of both oracles), but only as the story is told do we know that this was happening through the Philistines. Because of the prominence given to Samuel's word (1 Sam. 4:1a) immediately before this account, it is his oracle that is particularly stressed. Samuel has been unmentioned throughout, but his word to Israel is brought about through foreigners who now bring judgment.

---

[10] Cf. Spina 1991.

Following the ark's return, the narrative moves forward twenty years (1 Sam. 7:2). Whereas Samuel was a lad in the opening chapters, he is now Israel's key leader, though his role is marked as being akin to that of the judges (1 Sam. 7:17). The similarities between Samuel and the judges are evident in the events recounted in 1 Samuel 7:3–17, especially with Deborah, who was also both a prophet and a judge.[11] His opening speech here (1 Sam. 7:3) is also reminiscent of the judges, evoking earlier references to sin (Judg. 2:13–14), while Israel's response alludes to events in the Jephthah story (Judg. 10:16); except this time Yahweh does act for Israel. Israel's repentance in this instance is demonstrated by a gathering at Mizpah, where Samuel is said to have 'judged' Israel (1 Sam. 7:6). Yet while Israel are worshipping, they are attacked by the Philistines. But just as the preceding story of the ark demonstrated that Yahweh could conquer foreign powers without human intervention, so Yahweh defeats the Philistines in response to Samuel's prayer, acting while Samuel is in the act of offering a sacrifice (1 Sam. 7:10). At this point Yahweh 'thundered' and so threw the Philistines into confusion. In this, the promise of Hannah's song, that Yahweh would defeat his enemies by 'thundering' against them, is confirmed (1 Sam. 2:10).[12] Once the Philistines were routed the Israelites pursued them, but the emphasis on the victory being Yahweh's is shown when Samuel establishes the rock Ebenezer, noting that to this point it is Yahweh who has helped (1 Sam. 7:12). Hence, although Samuel 'judged Israel' (1 Sam. 7:15), he is distinguished from the earlier judges whom Yahweh raised up to save Israel in that he was not the one who led Israel in battle. Yahweh could overcome Israel's foes without a human leader.

This background is important for the story in 1 Samuel 8 – 12 of how Saul became Israel's first king. Along with the failings of Samuel's own sons (1 Sam. 8:1–5),[13] a desire to be like the nations and have a king lead them in battle were pivotal elements in the request of Israel's elders for a king (1 Sam. 8:4–5). Despite Samuel's protests, and Yahweh's apparent displeasure at the form of the request (1 Sam. 8:7–9), he was instructed to grant them a king (1 Sam. 8:19–22).

[11] Garsiel 1983: 55.

[12] The passages are linked by the verb *r'm*. Apart from Hannah's response to Peninnah (1 Sam. 1:6), the verb occurs elsewhere in Samuel only in David's song (2 Sam. 22:14), again pointing to the means by which Yahweh defeats his adversaries. The balancing of key terms such as these points to the integration of these poems into the overall structure of the book.

[13] In this, Samuel is shown to be similar to Eli, who also was said to have 'judged' Israel (1 Sam. 4:18). Dynastic structures are a constant problem in this period (cf. Green 2003: 180–181).

Throughout 1 Samuel 4:1b – 7:17 Yahweh had demonstrated that Israel did not need a king to fight their battles, though he was clearly preparing to work with a king (1 Sam. 2:10, 35). But that Yahweh could do this without a king points to the nub of the problem in Israel's initial request for a king. A king who guided the nation to understand Yahweh's will was not problematic (Deut. 17:14–20), but when Israel projected their desire to defeat enemies onto their king rather than Yahweh, they fundamentally subverted the nature of their relationship with Yahweh. Such a king was always a danger to Israel, a king who would take continually from them (1 Sam. 8:10–17). Yahweh, not a human, was king, and overcame their enemies. Nevertheless, although Israel had asked for a king, by the end of 1 Samuel 8 Yahweh claimed the initiative, providing Israel with the means necessary for appropriate kingship.[14]

Much of the process by which Saul was proclaimed king need not detain us here, beyond noting that after his initial recognition some 'worthless men' (*běnê běliyya'al*)[15] had asked how Saul could 'save' (*yš'*) them (1 Sam. 10:27). The observation itself not only rejected Yahweh's choice of Saul, but also still understood the role of the king in terms of military success. Perhaps more importantly, the process by which Saul was proclaimed king (1 Sam. 10:17–26) seems to echo the Achan narrative (Josh. 7:1–16), as well as anticipating the taking of Jonathan during battles with the Philistines (1 Sam. 14:36–42). These allusions indicate a continued tension within Israel about the role of the king and how they were to live as a distinctive people. Choosing a king who was not on Yahweh's pattern could see Israel heading down the path of becoming Canaanite (as with Achan). But that Yahweh has given Israel Saul as a king means that Saul always has the chance to succeed.[16] This tension is also evident in the account of the capture of Jabesh-gilead by Nahash the Ammonite (1 Sam. 11:1–11),[17] an event that leads

---

[14] Fokkelman 1993: 354.

[15] Cf. 1 Sam. 2:12, where the same term describes Eli's sons.

[16] It is beyond the scope of this study to examine the supposed pro- and anti-monarchic sections of 1 Sam. 8 – 12. However, in general it seems better to adopt tension as the literary key, a tension that is not resolved within these chapters between what a king may be and what Israel keeps trying to make the king. This seems preferable to attempts to isolate conflicting sources. Cf. Firth 2009: 111; 2017a: 58–60; and the literature cited there.

[17] 4QSam[a] offers a much longer text after 1 Sam. 10:27, providing potential background to this narrative, and this reading is adopted by the NRSVA. However, with Kallai (1996) it is more likely that the longer reading is an attempt to fill the terse form of the MT rather than being original material accidentally omitted.

to Saul's wider recognition.[18] At one level this chapter recounts a victory that Saul, empowered by the Spirit like the judges (most especially Samson, Judg. 14:6; 15:14[19]), achieved over the Ammonites, showing that he could deliver the nation. Along with Spirit empowerment there are elements that read very positively, notably the fact that his plan for the victory also echoes the victory won at Ai once Yahweh has established the plan (Josh. 8:1–29) in his division of his forces into three groups. But against this, the division of one of the oxen into twelve pieces also alludes to the account of the Levite and his concubine (Judg. 19:29). These allusions are strengthened when we note that Saul returned to Gibeah (1 Sam. 11:4), a town central to the events of Judges 19, events that finally contributed to Israel's earlier destruction of Jabesh-gilead (Judg. 21:8–12), the town now central to the conflict with Nahash. Perhaps it is best to allow these tensions to remain unresolved within 1 Samuel 11 because their presence explains the need for Samuel to lead the nation to Gilgal to renew the kingdom (1 Sam. 11:14).

This renewal was achieved through the offering of sacrifices and Samuel's final national address (1 Sam. 12).[20] Importantly, in raising the issue in his speech of how Israel has related to foreign powers, Samuel stresses that Yahweh previously delivered Israel. He did this through various figures such as Moses and Aaron in Egypt, or later through the judges, but it was still Yahweh who acted. Israel's error when confronted by Nahash was to seek a king so that the king, not Yahweh, was seen as the deliverer. But if Yahweh was king, there was no need for Israel to understand a king as a deliverer. This did not mean that Israel was prevented from having a king – as Samuel makes clear, this is entirely possible, but the key issue for Israel is to continue living under Yahweh as king.[21]

The period up to the renewal of the kingdom under Samuel was thus marked by the rise of kingship within Israel along with the pressures brought about by foreign powers. Unlike key texts noted earlier in Joshua and Judges, at no point are we told of any foreigners who became part of Israel. However, interaction with foreigners (as military powers opposed to Israel) is crucial for understanding these

[18] With V. P. Long (1989: 183–190) it is better to see the events of this chapter as part of a process by which kingship was gradually established.
[19] See also Han 2015: 106–107.
[20] Most English Bibles head 1 Sam. 12 as 'Samuel's Farewell Address', but given that he was active in the early days of David's reign, this is hardly appropriate. Rather, it is offering a way forward for kingship. Cf. Firth 2009: 144.
[21] Vannoy 1978: 178.

chapters, as it is through this that the narrative demonstrates the tension Israel faced in moving towards kingship even though Yahweh had already prepared for it. Concern about foreign powers tempted Israel to seek a king who would be a military saviour. But although Israel could have a 'king like the nations' if that meant a political structure, they could not have a 'king like the nations' if that meant that the king would claim the status of national deliverer. Only Yahweh could truly be Israel's king, though in Samuel David will emerge as the ideal representation of this.[22]

Saul: 1 Samuel 13 – 15

By the end of 1 Samuel 12 Saul is established as Israel's king. However, even though the Philistines are subdued in the time of Samuel, along with there being peace with the Amorites (1 Sam. 7:14),[23] the pressure from foreign powers that triggered Israel's request for a king has not abated, and Saul is shown in conflict with two foreign groups – the Philistines (1 Sam. 13 – 14) and the Amalekites (1 Sam. 15). It is through interaction with these powers that Saul loses first the right of a dynasty (1 Sam. 13:14) and then ultimately his legitimacy as king (1 Sam. 15:28). At both these points there is an oblique reference to David; but even before his introduction, foreigners are used as a central mechanism for evaluating Israel's leadership.

Saul's loss of dynasty is reported in 1 Samuel 13. The tragedy this implies becomes clear only in 1 Samuel 14, where Saul's son Jonathan is introduced, since he appears to be the sort of king Israel needs.[24] The account here builds on an unresolved element from 1 Samuel 10:7, where Saul has not carried out an expected attack on a Philistine garrison.[25] Saul moved to Gilgal, but was faced by a massive Philistine force, which resulted in his losing some of his forces (1 Sam. 13:2–7). Samuel had earlier indicated that Saul should wait there for seven days (1 Sam. 10:8), at which point he would show him what to do. As the narrative has developed to this point, Saul was king of a renewed kingdom, but the challenge was now for him to live out that renewal, where Yahweh, not Saul, was the deliverer. With the seven days

---

[22] Cf. Lee 2017: 70.

[23] These Amorites must be understood as living outside Israel's territory.

[24] Mommer (1991: 135) is typical of many critical scholars who bracket 13:7–15 on the basis that it is a doublet of the second rejection, but this misses the importance of repetition within Samuel and the development between the two accounts.

[25] With V. P. Long (1989: 43–66) and van Zyl (1988: 169).

seemingly having passed and the people scattering, Saul orders that the burnt and peace offerings be brought to him; but just as he offers the burnt offering Samuel arrives (1 Sam. 13:10). Samuel's arrival is within the seven days, but Saul has not waited until the end of the time. Rather, he has made the offering to obtain Yahweh's favour, even though Samuel had already outlined the process by which Saul would have this. It is this that triggers Samuel's famed observation of Yahweh's having sought a 'man after his own heart' in the context of Saul's losing the right of dynasty (1 Sam. 13:13–14). Pressure from foreign nations revealed the extent to which Saul was no longer true to Yahweh's purposes.

None of this meant that Yahweh could not deliver Israel from a seemingly impossible position. Indeed, in 1 Samuel 14:1–23 we see how Yahweh did defeat the Philistines, but with this happening through Jonathan. To this point the narrative has held back from indicating that Saul had any sons, but Jonathan is introduced as 'the son of Saul' (1 Sam. 14:1), though we do not yet know he is the eldest son. But it quickly becomes clear that he not only demonstrates a level of initiative that Saul lacked (as shown by the fact that he did not tell his father of his plan to attack the garrison); he does so from a clearly defined faith in Yahweh (1 Sam. 14:6). The tragedy of Jonathan's position is laid bare in his introduction – he is competent in ways Saul is not and with the humility his father lacks. But he can never be king. Saul finally joined in the battle after consulting Yahweh through either the ark or the ephod,[26] and it will ultimately be said that Yahweh delivered Israel. But in this context we see the tragedy of Jonathan's position, even if it is not a tragedy about which he complains, as we also see him consistently support David (1 Sam. 18:1–5; 20:13–17; 23:16–18).[27] Once more it is through conflict with foreign powers that Samuel offers insight into Jonathan.

The positive presentation of Jonathan is largely contrasted with that of Saul in the balance of 1 Samuel 14 because of his rash vow. What is striking is the wording of the vow, as he lays a curse on anyone who eats until 'I have been avenged on my enemies' (1 Sam. 14:24). Against the summary statement following the victory Jonathan initiated (1 Sam. 14:23), itself a clear reference to Exodus 14:30,[28] Saul's vow focuses on himself rather than Yahweh as the source of victory. In the ensuing confusion, a victory was still won, but again

---

26 Cf. the MT and LXX. For an integrating reading, see Fokkelman 1986: 58.

27 On the covenants sworn between Jonathan and David, see Wozniak 1983.

28 Youngblood (1992: 663) thus links this victory to the crossing of the Sea.

through the insight of Jonathan rather than Saul, something that even led to Saul's wanting to put Jonathan to death through a process of selection that seems to parody his own in becoming king (1 Sam. 14:36–46; cf. 1 Sam. 10:17–24). In spite of this, the closing notes of this chapter (1 Sam. 14:47–52) do acknowledge that Saul was a valiant soldier who won various battles and delivered Israel (1 Sam. 14:48). However, these events receive no detailed record because the key insights into Saul's character have already been shown. He lost the right to a dynasty because he had not understood the reality of Yahweh's reign, and foreign powers are the mechanism by which this is demonstrated.

But Saul's downfall is not complete. After the first stage of his rejection in 1 Samuel 13 he lost the right to a dynasty. He had not yet lost his legitimacy as king. It is this that is recounted in 1 Samuel 15,[29] and again it is through foreign powers that we see Saul's failings. In this case Saul was sent by Samuel to place the Amalekites under the ban,[30] a directive rooted in both his anointing as king and events recounted in Exodus 17:8–16, and Yahweh's enduring war with Amalek because of their actions then. Although some have suggested that the threat posed by Amalek was in the past,[31] accounts such as that reported in 1 Samuel 30 make clear that it was very much a present difficulty for Israel. This later story shows that the Amalekites were a semi-nomadic people living in the Negeb, the wilderness to the south of Israel.[32] Placing them under the ban was thus about enabling Israel to live out their life, though consistent with the application of this law in Joshua it remained the case that the victory ultimately belonged to Yahweh. In this case a particularly strict definition of the ban is provided (1 Sam. 15:3), one that has its closest parallel in the events at Jericho (cf. Josh. 6:21).

A crucial motif running through this chapter is the importance of obedience to Yahweh, something achieved by repetition of the verb *šm'*. This verb, depending on context, means 'to hear' or 'to obey', with both senses evident in its eight occurrences in this chapter (1 Sam. 15:1, 4, 14, 19, 20, 22 [twice], 24). This range is already evident in Samuel's opening words, where his call that Saul 'hear' Yahweh's

---

[29] For reasons why 1 Sam. 13 and 15 need to be seen as demonstrating an extended narrative of Saul's fall rather than doublets, see Firth 2009: 171.

[30] See the discussion of 'Language' in chapter 2, where the discussion of people and things 'devoted to destruction' (*ḥrm*) applies equally here.

[31] Brueggemann 1990b: 110.

[32] Edelman (1986) argues that a northerly group is meant here, but the main sites are all in the south.

word is also a summons to obedience. But Saul will finally admit to having listened to the voice of the people so that he heeded them rather than Yahweh. His claim that he kept the best of the Amalekite herds and flocks that he might sacrifice them to Yahweh after he was confronted by Samuel is thus shown to be an attempt to avoid the claim that Yahweh had on him. The flaw in his logic is directly rebuked in Samuel's famous response about the priority of obedience over sacrifice (1 Sam. 15:22). Even beyond the claimed influence of the people, Saul also delivered the Amalekite king, Agag. Although the Rahab story (Josh. 2) demonstrated the possibility of people under the ban changing their status, there is no evidence here of his committing himself to Yahweh, or even of following the pattern of the Gibeonites and choosing no longer to oppose Yahweh. The parallels to the Jericho story and the problems caused by Achan's unfaithfulness, a motif hinted at in 1 Samuel 14:29, find their continuation in Saul's disobedience here.[33] Saul's failure to reign as one under Yahweh is thus demonstrated through his engagement with foreign powers, and it is because of this that the kingdom is then torn from him (as symbolized by Saul's tearing Samuel's robe) and given to a neighbour who is 'better' than him (1 Sam. 15:28). It would be difficult to argue that David, the one obliquely referred to here, was morally better than Saul, but he did understand that Israel's king must reign under Yahweh and not as a king with final authority. Unsurprisingly, the book of Samuel will demonstrate this through David's engagement with foreigners.

Saul and David, Ish-bosheth and David: 1 Samuel 16:1 – 2 Samuel 5:16

David until his departure from Saul's court: 1 Samuel 16 – 20

Although one might expect that Saul's final rejection would immediately be followed by his replacement by David as king, Samuel takes a much longer narrative path to demonstrate this.[34] Although David

[33] Fokkelman (1986: 66) also points to ways in which 1 Sam. 14:25–30 evokes Samuel's condemnation in 1 Sam. 13:13–14, showing that the whole of this section of Samuel is a carefully integrated whole.

[34] By contrast, 1 Chr. 10:1 – 11:4 starts the account of monarchy with Saul's death and David's accession, thus telescoping this material. However, the genealogies involving Saul (1 Chr. 8; 9:35–44) indicate that those responsible for Chronicles were aware of a

is anointed as king over Israel in 1 Samuel 16:13, an anointing matched by his experience of the Spirit, he became king over Judah in 2 Samuel 2:1–4 only, and over Israel and Judah in 2 Samuel 5:1–5. However, throughout this extended stretch of text, which includes a long rivalry narrative with Saul (1 Sam. 16:1 – 2 Sam. 1:27) and then a short rivalry narrative with Ish-bosheth (2 Sam. 2:1 – 5:16), David is the legitimate king, even while others occupy the throne.[35] This structure is parallel to the long and short rebellion narratives recounted in 2 Samuel 9 – 20. It is notable that foreigners play a significant role in both the long rivalry and rebellion narratives, but not in the short rivalry and rebellion narratives. However, a more significant shift in these chapters is that whereas previously in Samuel foreigners are principally presented through hostile nations, there is now an increasing focus on individual foreigners and their relationship with Israel. This does not mean that foreign nations cease to be important, not least in that Saul will die in a battle with the Philistines, but that named foreign individuals gradually become the more important means by which Samuel evaluates its main characters.

This shift towards named individuals becomes evident in the opening chapters that are focused on David. Following the notice of his anointing (1 Sam. 16:1–13), attention switches to the means by which David was brought to Saul's court (1 Sam. 16:14–23) before reporting his pivotal encounter with Goliath (1 Sam. 17).[36] Obviously, the Goliath story occurs within the context of a larger conflict with the Philistines, but its focus on Goliath provides an immediate distinction between Saul and David. The story is situated at a strategically significant point, with the Valley of Elah (1 Sam. 17:2) controlling access between the highlands (controlled by Israel) and the coastal plain (controlled by the Philistines). When Goliath is introduced, the narrative is careful to do so in terms the Philistines

wider range of material about Saul, but chose to omit this because their goals differed from those of Samuel at this point.

[35] Within Rost's source analysis of Samuel these chapters are often treated as 'The History of David's Rise' (e.g. Grønbæk 1971). See Firth 2017a: 45–46 for weaknesses involved in treating this as a discrete source. With Short (2010) it is better to read this account within its literary framework within Samuel than as a source with discrete goals, not least since these goals are unclear once the text is removed from the context in which we find it. As such, these chapters function to provide a positive commendation of David, rather than as an apology that effectively distorts his presentation (for which approach, see McCarter 1980b; Halpern 2001; McKenzie 2000).

[36] On the chronological relationship between these narrative segments, see Firth 2005c. For a defence of reading the MT rather than the shorter LXX, an issue closely related to the chronology here, see Firth 2009: 194–195.

themselves would have wanted, showing him as someone of massive size[37] who is also equipped with the latest armour and weapons. Through this, readers are initially (like Saul and the rest of the Israelite army) lulled into a 'false sense of insecurity'[38] so that they accept his presentation as someone possessing military might who cannot be defeated. When Goliath indicates that he 'defied' (*ḥrp*) Israel's ranks (1 Sam. 17:10), he presents a challenge to Israel that leaves them dismayed, though in fact in this term he introduces a key word that will gradually be refocused through David (cf. 1 Sam. 17:45). But Saul, along with Israel's army, is left dismayed and afraid of him (1 Sam. 17:11).

David was not yet a professional soldier, and attended the battle lines only at the directive of his father to take some provisions and to enquire about the well-being of his brothers (1 Sam. 17:12–18). Seeing the troops in their daily march to the lines, David hears Goliath[39] 'defying' (*ḥrp*) Israel and the ensuing discussion among the troops about the reward for the man who will kill him (1 Sam. 17:19–25). What immediately distinguishes David within the story is that he is the one who reframes Israel's perceptions. Where everyone to this point has accepted Goliath's perspective, David wonders why he should have defied not Israel, but 'the armies of the living God' (1 Sam. 17:26). David is the first one to speak of Yahweh, and gradually reframes the perspective of each person he encounters in the balance of the chapter, though his brother Eliab apparently remained rather unimpressed with him (1 Sam. 17:28–30). Hence, when taken to Saul, David has to reshape his thinking – Saul sees individual combat here in Goliath's terms, claiming that David cannot fight him because he is a lad, whereas Goliath is an experienced warrior. But where Saul conspicuously makes no reference to God, David insists that just as Yahweh delivered him from both a lion and a bear, he will also deliver him from Goliath. Only after David makes this point does Saul speak of Yahweh (1 Sam. 17:37). But though Saul speaks of Yahweh, in

---

[37] In the MT he is 6 cubits (about 9 ft 9 in. [3 m]), but the LXX, Josephus and 4QSam[a] all put his height at 4 cubits and a span (about 6 ft 6 in. [2 m]). Given that the MT is our youngest textual witness here, the alternative reading is more probable. However, in either case he is considerably larger than any Israelites of the time, save of course for Saul, who was 'head and shoulders taller' than the other Israelites (1 Sam. 10:23), though given that his armour apparently fitted David (1 Sam. 17:38–39), David must also have been reasonably tall for an Israelite.

[38] Firth 2009: 193.

[39] More often in this chapter he is 'the Philistine', but for convenience I follow the convention of referring to him as 'Goliath' throughout.

dressing David in his armour he continues to act in a way that leaves Yahweh out, attempting to equip David in a way that matches Goliath. Instead, David takes only that with which he is familiar, the sort of equipment with which Yahweh previously delivered him.

David's reframing of the situation comes to a focus in his encounter with Goliath. Goliath despised David when he saw him because he too saw the battle in traditional terms, though there is surely irony in his comparing himself to a dog given David's earlier encounters with the lion and the bear.[40] Cursing David by his own gods takes this irony one step further given Dagon's spectacular failure to deal with Yahweh before (1 Sam. 5:1–4). But David will also reframe Goliath's perspective, claiming not only that Yahweh will grant him victory, but that he will do so without the normal structures of military might because it is not Israel whom Goliath has 'defied' (*ḥrp*) but Yahweh (1 Sam. 17:45). David's victory over Goliath will be so 'all the earth may know there is a God in Israel' (1 Sam. 17:46). In this statement, David provides the theological key to this story, demonstrating an understanding of Israel's role as a witness to the nations. This statement also echoes Joshua 4:24 in evoking the role of Yahweh's mighty acts in witnessing to the whole earth of his reality and power while anticipating similar statements in 1 Kings 8:60 and 2 Kings 19:19. The battle between David and Goliath can then be told briefly because the central point of the narrative is the demonstration of Yahweh's power over all the nations, and as soon as David casts his stone the job is done (1 Sam. 17:49). David prevailed, but not by might. He prevailed because he understood that Yahweh defeated Israel's foes. More than this, he demonstrated the reality of Yahweh as the one who was greater than all beyond Israel.

David in the wilderness: 1 Samuel 21 – 26

Although the Philistines are important in the subsequent chapters, they do not contribute significantly to the story in 1 Samuel 18 – 20 since the focus is on Saul's attempts to kill David. However, the reality of these attempts does lead David to flee to the Philistines (1 Sam. 21:1–9; MT 21:2–10), though this is only made explicit in 1 Samuel 21:10.[41] On the way he stopped at the priestly city of Nob, where he met the priest Ahimelech and convinced him to hand over both Goliath's sword and the bread of the presence. David is hardly

---

[40] Cf. Birch 1998: 1112.
[41] MT 21:11.

presented in a positive light here as he lies about the purpose of his visit. But David is not the only one at the sanctuary, because an Edomite named Doeg was also there (1 Sam. 21:7). Doeg was Saul's chief herdsman[42] and he is said to have been 'detained' before Yahweh. Exactly what this means is never made clear because the point is to place him at the sanctuary when David arrived so Doeg could later report events to Saul. As an Edomite, Doeg is from a people with a long history of antipathy towards Israel (Num. 20:14–21), whose access to the sanctuary was restricted (Deut. 23:7–8). His role as a witness to David's dissembling with Ahimelech is fraught with threat, though how this will play out is initially deferred until David has gone to the Philistines and unsuccessfully attempted to convince Achish to allow him to stay there (1 Sam. 21:10–15; MT 21:11–16) before he returns to the cave at Adullam (1 Sam. 22:1–5), perhaps a site near his battle with Goliath.[43]

The danger Doeg posed becomes clear after a rambling complaint about David by Saul, where he effectively suggested to his fellow Benjaminites that they should remain loyal to him because he would provide them with rewards whereas David would not (1 Sam. 22:6–9). In response, Doeg gave an abbreviated report of David's actions at Nob. This report notes that Ahimelech had provided food for David along with Goliath's sword, while also adding that Ahimelech had enquired of Yahweh for him (1 Sam. 22:9–10). Nothing in the previous chapter requires this, but Doeg might have misunderstood the removal of the sword from near the ephod, and interpreted this as an enquiry. Alternatively, he might simply have been malicious because he knew Saul would accept a report such as this. This second option is made more likely by the fact that he shaped his response around the themes Saul established in his initial complaint about David.[44] Although he never directly accuses Ahimelech of conspiring with David, his speech implies this, and this is how Saul took it when he summoned Ahimelech. In spite of Ahimelech's denial, his response is shaped by failing to understand the full import of Saul's charge, leading Saul to order his attendants to kill him and his fellow priests. Saul's attendants would not do this, so Saul directed Doeg to do it. He did so with bloody efficiency, killing eighty-five priests and all other people and livestock at Nob (1 Sam. 22:18–19). What Saul had failed to do to the

---

[42] Aster (2003) makes a plausible case for this being a military title, which would explain Doeg's ability to act against Nob (1 Sam. 22:18–19).

[43] Firth 2009: 237.

[44] Cf. Fokkelman 1986: 389.

Amalekites, he now achieves through Doeg at Nob since his actions effectively place the city under the ban. But where Amalek were Yahweh's enemies, Nob was a city of loyal priests. Saul's failure is marked by his association with a foreigner who does not understand what it means to be loyal to Yahweh.

Saul's assault on an Israelite city is immediately contrasted with David's actions at the southern city of Keilah (1 Sam. 23:1–5). Although fleeing from Saul, and perhaps recognizing his own error at Nob, David responded to news of a Philistine raid on the city's threshing floors, something that could lead to great hunger if they took the year's food production. In spite of his men's fear, David went at Yahweh's directive and defeated the Philistines, even taking their livestock so that the town had more food than before. David's loyalty to the town would not be repaid as they then conspired with Saul against him; though with the assistance of the surviving priest Abiathar, who had brought the ephod with him, David was able to flee (1 Sam. 23:6–14). Where Saul should have been battling the Philistines, and thus providing for the people, it was David who showed the leadership the nation needed.[45]

The accession narrative: 1 Samuel 27 – 2 Samuel 1

Issues concerning foreigners are less prominent until David flees to the Philistines for a second time in 1 Samuel 27, staying with them as a notional vassal until he claims the throne of Judah in 2 Samuel 2:1.[46] The David who emerges from these chapters is deeply ambiguous – he lies regularly to the Philistine king Achish, but these chapters are also careful to show that David never acted against Israel. Moreover, when Saul died, David was as far removed from the site at Gilboa as was reasonably possible while still remaining within Israel's general boundaries. This ambiguity is revealed almost immediately in his encounter with Achish, where he speaks of 'finding favour' with him (1 Sam. 27:5), though he uses this speech to dupe Achish into giving him Ziklag, a town that subsequently belonged to the kings of Judah (1 Sam. 27:6). David's care in obtaining this site is important because it enabled him to raid a range of sites in the Negeb that had foreign groups hostile to Israel (1 Sam. 27:8).[47] David's raids were violent, and have been interpreted as a form of placing these groups under

---

[45] Cf. Short 2010: 190.

[46] On the structure of this narrative portion, see Firth 2007.

[47] The Girzites are otherwise unknown (and this seems to have triggered some text-critical variants), but their inclusion here suggests they are to be read as a hostile group.

the ban,[48] though the absence of any overtly religious language here could also mean it was a practice borne more from political expediency than anything else. If it was an application of the ban, then it represents the more limited form in which spoil could be claimed.[49] On his return with the booty he would claim to have been raiding territories hostile to the Philistines, including regions of Judah, and through this he convinced Achish of his loyalty, so that he believed David had so damaged his relations with Israel that he could not return (1 Sam. 27:12). Unfortunately for David he had done this so well that as battle with Israel loomed, Achish decided to include him in his elite troops (1 Sam. 28:1–2). The irony of David's position here has been carefully framed – his lies left him vulnerable to being on the wrong side of a conflict with Israel even though his actions have been against Philistine interests. It is notable that God is never mentioned in these dealings with Achish, a subtle hint that David is relying rather too much on his own intuition.

A feature of these chapters is that they recount the stories of David and Saul in parallel,[50] usually leaving each on a point of unresolved tension until the point of Saul's death.[51] While David was with Achish, Saul had seen the Philistine army and although he had previously attempted to remove all mediums and necromancers, the absence of any other answer from Yahweh led him to seek one out. On the advice of his attendants (who were clearly better informed than him) he went in disguise to one at En-dor with the intention of enquiring through Samuel's ghost (1 Sam. 28:3–7). Although the woman was initially suspicious, following Saul's oath that she would not be punished she summoned Samuel's ghost. Samuel then announced Saul's downfall, affirming that the kingdom had been given to David because of Saul's failure against Amalek.[52] Saul stood condemned because he reverted to a Canaanite practice, something he knew was prohibited in Israel. Although the woman is active within Israel, her approach is more

[48] So Bergen 1996: 262.

[49] As at Ai, Josh. 8:27.

[50] Fokkelman (1986: 594) provides a helpful chart of the synchronisms in the narrative.

[51] As with other parts of Samuel, the narrative is dischronologized, so that the events of 1 Sam. 29 preceded those of 1 Sam. 28:3–25, but are recounted after them to leave both David and Saul at a narratively unresolved point. See Firth 2007: 70–71.

[52] Exactly what happened here lies beyond our purposes. For the view that the woman did contact Samuel, see Bergen 1996: 267. For the view that the woman convinced Saul of something that had not happened, see Kent 2011: 159–204, or, more briefly, Steinmann 2016: 528–534. However, on either interpretation Saul acts as if it were a genuine event.

consistent with someone from outside Israel. Once again parallels between Saul and Achan emerge as Saul's leadership becomes indistinguishable from Canaanite practice.

By contrast, although David's position with Achish seemed impossible, when the Philistine forces gathered at Aphek, their leaders saw David as a threat (1 Sam. 29:1–5), citing the song sung by the Israelite women on his return from the defeat of Goliath (1 Sam. 18:7), a song also noted when David first went to the Philistines (1 Sam. 21:12; ET 21:11). From their perspective having David in their forces was too great a risk, and Achish accordingly (but unwillingly) sent him away (1 Sam. 29:6–11). David's dissembling with Achish is still evident, though his speech on being sent away is carefully ambiguous.[53] The reality of this is that the perspective of the other Philistine leaders is validated, but more importantly when the Philistines were engaging Saul, David and his men were in the far south, deep in the Negeb. This is because on their return to Ziklag (a three-day journey), they found the city had been raided and burnt by the Amalekites, with all the town's residents taken captive, including David's two wives. As a result, some even spoke of stoning David. But the narrative makes one of its few direct comments, noting that David 'strengthened himself in Yahweh his God' (1 Sam. 30:1–6). Following this, and enquiring of Yahweh through Abiathar and the ephod, David led his men further south to recover both the people and their possessions, though some who were exhausted from the length of the march to this point went only part of the way (1 Sam. 30:7–10).

The central place of the Amalekites in this account reminds readers of Saul's earlier failure (1 Sam. 15), so that this story becomes an important mechanism for showing how David (in spite of his other failures) did deal with these Amalekites appropriately.[54] Intriguingly, it is noted that as David and his men followed the Amalekites, they found an Egyptian man who had been abandoned by the Amalekites when he became ill. David treated this man well, consistent with the law's requirements for aliens (Exod. 22:21; 23:9; Lev. 19:34; Deut. 23:7). The narrative thus again contrasts him with Saul – Saul engaged in forbidden practices foreign to Israel, but David engaged with a foreigner and demonstrated the concern for the alien Israel was meant to demonstrate. The Egyptian not only told David what the Amalekites had done, raiding the territory of Judah as well as some Philistine

---

[53] Cf. Firth 2009: 300.

[54] Birch (1998: 1191–1192) points out that it also provides a contrast with Saul's actions at En-dor, which are happening about the same time.

lands;[55] he also led David and his men to their camp, enabling David's forces to defeat them and recover everyone and everything they had taken, with only 400 Amalekites able to escape (1 Sam. 30:16–20).

When David and his men had returned to those too exhausted to continue the pursuit of the Amalekites, those who had gone with him suggested that these men be excluded from the return of their spoil, save their wives and children. But David, having earlier strengthened himself in Yahweh, declared that it was Yahweh who had preserved them and given them everything back. Therefore, all the spoil was still to be shared equally because it was not won by individual Israelites: it was recovered by Yahweh, who had given it to them. This became a statute in Israel, even though at that stage David was not yet king (1 Sam. 30:21–25). The story does not say exactly how Yahweh had done this, but the implication seems to be that it was a combination of his direct guidance to David through Abiathar and the ephod, and through the existence of laws requiring the fair treatment of foreigners, especially foreign slaves, that encouraged the Egyptian to share important information with David. Throughout this, David thus deals with foreigners in appropriate ways – those who are opposed to Israel (the Amalekites) are confronted in battle, while those prepared to work with Israel (the Egyptian) are treated justly – and it is this that shows David as a positive king, even establishing statutes before he is king.[56]

All this is contrasted once more with Saul, whose death is reported in 1 Samuel 31. The battle for which readers have been waiting since 1 Samuel 28:1 is finally recounted, though as is typical for Samuel it is passed over fairly quickly. Attention is instead directed to Saul and his sons as they are overtaken by the Philistines on Mount Gilboa. There, with the death of three of his sons noted, the wounded Saul asks his kit bearer to kill him. When the lad refuses to do this, apparently fearing that he will be a regicide, Saul commits suicide by falling on his sword, something the kit bearer also does after Saul (1 Sam. 31:1–6). After this, a significant portion of Israel's territory fell under Philistine control, especially the key trade routes through the Jezreel Valley, with Saul's humiliation completed as the Philistines beheaded

---

[55] The Negeb of the Cherethites is distinguished from Judah's territory (1 Sam. 30:14). Cherethites will also be noted as forming part of David's standing military forces (2 Sam. 8:18; 15:18).

[56] Fokkelman (1986: 590) points to a further contrast with 1 Sam. 15. There Saul sins because he listened to the people, whereas here David enacts justice because he does not listen to them.

him, stripped[57] his armour to send it to the temple of their gods in Ashtoreth, leaving his body impaled on the wall of Beth-shan, a town only a few miles from Gilboa. Though his body would be recovered by the men of Jabesh-gilead, who also buried his ashes, Saul's death at his own hand as Israel lost control of key territory marks a low point in the early days of Israel's monarchy. A king like those of the nations cannot win Israel's battles; though, as David has shown in his conflict with Amalek, a king who understands Yahweh's authority over rulers can win.

The contrast with David is developed as he hears a report of Saul's death from an Amalekite (2 Sam. 1:1–16).[58] A key concern here is to show that David was completely removed from the battle where Saul and his sons died and to make clear that he was given Saul's badges of rank by the Amalekite rather than claiming them for himself.[59] Nevertheless, Samuel again uses an encounter with a foreigner to demonstrate the legitimacy of David's ascent towards the throne. As the man is introduced, we do not know he is a foreigner – this emerges only through the encounter with David so that as readers we discover information at the same rate as David. We may also miss the fact that the man is carefully ambiguous in his initial response to David's question about where he has come from. Should we read the verb *mlṭ* as 'escape' (cf. 1 Sam. 19:10, 12, 17–18) or 'slip away' (cf. 1 Sam. 20:29)? That is, the man could be claiming that he was a genuine escapee from the battle or that he saw his opportunity to depart and took it, an ambiguity reinforced by his statement that he had come from 'the camp of Israel' since this could mean either the site of the

---

[57] There is a high concentration of the root *pšṭ* in these chapters (cf. 1 Sam. 27:8, 10; 30:1, 14), more often translated 'raid'. Its repetition here thus directs readers back to these earlier passages, providing a further contrast between Saul and David.

[58] Many scholars have treated this passage as a doublet with 1 Sam. 31, with discussion focused on which provides the more accurate record of events, often in the belief that they are contradictory (cf. Smith 1899: 251; Robinson 1993: 155–156). However, the Accession Narrative is marked by its use of repetition (Firth 2007: 73–74), so that a doubling of information is a key narrative technique. Moreover, 1 Sam. 31 is reported by the narrator of Samuel, whereas 2 Sam. 1:1–16 is the report of an Amalekite – an obviously suspicious figure within the book, who clearly has matters of self-interest he is seeking to promote. Moreover, as Arnold (1989) has demonstrated, the various elements are capable of reasonable reconciliation, especially once one grants that the Amalekite may not be an entirely reliable narrator. Even those not persuaded of this have long found ways to reconcile these accounts; cf. Bergen 1996: 288, who follows Josephus (*Ant.* 6.370–372).

[59] In analysing this passage Lee (2017: 124) finds several redactional layers, but much of this depends on supposedly unintended contrasts. If, as noted above, the Amalekite may be an unreliable witness, much of this becomes unnecessary.

battle itself, or the area behind the lines. David's own concerns are focused in his second question when he asks how the battle has gone, after which the man reports the deaths of Saul and Jonathan (though not the other sons) in the context of Israel's defeat. David's concern is then with how the man knows Saul and Jonathan have died, at which point he claims to have been present on Mount Gilboa and to have seen Saul leaning on his spear. Reporting a question from Saul in which the man indicates he is an Amalekite, he then claims he killed Saul at his own request. Intriguingly, he never addresses the question of how Jonathan died, though this was part of David's question. But without addressing any question from David, he then presents Saul's crown and armlet to David, even though nothing to this point has prepared us for such a disclosure. Might he be telling the truth? Perhaps, though even if we grant this as a general point, it is clear that he has presented the account in as positive a light as he can to ingratiate himself with David, and as such one should not push the details of his claims. But we are equally entitled to think of the man as an opportunist who reconstructed a story from the bodies he found on Mount Gilboa, and given the general presentation of Amalekites in Samuel we are probably intended to think the latter is more likely.

David's immediate response is to mourn both Saul and Jonathan. But he then asks the man about his identity, another point the latter has offered in his account that is not necessary to answer David's questions. David's question does not ask about his ethnicity (since that has already been disclosed) but rather where he has come from. This is because he needed to know if the man was subject to Israelite law. By indicating that he was from a 'sojourner' (*gēr*) family the man thus revealed he was subject to Israelite law since sojourners were subject to Israelite law in the same way as the native born. Whether or not he had killed Saul, he claimed he had, and David therefore ordered his execution.[60] David had consistently indicated he would not claim the throne by killing Saul (1 Sam. 24:12; 26:9–11), since killing him would incur guilt. David's encounter with the Amalekite thus demonstrates that he not only refused to claim the throne through violence, but also that he acted with justice against someone who claimed to be a regicide. Moreover, he understood that a foreigner who had joined Israel, even from a people like the Amalekites, was meant to live in a manner consistent with what was expected of

[60] The verb *pg'* can have the sense of 'execute' rather than the more general 'strike', even though it is usually translated this way (cf. Hubbard 1984).

an Israelite. An Israelite like Achan, who rebelled against Yahweh's commands, was executed, and the same was true for a sojourner such as this Amalekite.

David and Ish-bosheth: 2 Samuel 2:1 – 5:16

The structure of Samuel shows several similarities between the short rivalry narrative and the short rebellion narrative, indicating that we are to read these in the light of each other.[61] For our purposes the most important is that neither has a significant interest in foreigners, both being more concerned with matters internal to Israel.[62] This is because the conflict between David and Ish-bosheth was apparently focused on the central highlands. Ish-bosheth's realm covered much of the area east of the Jordan (though claiming much to the west), whereas David was king over Judah. But with his base in the far south at Hebron, David's access to the more northerly points was limited. Hence the main conflict between their forces occurred at Gibeon, though of course this was a town with important foreign associations (Josh. 9). However, these do not play a significant role in the battle there, a battle won by David but that also established enduring conflict between David's commander, Joab, and Ish-bosheth's uncle (and power behind the throne), Abner (2 Sam. 2:12–32). However, as the rivalry is resolved, interest in foreigners resumes.

In spite of this general lack of interest in foreigners, 2 Samuel 3:2–5 does provide a list of sons born to David while he was based in Hebron. As only one child is listed per mother it is likely that this list is representative rather than comprehensive, showing that he was indeed blessed while in Hebron. Six sons and their mothers are listed. Of these, the first two (Ahinoam and Abigail) had previously been noted in the Nabal story (1 Sam. 25), while nothing more is known about the last three mothers. However, the third son was Absalom, and he receives a slightly extended note that records that his mother Maacah was a daughter of Talmai, king of Geshur. This was a small kingdom immediately north of the territory Ish-bosheth claimed. Since his marriages to Ahinoam and Abigail were both clearly political, it is no surprise that this one was too. Perhaps this already

---

[61] One intriguing crossover between these two narrative portions is that both sections note points where deaths occur when someone is struck in the belly (2 Sam. 2:23; 3:27; 4:6; 20:10), an unusual idiom that occurs nowhere else in the OT.

[62] 2 Sam. 2:9 claims that Ish-bosheth's realm included the otherwise unknown Ashurites, but since all the other regions claimed for him are Israelite, and indeed he claimed to rule 'all Israel' (2 Sam. 2:9), we are probably to understand this as an Israelite clan, perhaps in the region of Mahanaim.

demonstrates signs of David's living in breach of the requirement that Israelite kings not marry many wives, though there is possibly also a sense of *Realpolitik* here. However, although there appears to be no legal problem with David's taking at least one foreign wife, this note also lays the foundation for Absalom's flight to Geshur after he killed Amnon (2 Sam. 13:37–38), the first son mentioned on this list. This pattern is continued in the second list of sons that closes this section, though there are no clear references to foreigners there (2 Sam. 5:13–16).[63]

Although it is possible that Ish-bosheth's assassins (2 Sam. 4) have some foreign heritage (in that according to Josh. 9:17 the town of Beeroth is associated with Gibeon), they are both explicitly said to be Benjaminite (2 Sam. 4:2). However, since they too were executed by David after confessing regicide (2 Sam. 4:9–12), and so parallel the Amalekite who claimed to have killed Saul (2 Sam. 1:1–16), they could be considered another example of Israelites who effectively placed themselves in the position of foreigners. This does not, however, appear to be a significant element in the story. As such, foreigners begin to emerge as important figures in the book only following the point where David takes the throne of all Israel and Judah (2 Sam. 5:1–5).

This focus is initially reintroduced with the report of David's capture of Jerusalem from the Jebusites (2 Sam. 5:6–10), a Canaanite people who continued living among Israel. This had been noted in Judges 1:21 (cf. Josh. 15:63), and had also played an important part in the account of the Levite and his concubine (Judg. 19:10–12). In that account, staying with Jebusites might have been preferable to going to Gibeah. In 2 Samuel 24:18–25 Araunah the Jebusite emerges as a significant figure, indicating that even though the account of Jerusalem's capture indicates some rivalry between Israel and the Jebusites, the city's capture did not prevent continued positive relations with at least some Jebusites. But at the point of the city's capture the fact that the Jebusites are noted as 'inhabitants of the land' (2 Sam. 5:6) makes clear that they were a remnant Canaanite group. Unfortunately, many of the details of the city's capture are obscure,[64] so it is unwise to draw too many conclusions beyond noting that David has now dealt with an issue that remained unresolved since the time

---

[63] That said, it is possible that the note that David 'took more concubines and wives from Jerusalem' may, depending on how we read the preposition *min*, mean that he took Jebusite concubines; see Hill 2006.

[64] See Firth 2009: 363–365.

of Joshua, and that this is proof of Yahweh's presence with him (2 Sam. 5:10).

Jerusalem's capture was understood as external evidence of Yahweh's presence with David, and this is matched with his own awareness from his dealings with Hiram, king of Tyre.[65] Tyre was a town to the north of Israel. According to Joshua 19:29, Asher's border had reached Tyre, but it fell outside the territory allotted to Israel. Interaction with Hiram was an important element in Solomon's reign, and it is clear from this that the note here reflects a point late in David's reign, whereas Jerusalem's capture was relatively early. The problematic elements of the association with Hiram are not raised here because within Samuel he becomes an early witness to David's claim to Goliath that all the world will know there is a God in Israel (1 Sam. 17:46), making this an important element in summarizing David's reign. Foreign kings may be a problem, but they can also show Yahweh at work. The focus on Hiram here also highlights the important shift that has been developing within Samuel, where concern gradually moves away from foreign powers and onto named individuals (though without entirely forgetting foreign powers) who come to understand something of Yahweh's nature through their encounter with Israel. Yahweh's choice of David as king is thus not only something recognized within Israel; it is recognized more widely within the region, pointing to the fact that Israel's life was intended to point to the character of Yahweh.

David as king: 2 Samuel 5:17 – 24:25

Summary I: 2 Samuel 5:17 – 8:18

For the balance of Samuel, David is king of all Israel, though his reign is marked by conflict. The report of the reign itself is composed of four main sections – two summaries of David's reign (2 Sam. 5:17 – 8:18; 21:1 – 24:25) that are placed around the two rebellion reports (2 Sam. 9 – 19, 20). The rebellion reports are linked by notes about David's court that provide bridges between these sections (2 Sam. 8:15–18; 20:23–26). Both summaries are presented as closely matching chiasms that cover the whole of David's reign and provide a generally positive assessment of him, while the rebellion reports are extended narratives exploring events within his reign that show more negative

---

[65] Cf. Frisch 2004.

sides to his reign.[66] Both summaries principally deal with foreigners outside Israel, whereas the rebellion narratives deal with foreigners within Israel. However, as is typical for Samuel as a whole, attention is given to foreigners as a mechanism for evaluating Israelites, especially David.

Summary I is presented with the following structure:

A Military victories with Yahweh's help, 2 Samuel 5:17–25
  B Worship of Yahweh: bringing the ark, 2 Samuel 6:1–23
  B' Worship of Yahweh: Nathan's oracle, 2 Samuel 7:1–29
A' Military victories with Yahweh's help, 2 Samuel 8:1–14[67]

Where comparatively little attention is given to foreigners in the chapters focused on Israel's worship, it is clear that the military victories do require a focus on foreigners. This is immediately apparent in the initial report of military victories, where two defeats of the Philistines are noted (2 Sam. 5:17–25). Given the summary nature of this section, it is unsurprising that both these reports are quite brief. They are clearly intended to be read as a pair since they even include similar wordplays.[68] Right from the outset they point to the problem posed by the Philistines as they responded to the news that David had been anointed king of Israel (2 Sam. 5:17) – that is, he was no longer king only of Judah but now reigned over the whole nation. Given David's previous relationship with Achish (1 Sam. 27:1 – 28:2) they might have regarded him as a client king while he reigned over Judah. But if he reigned over a united Israel, then he posed a greater threat, which is why they came in search of him. In effect, they were seeking to keep him under their control as they gathered near Jerusalem. But David sought Yahweh's guidance and defeated them at Baal-perazim (2 Sam. 5:19–21).[69] Although there are some variations, David was also able to defeat the Philistines the second time they gathered in this area because of Yahweh's guidance. The crucial point is that although David led Israel in battle, it was Yahweh who overcame the Philistines. From here on the Philistines cease to be an issue for Israel.

[66] On the rhetorical goals of this structure, see Firth 2001.
[67] Firth 2001: 212. Cf. Flanagan 1983. For a slightly variant form that includes elements here regarded as bridging elements, see U. Kim 2008: 106.
[68] Fokkelman 1990: 169–176.
[69] The place name means 'Lord of bursting through' and is one of the few places in Samuel where a name based on *baal* is not changed to a form with *bosheth* (shame), acknowledging that although this form could refer to a storm god, it could also have a more general meaning.

Foreigners play only a limited role in the two chapters focused on worship, with the only possible foreigner being Obed-edom. David had delivered the ark to his house after his initial attempt to bring the ark to the city of David (2 Sam. 6:1–11). The designation 'Gittite' could mean that he came from Gath, as is clearly the case with Ittai the Gittite (2 Sam. 15:18–23). However, 1 Chronicles 15:17–19 indicates that Obed-edom was a Levite. Given that the noun *gath* can also mean 'wine press' and is a common element in toponyms,[70] it seems wisest to exclude him from this discussion, especially since the other references to Gittites in Samuel make clear that they are foreign.

Within Summary I it is possible that 2 Samuel 8:1 follows on from 2 Samuel 5:17, a mechanism for highlighting the internal relationships within the chiasm. However, that the battle reported here occurred within Philistine territory means it is later than those already noted. 'Metheg-ammah' is not otherwise known, but may be another name for Gath.[71] The balance of 2 Samuel 8:2–14 reports other victories David achieved outside what was then Israelite territory, covering Moab (2 Sam. 8:2), Hadadezer of Zobah (a region north of Israel, but south of the Sea of Galilee, 2 Sam. 8:3–4), the Arameans who had helped Hadadezer (2 Sam. 8:5–6)[72] and Edom (2 Sam. 8:13–14). Beyond this, David also gained the support of Toi, king of Hamath, a neo-Hittite city north of Zobah. All this is reported in an annalistic way with as little colour as possible. In spite of this, twice we are told that David achieved these victories with Yahweh's assistance (2 Sam. 8:6, 14), these two references matching the two accounts of Yahweh's giving victory in 2 Samuel 5:17–25. Along with this, David received a considerable amount in tribute, both as a result of victory (2 Sam. 8:6–8) and from those who allied themselves with him as a result of these victories (2 Sam. 8:10–12).

Summary I thus demonstrates that David, with Yahweh's assistance, drove out foreign forces that were hostile to Israel and that he also brought great wealth to Israel as a result. Along with this, by the end of Summary I Israel controlled the land Yahweh had promised to Abram (Gen. 15:18–21). That is, although the accounts are telescoped in time because they cover the whole of David's reign, they continue to demonstrate the reality of David's claim to Goliath – that there is

---

[70] E.g. Gath-rimmon. See also Anderson 1989: 105.

[71] So 1 Chr. 18:1, perhaps understanding it as a common noun ('control of the mother city'; Driver 1913: 306).

[72] David would have had to pass through Aramean territory to reach Zobah, making this necessary.

a God in Israel, and he gives victory to his people, even when others seem more powerful (1 Sam. 17:46–47). David's encounters with foreign powers are thus a key mechanism within Summary I of demonstrating the significance of Yahweh's presence.

Long rebellion narrative: 2 Samuel 9 – 19

These chapters (with 2 Sam. 20) have long been considered as part of a so-called succession narrative, and are often examined in these terms.[73] However, Keys has demonstrated that there are significant problems with this approach, not least that 1 Kings 1 – 2 (which is usually treated as its conclusion) appears to have come from a different source from the material in Samuel, one that was written in knowledge of it but nonetheless still separate.[74] Once we separate 1 Kings 1 – 2 from this material, then it is difficult to see how it is about succession to the throne,[75] and Keys's preferred theme of sin and punishment is more consistent. However, moving beyond Keys, although the two rebellion narratives are clearly linked, there is value in separating them for analysis, provided their integration is also noted.

The long rebellion narrative is where we most clearly see a focus on named foreigners who have been integrated into Israel, some of whom appear to be part of the remnant Canaanite population, while others are Philistines. Consistent with the general emphasis in Samuel, these foreigners are used to assess the book's main characters, though they also develop the insights developed in Joshua and Judges about the possibilities of foreigners being included within Israel. This does not mean that foreign powers are ignored, but they do play a lesser role.

The long rebellion narrative has a doubled introduction,[76] noting David's dealings with potential internal problems (Mephibosheth as a descendant of Saul, 2 Sam. 9) and[77] his interactions with the Ammonites (2 Sam. 10). In this case problems were triggered when he sent emissaries to console Hanun, the new Ammonite king, following the death of his father.[78] David's attempted expression of

---

[73] Most notably, following the lead of Rost (1982). See also Seiler (1998), who continues the pattern established by Rost of tracing this through to 1 Kings, though ignoring 2 Sam. 21 – 24.

[74] Keys 1996. Cf. McCarter 1980a: 361–362.

[75] For more on why this source theory is unpersuasive, see Ackroyd 1981 and Firth 2017a: 46–48.

[76] On links between these chapters, see Youngblood 1992: 921.

[77] 'After this' (2 Sam. 10:1) is not necessarily indicating a close chronological connection; see Bailey 1990: 54–57.

[78] His father, Nahash, had been a pivotal figure in the events of 1 Sam. 11:1–11.

'kindness' (*ḥesed*) was interpreted by Hanun's advisors as a spy mission, as a result of which they insulted David through their crude treatment of the emissaries. The narrative withholds any insight into David's response[79] and instead focuses on the actions of the Ammonites who realize they have offended David and therefore bring in troops from regions to the north (2 Sam. 10:6–9). Somewhat surprisingly, the narrative initially focuses on Joab and the arrangements he makes with his brother Abishai (2 Sam. 10:9–14), arrangements that not only result in victory but that show Joab in a somewhat more positive light than elsewhere. The Arameans who have allied themselves with the Ammonites then launch their own attack, but are defeated, this time with David involved (2 Sam. 10:15–19).

The report of the defeat of the Arameans does not lead to the end of the Ammonite war, and this will be resumed in 2 Samuel 12:26. But interwoven with this battle is one of the darkest moments of David's reign. In 2 Samuel 11:1, David stayed in Jerusalem while Israel's forces besieged the Ammonite capital of Rabbah.[80] This is often understood as a criticism of David, though this is muted if we recognize that 2 Samuel 10:9–14 has shown that the king need not be present at every battle, while also preparing for Joab's invitation to David to be present for the final capture of Rabbah (2 Sam. 12:26–28). If there is criticism of David here, it is perhaps seen in retrospect rather than directly through this observation. Nevertheless, as the narrative unfolds it quickly becomes clear that David's actions in Jerusalem are indefensible,[81] as he engages in an illicit sexual relationship with Bathsheba, even though he knows she is married to Uriah the Hittite (2 Sam. 11:3). Following the report of her pregnancy (2 Sam. 11:5), the balance of 2 Samuel 11 is given over to his dealings with Uriah.

Uriah is immediately noticeable as a foreigner. His name 'Uriah'[82] indicates that he came from a Yahwist family, but one that was still known as Hittite. It is unlikely that he descended from the

[79] Cf. Fokkelman 1981: 45.

[80] Most English Bibles translate this verse as indicating that spring was the time of year 'when kings go out to battle'. But the MT would suggest 'messengers' go out to battle. With Fokkelman (1981: 50–51) the MT is here followed, especially since messengers are a key motif through the chapter; though Bodner (2005: 80–84) may be right that there is intentional ambiguity.

[81] My own view is that this chapter is even more critical of David than the traditional reading (that much of it is a botched attempt at covering up his adultery with Bathsheba); see Firth 2008b. However, the conclusions above do not depend on this.

[82] Perhaps 'Yahweh is light'.

better-known Hittites (from Anatolia) but that rather he was a member of the Canaanite group to whom this label was given who were perhaps descendants of Heth (Gen. 10:15).[83] As such, he represented those Canaanites who had integrated themselves into Israel, including committing themselves to the worship of Yahweh. His Canaanite background could still be recognized in his name, just as 'Uriah' indicated faith in Yahweh on the part of his parents. As the narrative unfolds, it is this faith that emerges with great clarity as he becomes an exemplary case study of how a Canaanite can become part of Israel even as Israel's great king demonstrates a remarkable level of fallibility.

Throughout the chapter there is a carefully drawn contrast between David and Uriah. Initially, David sent Uriah back to his house with the suggestion that he 'wash his feet'. This may be a euphemism:[84] Uriah certainly took it this way. But, rather than returning to his house and having sexual relations with his wife, Uriah sleeps at the door to David's palace, though no reason is initially given (2 Sam. 11:6–9). When informed of this, David asks Uriah why he has not gone to his house. This leads to Uriah's only speech, one that expresses a clear understanding of and commitment to Israel's faith, something notably absent from David. Uriah was a soldier who understood the requirements of holiness, especially in a war where the ark was with the army. He refused to sleep with his wife or even engage in any activity that might compromise that holiness (Deut. 23:10; ET 23:11). David's response was to get him drunk, but he still did not sleep with his wife. 'Uriah drunk is more pious than David sober.'[85] As a result, David arranged for Joab to kill Uriah, with Uriah even carrying back the letter that ordered this (2 Sam. 11:14–15). Joab was astute enough to know he could not follow David's orders precisely,[86] but when sending back his report he knew he needed to ensure that he foregrounded Uriah's death, something the messenger who reported this also realized (2 Sam. 11:16–25).

Throughout this chapter the contrast with Uriah shows the heinousness of David's actions. What is most striking is that it is not only a foreigner, but a descendant of the Canaanite population who is righteous. Uriah is destroyed by the power David demonstrates, but the concluding note to the chapter (2 Sam. 11:27b) along with the

---

[83] On the wider questions, see Wood 2011.
[84] Cf. Yee 1988: 248.
[85] Ackroyd 1977: 102.
[86] See Bodner 2002.

encounter with Nathan (2 Sam. 12:1–15a) shows that Yahweh will not tolerate such actions: indeed, he acts on behalf of a Canaanite. The war with Ammon is later concluded (2 Sam. 12:26–31), but it is a victory forever tainted by David's treatment of a foreigner.

In his ensuing encounter with David, Nathan announced that the sword would not depart from David's house. Indeed, it was particularly because of his treatment of Uriah the Hittite that this would come about (2 Sam. 12:7–15a). The two rebellion narratives then work out how this happens, reporting the conflicts within David's family that ultimately triggered civil war within Israel. Because much of this was internal to David's family and Israel more generally, one might expect that there would be little interest in foreigners. But perhaps we should not be surprised that an account triggered by the murder of a foreigner also includes important cameos by other foreigners.

The next mention of foreigners is brief, though it picks up on the note in 2 Samuel 3:3 about Absalom's mother being from Geshur. Following the murder of Amnon for raping his sister Tamar (2 Sam. 13:1–33), Absalom fled to Geshur, presumably as a place of safety. David perhaps longed for him (2 Sam. 13:39)[87] but he did nothing about bringing Absalom back until Joab intervened (2 Sam. 14:1–24). Not all foreigners were supportive of Israel, but there must have been a positive enough relationship with Geshur so that Absalom could be brought back.

Absalom's return did not resolve the relationship with David, and Absalom ultimately engineered a rebellion against David, having himself recognized as king in Hebron and even drawing in Ahithophel, David's counsellor (2 Sam. 15:1–12). This rebellion dominates everything up to the end of the long rebellion narrative, and is a carefully structured unit.[88] Much of it is focused on David's flight from Jerusalem as Absalom's forces approach and capture the city, the point where David seems furthest from remaining as king (2 Sam. 15:12 – 17:29). Yet at crucial points within this it is David's encounters with foreigners that are pivotal in his ultimate restoration to the throne.

Fleeing from Jerusalem, David met various groups and individuals as he went up the Mount of Olives (2 Sam. 15:12 – 16:4). As he went, he left the concubines he had taken from Jerusalem, women who would become pawns in the conflict between David and Absalom

---

[87] Here following 4QSam[a] and the LXX, and as represented in most English Bibles (e.g. the ESVUK).
[88] Cf. Conroy 1978: 89.

(2 Sam. 16:20–23; 20:3). If these women were Jebusites, then they are a further example of how an Israel that forgot its mission mistreated foreigners, though perhaps the ambiguity over their status is appropriate here because no women should have been treated as they were, joining Tamar (2 Sam. 13:1–22) and Bathsheba (2 Sam. 11:1 – 12:25) among the abused women of these chapters.

The first encounter on David's departure is, however, with foreigners, and they play an important role in challenging David's perspective on these events. David's departure was apparently sufficiently ordered for his troops to pass before him, and those mentioned are the Cherethites, Pelethites and 600 Gittites, who are said to have come from Gath. The Cherethites are also identified with the Philistine territory in the Negeb (1 Sam. 30:14; cf. Zeph. 2:5), while the Pelethites might also have been Philistine since they were always associated with the Cherethites. If so, David had a significant Philistine force that was part of his standing army. Although Benaiah, an Israelite, commanded the Cherethites and Pelethites (2 Sam. 8:18), the Gittite contingent apparently remained under the command of another Philistine, Ittai the Gittite. When David saw him marching past, he suggested that as a foreigner he would be better off returning to his home region, even as David expressed a hope that Yahweh would 'deal faithfully' (*ḥesed*) with him. But here there is a remarkable reversal to the events of 1 Samuel 17. There it was David who reshaped Israel's perspective as they dealt with a Philistine to see what Yahweh was doing. Here a Philistine reshapes David's perspective, swearing an oath of loyalty to David not dissimilar to that sworn by Ruth to Naomi (2 Sam. 15:21; cf. Ruth 1:16–18), except where Ruth indicated that Naomi's God would be hers, Ittai can already swear by Yahweh. Where David's flight was initially expressed only in military terms, it was a foreigner who was the first to indicate that loyalty to Yahweh in this instance also meant loyalty to David. It was a foreigner who more truly embodied the life that Israel were meant to live, and it is this that began the long process of permitting David to develop a more positive strategy in response to Absalom.

The crucial moment in the initial phase of David's flight was the brief prayer he offered when he heard that Ahithophel had joined Absalom, asking that Ahithophel's counsel be turned to foolishness (2 Sam. 15:31). As well as his encounter with Ittai the Gittite, David had by that stage also met Abiathar and Zadok, along with some Levites and the ark. He had chosen to send the ark back, reasoning that if he found 'favour' (*ḥēn*) with Yahweh, then Yahweh would bring him back. We see in these encounters that David had learnt the lesson taught by Ittai, that he needed to focus on the presence of Yahweh (2 Sam. 15:24–29). David's group were in mourning as they journeyed,[89] but at the same time there was a change in focus, indicated by his prayer. Immediately after the prayer, as he approached the summit (where there was a shrine), he met Hushai the Archite. Hushai would play a significant role in David's return, and would later be described as David's 'friend' (2 Sam. 15:37). But at his introduction we know only that he was an Archite and that he too mourned.

As an Archite, Hushai was (like Uriah) a descendant of one of the remaining Canaanite groups,[90] though they seem to have been regarded slightly differently from some of the other Canaanites.[91] Nevertheless, it is his status as a foreigner within Israel that is immediately flagged, a status that is contrasted within the narrative by the fact that David's next two encounters are with Saulides, one of whom may well have been manipulating things to his own advantage,[92] while the other chose to curse David.[93] In the account of David's flight it is thus the loyalty of foreigners that is particularly stressed. In Hushai's case this involved the perilous task of going to Jerusalem and acting as David's agent there. David thought of this in terms of providing information through his other agents, perhaps seeing this as how he would defeat Ahithophel's counsel, but Hushai's role quickly becomes more complex as he returns to Jerusalem just as Absalom enters the city (2 Sam. 15:32–37).

Hushai remains outside the narrative in 2 Samuel 16:1–14, though since there is a chronological correlation between the point of his arrival (2 Sam. 15:37) and that of Absalom (2 Sam. 16:15) this is partly because of the need to complete the reports of David's encounters as he fled. But once the timeline for both has been joined, the narrative immediately reports Hushai's encounter with Absalom, where he needed to convince Absalom that he would serve him. Once again Hushai's foreign status is stressed by noting that he is an Archite, though now his status as David's friend is joined to this (2 Sam. 16:16). An additional element is also established in his opening encounter with Absalom, that he is rather loquacious, as is evident

---

[89] See Seiler 1998: 145; Bodner 2014: 68.

[90] Josh. 16:2.

[91] See above, 'Caleb, the surviving Canaanites and the cities of refuge (Josh. 13 – 21)', in chapter 2.

[92] Ziba, 2 Sam. 16:1–4; cf. 2 Sam. 19:24–30.

[93] Shimei, 2 Sam. 16:5–13; cf. 2 Sam. 19:16–23; 1 Kgs 2:8–9.

from his doubled declaration of 'Long live the king!' (2 Sam. 16:16). Absalom, unsurprisingly, is suspicious, asking if this is the loyalty he shows to his friend (2 Sam. 16:17). But this leads into a longer speech from Hushai, one that is careful in its use of ambiguity[94] so that he leads Absalom to interpret his words as if they support him while leaving open the reality that he is supporting David. This ambiguity was already evident in his opening declaration: Who was the king to whom he wished long life? Absalom might have thought this meant him, but technically only David was king. Similarly, when he averred that he would serve the one chosen by both Yahweh and all the people of Israel then he could again mean only David (2 Sam. 16:18–19; cf. 2 Sam. 5:1–5). That he served David while letting Absalom think he served him is evident from the fact that his words about serving the son like the father are drawn from David's earlier directives (2 Sam. 16:19; cf. 2 Sam. 15:34). We are given no response from Absalom at this point, so from here on Hushai can stay in Jerusalem.

But Hushai's place at Jerusalem is not altogether secure, and this becomes quickly apparent in 2 Samuel 17:1–14, when he is brought in to give advice against that of Ahithophel. Given the earlier characterization of Ahithophel's advice as being as though one enquired by the word of God (2 Sam. 16:23) it is quickly apparent that Hushai faces a great challenge, though we also remember David's prayer for Ahithophel's advice to be turned to folly (2 Sam. 15:31). Where Absalom initiated his conversation with Hushai and asked Ahithophel for counsel on his arrival in Jerusalem, in this instance Ahithophel offers advice that has not been requested (2 Sam. 17:1–4).[95] That this is unrequested may be significant: it comes at a point at which Absalom, whose vanity is never in doubt (2 Sam. 14:25–27), may feel he has overstepped proper boundaries. In addition, where Hushai was carefully ambiguous about the king's identity, Ahithophel here refers to David as 'the king'. This, admittedly, is in the context of explaining how he will kill him and so bring the people over to Absalom's side,[96]

---

[94] Bodner (2014: 73) observes that his speech is 'flowing with misdirection'.

[95] Some English Bibles (e.g. the ESVUK) render the conjunction at 2 Sam. 17:1 as 'Moreover', giving the sense that this was perhaps a continuation of the previous advice, but the conjunction can imply a weaker link, merely suggesting that this was subsequent to the earlier advice. Auld (2011: 521) notes that Ahithophel had not been asked for his advice, but does not develop this point.

[96] The LXX (followed by the ESVUK, NRSVA) has a significant plus in Ahithophel's speech here, but preference should be given to the shorter MT (cf. Fokkelman 1981: 456–457).

but it is a comment that implicitly questions the legitimacy of Absalom's position. In addition, Ahithophel's advice focuses not on Absalom but on what Ahithophel will do, and this too could sit uneasily with Absalom, especially if it suggests that Ahithophel is more concerned with defeating David for his own reasons rather than promoting Absalom.[97] Yet, considered only from a military perspective, the advice he gives seems entirely reasonable, recommending a quick and surgical strike before David has the chance to establish himself. Given the rather disorganized nature of David's flight, readers have additional reason to think that this advice will succeed.[98]

At first Absalom joins with the other elders in considering this advice to be valid,[99] but that he has concerns is immediately evident from the fact that he asked Hushai to give his advice (2 Sam. 17:5–13). Hushai's speech follows the loquacious pattern already hinted at in his previous encounter with Absalom, though it opens with the startling declaration that Ahithophel's counsel is 'not good' (2 Sam. 17:7). In saying this, Hushai does not deny that it may be valid in general, but focuses on the instance of David's flight. Beyond this, Hushai's speech is short on military particulars, focusing on the threat that David posed to an Israelite force that pursued him because of his military experience. The comparison of David to a bear provides an echo for readers back to David's encounter with Goliath, where his previous deliverance from a bear gave him confidence to assure Saul he could meet Goliath (1 Sam. 17:34–37). Throughout Hushai stresses the threat that David poses, so when he finally offers military advice it is a process that will take a considerable amount of time because of the need to gather troops from across the country. But where Ahithophel put himself at the centre of the proposed battle, Hushai ensures that Abaslom is the one who is to lead. It is a speech that is full of bluster rather than the precise detail Ahithophel offered, and readers may well wonder if it is even valid. And yet Absalom, and his associates, declare that Hushai's advice is better than that of Ahithophel. Readers are meant to be surprised by this, which is why the narrator then points out that Yahweh has determined to thwart

---

[97] According to 2 Sam. 23:34, Ahithophel's son Eliam was one of David's elite soldiers. If the same Eliam was Bathsheba's father (2 Sam. 11:3), then Ahithophel might well have had his own grudge against David for the treatment of his granddaughter, something that would also explain his advice to Absalom in 2 Sam. 16:20–22. See also McKenzie 2000: 168.

[98] Cf. Bodner 2014: 79.

[99] This is perhaps a better way of understanding *wayyîšar* here than rendering it as 'good' or 'right', as is often done; e.g. the NIV, ESVUK or Firth 2009: 462.

Ahithophel's good advice in order to bring harm onto Absalom (2 Sam. 17:14). Although it may look to some extent as if the narrative has just reported a conflict between counsellors, the narrator insists that this is a point where Yahweh is at work, a point where David's prayer is being answered, and answered through the commitment of a foreigner.

Only one other foreigner features in the long rebellion narrative, a Cushite who brings the news of Absalom's death to David (2 Sam. 18:19–32). The characterization in this vignette is not particularly developed, but it seems that Joab might have thought it best that David heard the bad news from the Cushite rather than Zadok's son Ahimaaz, who had been anxious to deliver it. Perhaps, given some of David's earlier encounters with messengers reporting royal deaths (2 Sam. 1:1–16; 4:9–12), Joab felt that the Cushite was a more disposable figure. If so, it quickly becomes apparent that he need not have worried because although David immediately mourns for his son, he does not act against the Cushite.

The long rebellion narrative is thus notable for its careful deployment of foreigners throughout. Although it still allows scope for foreign powers who oppose Israel, it is more remarkable for the fact that it uses individual foreigners who for various reasons live within Israel to characterize David and to show how Yahweh is at work. The Canaanite remnant who have committed themselves to Yahweh prove more faithful than Yahweh's anointed king, and it is a Philistine who helps David see how Yahweh is continuing to act. Foreigners are thus pivotal throughout.

Short rebellion narrative: 2 Samuel 20

Where foreigners play a significant role in the long rebellion narrative, they have only a minor part in the short rebellion narrative when Sheba leads at least some of the northern tribes in a further revolt against David. In this narrative it is clear that Judah remained loyal to David (2 Sam. 20:2) and those who joined Sheba were all from the north. In the midst of a degree of chaos in which Amasa was initially appointed head of the army, but could not gather them in time, Joab eventually took control after murdering Amasa (2 Sam. 20:4–10). Joab apparently took some of the standing army, including the Cherethites and Pelethites who had previously been prominent in offering David support as he fled from Absalom (2 Sam. 15:18). As noted above, the Cherethites were originally Philistine and the same is probably true of the Pelethites, indicating that these foreign mercenaries continued to be loyal to David. After Joab returns, it is noted that Benaiah continues to command them (2 Sam. 20:23; cf. 2 Sam. 8:18).

Summary II: the Samuel conclusion: 2 Samuel 21 – 24

As with Summary I, Summary II is presented as an extended chiasm,[100] and one that shows considerable similarity to that in Summary I:

A   Famine, 2 Samuel 21:1–14
   B   Warrior stories, 2 Samuel 21:15–22
     C   Psalm, 2 Samuel 22
     C' Psalm, 2 Samuel 23:1–7
   B' Warrior stories, 2 Samuel 23:8–39
A' Plague, 2 Samuel 24:1–25

Although these chapters are often treated as an 'Appendix',[101] there are good reasons for seeing them as an intentional conclusion to Samuel, not least because the two psalms at their heart match Hannah's Song (1 Sam. 2:1–10) so that the whole book is bounded by songs that reflect on kingship.[102] These psalms are also private expressions of worship by David that match the central focus on worship in Summary I. Summary I was bounded by tales of David's winning battles with Yahweh's help, and here the sections around the psalms also reflect on how battles were won, but this time pointing to the warriors who joined David. It is the famine and plague narratives that add a distinctive element. Apart from the two psalms, there is again a close focus on foreigners[103] through these chapters as a mechanism for assessing David, though these narratives are more difficult to interpret. As a summary of the whole of David's reign it is not always easy to tie these narratives into the chronology of the rest of the book.

The famine story (2 Sam. 21:1–14) is the first of three elements in the conclusion that offer a critique of Saul.[104] It reports a famine that lasted three years. On seeking guidance from Yahweh, David was

---

[100] This structure was recognized at least as early as Budde (1902: 304), but its significance has been explored only more recently; most notably by Klement (2000), who explores its significance for the whole of Samuel.
[101] Even an author as aware of literary links as Fokkelman (1990:11) finds these chapters aesthetically displeasing.
[102] See more fully Firth 2009: 501–503; Ko 2018.
[103] Foreigners are mentioned in 2 Sam. 22:45–46, but as stereotyped enemies.
[104] Klement 2000: 165–166.

informed of bloodguilt incurred by Saul and his family because of an otherwise unreported time when he put some of the Gibeonites to death. This connects with the arrangements made with them by Joshua (Josh. 9:3–27) that had guaranteed their safety along with assigning them a place at the sanctuary. A key focus in this account is to contrast David's approach with Saul's in that David asked the Gibeonites for their input into the question of how to address this bloodguilt. As Kim has argued, although there are numerous obscure elements within the story that cannot be examined here, its central aim is to show that David honoured a Yahweh oath concerning these foreigners, whereas Saul acted against it.[105] The Gibeonites are a Canaanite remnant living within Israel, and their status is such that the king cannot act against them. Rather, the king's responsibility is to promote the well-being of these people.

The conclusion recognizes that there will still be foreign powers opposed to Israel, and this is evident in the first of the warrior accounts (2 Sam. 21:15–22). As with Summary I, we begin with conflict with the Philistines, and this time focus on four other giants.[106] Where 1 Samuel 17 showed David as a giant-slayer, now it is his men who do this, even needing to ensure that David is kept out of harm's way.[107] Although David is associated with these victories, it is his men who do the fighting in a series of reports that are remarkably silent on Yahweh's role. However, since both the conclusion's psalms point to the importance of the king's dependence on Yahweh (e.g. 2 Sam. 22:1–4; 23:3b–4), it is likely that overt theological evaluation is omitted in the battle reports in order to focus on the psalms.

Although less prominent, foreigners are also important in the records of David's warriors (2 Sam. 23:8–39). The most evident of these is Uriah the Hittite, who is the last one listed among the Thirty, an elite group of soldiers closely associated with David.[108] But he is not the only foreigner to serve in David's elite forces since Igal is from

[105] J.-S. Kim 2007: 171–176. Note that David also kept his oath to Jonathan (2 Sam. 21:7).

[106] McCarter (1984: 449–450) suggests that they are devoted to the god Rapha, not that they are giants; but the numerous references to the Rephaim as giants (e.g. Josh. 12:4) makes this the more likely interpretation.

[107] Although it is often argued that this passage indicates that the true killer of Goliath was Elhanan; see Firth 2009: 509 for the view that it was Goliath's brother Lahmi who was killed here.

[108] There were apparently thirty-seven members of the Thirty, though exactly how the text is to be arranged to achieve this is not clear (see Simon 2000: 188–189; Firth 2009: 532–533). However, if we understand that 'Thirty' reflects a rank rather than a specific number of soldiers the issue is not especially pressing.

Zobah (2 Sam. 23:36), while Zelek is an Ammonite (2 Sam. 23:37). Both Ira and Gareb are said to be Ithrites, which may make them descendants of Canaanite peoples, but this is not clear.[109] The place of continuing Canaanites within Israel is picked up as an important theme in the plague narrative with which Samuel closes (2 Sam. 24). Whether or not the opening 'again' here points to an original link with 2 Samuel 21:1–14, it seems clear within the conclusion that we are to read these narratives in the light of each other. As with that narrative, there are numerous difficulties in the interpretation of this account that need to be set aside for this investigation. It is enough to note that following a census David was presented with three options after he had confessed his sin to Yahweh, with the seer Gad acting as the go-between. After David chose to fall into Yahweh's hands (though perhaps trying to avoid any of the options), a plague was sent on Israel that resulted in significant death until Yahweh relented at the point where the destroying angel was at Jerusalem, by the threshing floor of Araunah the Jebusite (2 Sam. 24:14–17). However, although the link between the famine and the plague has often been noted, the continued interest in foreigners, and especially continuing Canaanites, has not been a notable feature of research on this chapter.[110]

Araunah's introduction (2 Sam. 23:16)[111] is initially unexpected. But through Gad's intervention David is gradually transformed within this narrative from being a king who takes, and thus stands condemned in terms of 1 Samuel 8:10–18, into one who understands that his role is to serve and lead his nation in worship. From Gad David discovers he is to learn this through his interactions with Araunah. Hence David is initially ordered to erect an altar at Araunah the Jebusite's threshing floor, Araunah's ethnicity thus being stressed, which points to the surprising element that the place where Yahweh was to be worshipped belonged to a Canaanite. In his encounter with

[109] 1 Chr. 2:53 places the Ithrites within Caleb's clans, but their level of integration makes it harder to be sure of their status.

[110] See Simon 2000: 122–126 for an overview of diachronic approaches that have seen the Jebusite element here as linked to a myth concerned with the foundation of the temple. The difficulty with all such interpretations, however, is that there is nothing in Samuel (or Kings) to indicate that this site would later be where the temple was built, even though David does build an altar. This is to bring in themes from Chronicles. With Schenker (1982: 33) a more unified reading of this chapter is required.

[111] Note that at this point he is 'the Araunah', suggesting that this is a title rather than a proper name. Given that the Kethib varies in different ways at 2 Sam. 24:16 and 24:18 from the other occurrences of the name it seems that there remained considerable uncertainty about how to represent this name, which becomes Ornan in 1 Chr. 21.

131

David Araunah behaves in an exemplary manner, initially prostrating himself before David and then offering the threshing floor and the implements necessary for the sacrifice as a gift, before expressing the wish that Yahweh accept David. But David has been changed, and the figure who once would have taken now insists on paying the full price.[112] Where Saul had sinned against continuing Canaanites in the famine narrative, and David had sinned against a continuing Canaanite in his dealings with Bathsheba and Uriah, here it is a Canaanite who becomes a key figure (along with Gad) in reshaping David's perspective so that he is a king who leads his people in worship.

Conclusions: Samuel and understanding the people of God

Foreigners play a significant role throughout Samuel. In particular, they are used to shine light on the character of Israelites and to demonstrate how foreigners can continue to be integrated into Israel's shared life. In Israel's encounters with foreign powers there is a consistent element in their portrayal – where they fight Israel, they are not simply advancing their own interests: they are opposing Yahweh's purposes. Although Samuel and David are able to see this, as is Jonathan to some extent, Saul never fully grasps this element. But Samuel also gives particular attention to individual foreigners who have become part of Israel's shared life. In the case of figures like Doeg, their willingness to oppose Yahweh's work and attach themselves to traditional models of royal power shows up those for whom they work. In particular, Saul is not the king Israel needs, because he continues to be drawn to this type of power model, and thus (like Achan) moves towards what was flawed in the old Canaanite model. In his encounter with Goliath David is able to see things differently, and in the two summaries of his reign his interaction with foreigners who are within Israel shows how seriously Yahweh takes those who have been joined to his people. Although these foreigners are descendants of Canaanites, they are able to teach Israel what it means to be faithful, and both David and Saul need to learn this.

There is, however, in the rebellion narratives the most sustained interest in foreigners, and here it is often the case that foreigners, particularly those descended from Canaanites, most truly live out what

---

[112] On the variation in price between Samuel and Chronicles, see Firth 2009: 548.

it is to serve Yahweh. It is the exemplary lifestyle of a foreigner like Uriah that shows the depths to which David has sunk, and it is through foreigners like Ittai and Hushai that Yahweh demonstrates he is continuing to work with David, in spite of the king's manifest faults. Throughout, Samuel shows the possibilities involved in the integration of foreigners into the people of God.

Chapter Five

The books of Kings: foreigners beyond the borders of Israel

Initial orientation

As with Samuel, the division of Kings into two books is a matter of historical practicality, most likely to provide a pair of scrolls that could be handled easily. This is evident from the fact that 2 Kings 1:1 picks up immediately on the closing verses of 1 Kings (1 Kgs 22:51–53), meaning the report of Ahaziah's injury that follows depends on readers knowing of his accession, something only introduced by the close of 1 Kings. In addition, as with Samuel, the Masoretes provided their notes only at the end of 2 Kings and these cover the whole of Kings. Hence, although there is diverse material within it, we need to read Kings as a single book.[1]

Granted this, there are still important questions to answer in terms of Kings's relationship to Samuel. Readers will often recognize this from the fact that 1 Kings opens with David's final days, recounting the process by which Solomon became king (1 Kgs 1 – 2). David's 'Last Words' are reported in 2 Samuel 23:1–7 and though these are probably intended as a final public declaration rather than as a deathbed statement, it is clear that 2 Samuel 23 (at least) presents an elderly David.[2] However, although there were hints of a David in decline there, none of that prepares readers for the infirm figure who needs Abishag to keep him warm at night.[3] On the other hand, almost all the major characters in 1 Kings 1 – 2 were introduced in Samuel,

---

[1] Similarly, Provan 1995: 1.

[2] Given the uncertain chronological relationship of the rest of the Samuel conclusion (2 Sam. 21 – 24) to the rest of Samuel we cannot conclude that 2 Sam. 24 is later than 2 Sam. 23. However, 2 Sam. 21:15–22 also seems to indicate that it came from a period when David was much older.

[3] As Wray Beal (2014: 69) notes, the language here can suggest sexual activity, but in this case David's infirmity is stressed by noting that he does not have sexual relations with her.

though very few of them feature in the Samuel conclusion. So strong are the links between Samuel and Kings that the LXX treats them as 1 – 4 Kingdoms.[4] Indisputably then Kings is to be read in the light of Samuel and, from this, the wider canon. But where the dominant trend has been to regard the division between Samuel and Kings as no more significant than the division between 1 and 2 Kings, we have noted above that there are good reasons for treating Samuel as an intentional work. Indeed, one effect of seeing only a minor break between Samuel and Kings has been an effective marginalization of 2 Samuel 21 – 24, seeing it as an appendix, so that the body of Samuel effectively finishes at 2 Samuel 20. But as noted in the previous chapter, there are reasons for seeing these chapters as the intentional conclusion to Samuel. With Keys,[5] it seems better to see 1 Kings 1 – 2 as material written with full knowledge of the material in Samuel, but rather than being the intended conclusion of a so-called succession narrative it functions to introduce the narrative of the kingdoms of Israel and Judah. Completing David's story from Samuel is an important task, but the primary goal is to introduce a new story, not to complete an old one. As with each of the other books of the Former Prophets, Kings too was intended to be read as a literary unit, albeit one that makes frequent reference to at least some of the sources used in its compilation,[6] while also expecting readers to make wider canonical connections.[7]

Seeing Kings as a distinct literary work helps to open its own presentational and theological emphases. The importance of this should not be understated. For example, in terms of narrative technique it is evident that Kings does not operate with the same models as Samuel – there is, for example, no attempt to provide the sorts of extended narratives that marked Samuel, and neither is there

---

[4] The divisions between Samuel and Kings are not uniformly presented in the LXX, with some Lucianic MSS placing the division between the books at 1 Kgs 2:11. But the most common divisions match those found in the MT and represented in English Bibles.

[5] Keys 1996: 54–70.

[6] E.g. 'The Book of the Acts of Solomon' (1 Kgs 11:41), 'The Book of the Chronicles of Israel' (1 Kgs 14:19) or 'The Book of the Chronicles of the Kings of Judah' (1 Kgs 15:7). Undoubtedly, other source materials were used (e.g. the stories of Elijah and Elisha), though many of these might have been integrated into a more complete document such as the 'Prophetic Record' proposed by A. F. Campbell (1986). With Provan (1995: 4) it is fair to believe that many authors were involved in the book's formation, though this does not lead to incoherence.

[7] Dharamraj (2011: 4–5) makes the key point that to understand the Moses typology applied to Elijah we must read Kings with an awareness of almost the whole of the Pentateuch and Former Prophets to this point.

any attempt to provide the parallel panels that Samuel employed. In part, this is dictated by the nature of the material covered; especially the need to provide a synchronized account of the kingdoms of Israel and Judah from the division of the kingdoms after Solomon's death (1 Kgs 12:1–24) through to the fall of the northern kingdom little over two centuries later (2 Kgs 17:6–23). The absence of some of the key features present in Samuel does not mean that Kings is somehow less sophisticated as a narrative text; merely that it works differently from Samuel with the palette of narrative techniques available to the narrators of the Old Testament.[8]

For the goals of this study this also opens the possibility of seeing Kings as having a distinctive contribution to the understanding of foreigners within the Former Prophets. On the one hand, because Kings is self-consciously presented as a continuation of the earlier works in this collection, it can presume readers are aware of themes developed in the earlier books. Hence in 1 Kings 15:4–5 it is possible to note David's murder of Uriah so that readers are reminded of it, but also to stress Yahweh's continued commitment to David as expressed in his promise to him. Likewise, 1 Kings 16:34 can look back to Joshua's cursing the one who would rebuild Jericho (Josh. 6:26), and thus contrast Ahab's story with Rahab's. But Kings also introduces new material relative to foreigners. Whereas each of Joshua, Judges and Samuel were (to some extent) concerned with foreigners who were in Israel, with foreigners outside Israel being largely foreign powers opposed to Israel, Kings now develops a focus on foreigners who live outside Israel but who discover Yahweh at work in their lives. Indeed, within Kings it emerges that one of the key functions of the temple is to provide a place to which a foreigner who continues to dwell outside Israel can turn and seek forgiveness; indeed, Naaman the Aramean is the only person within Kings said to receive forgiveness (2 Kgs 5:18–19). There is thus continuity in the treatment of foreigners with the earlier books of the Former Prophets, yet also some distinctive elements that demonstrate awareness of how Yahweh works in the lives of people even outside Israel. Kings differs from Samuel, though, in that it does not use foreigners as an evaluative tool for Israelites, though it continues to

---

[8] E.g. Paynter (2016) has demonstrated that the Elijah and Elisha stories are marked by 'seriocomic features', a technique not particularly evident in Samuel. Although Paynter draws this concept from the work of M. Bakhtin, her work is careful to demonstrate that it is a feature of the text itself, not something projected onto it by her as a reader.

demonstrate that foreigners who do not express faith in Yahweh can cause Israel to stumble.

Solomon: 1 Kings 1 – 11

In many respects the key elements of Kings's presentation of foreigners can be seen in the Solomon story, a narrative that although containing diverse elements now appears as a carefully constructed whole.[9] His story demonstrates both the possibilities offered to foreigners by Yahweh and the ways foreigners can cause Israel to stumble. The only element in Kings's overall presentation to be muted (at least relatively) here is the threat posed by foreign powers that are hostile to Israel.

Since 1 Kings 1 – 2 depends on some knowledge of 2 Samuel 9 – 20, it is notable that key foreigners continue to play important roles. In this they continue the pattern established in Samuel, though certain elements are developed. Most importantly, although Benaiah's status as the commander of David's foreign soldiers (the Cherethites and Pelethites) was noted in Samuel (2 Sam. 8:18; 20:23), as were some of his acts of valour (2 Sam. 23:20–23), he was a relatively minor character. But here he takes a pivotal role in the process by which Solomon both claims and secures the throne, as both a key figure among Solomon's supporters and then as his executioner. Most notably, when Adonijah heard that David had made Solomon king, it is reported that Benaiah took the Cherethites and Pelethites with him as part of the retinue that demonstrated his position as king (1 Kgs 1:44). Clearly, their presence with Solomon was intended to demonstrate to Adonijah that he should accept Solomon as king, relinquishing his own claim. Beyond this, their role was small. However, that David and Solomon were thus co-regents at this time introduces a new factor, even if David's position was increasingly feeble,[10] and might well have been modelled on earlier Egyptian patterns.[11] If so, this may be an initial subtle hint of the problems that Solomon will, despite his wisdom, have because of his close links with Egypt. However, as Seow has pointed out,[12] it is ultimately Yahweh who establishes Solomon on the throne, notwithstanding the political manoeuvring involved in bringing this about.

---

[9] See D. S. Williams 1999, though with modifications from Olley 2003.
[10] So DeVries 1985: 19.
[11] Ball 1977.
[12] Seow 1999: 36. Knoppers (1993: 67) sees it as 'providential'.

If the co-regency with David hinted at possible Egyptian links with Israel's court, this matter is brought to greater prominence once the kingdom is established in Solomon's grasp (1 Kgs 2:46). This is made explicit in the note about Pharaoh's daughter that initiates the main presentation of Solomon's reign in 1 Kings 3 – 11 (1 Kgs 3:1). Although at least 1 Kings 3 – 10 has usually been read as a positive presentation of Solomon,[13] Olley notes that this introduction of Pharaoh's daughter raises questions about Solomon even before the rest of the story unfolds.[14] As such, with Hays,[15] it seems likely that the narrator is writing a work that is always intended as a criticism of Solomon, though its components are subtly deployed.[16] This means that a first-time reader may be unable to determine how to interpret the reference to Pharaoh's daughter: Will she be like Rahab, a foreigner who will embody Israel's values more effectively than even the Israelites did? Or, as Hays claims, will this note 'explode like a bombshell in the reader's mind'?[17] Certainly, reference to an alliance with Egypt ought to be troubling, but when read in the context of the Former Prophets to this point it is not immediately clear that this is the correct reading.[18] But when she is reintroduced (1 Kgs 7:8; 9:24) the text reports both on the extent of Solomon's own palace relative to the temple and his trading activities, pointing to levels of wealth that are worrying in the light of Deuteronomy 17:17, an element that becomes more troubling in the following chapter. As such, it seems that reference to Pharaoh's daughter is employed within an emerging critique of Solomon, and though this marriage alliance can be recognized as flawed only from the end of the story, a second-time reader should indeed note that this concern with inappropriate marriage alliances is flagged up as a problem from the beginning. Walsh[19] also notes that in 1 Kings 9:16 Pharaoh seizes Gezer, a town not that far from Jerusalem, giving it to his daughter. Although he takes it from some continuing Canaanites, the implication is that Pharaoh is the dominant power in this relationship, though again readers appreciate the implications of this only at the second reading of 1 Kings 3:1.

---

[13] E.g. Parker 1992.

[14] Olley 2003: 365.

[15] J. D. Hays 2003b.

[16] Joseph (2015: 168) misses this element, seeing the wealth Solomon gains as a reward.

[17] J. D. Hays 2003b: 161. See also Schmid 2000: 110.

[18] Josh. 23:12, however, warns against such marriages; so even within the context of the Former Prophets this note is at best ambiguous.

[19] Walsh 1995: 70.

Moreover, at this point we can still be assured that Solomon loves Yahweh (1 Kgs 3:3), and this, combined with the anticipatory references to the building of both the temple and his palace, means that we do not yet have to read Solomon's story negatively. We have, however, a hint of the problems that will emerge and that 1 Kings 11:1 will make explicit, again by reference to Pharaoh's daughter.

Solomon's interaction with foreign women is thus a potential, but not necessary, problem. Its significance depends on how the motif is developed. However, given that the ensuing references to Pharaoh's daughter are in the context either of Solomon's wealth or the relative power of Pharaoh, readers are being prepared for the final problem of his many foreign wives. Before this there is a vital encounter with an important foreign woman, the Queen of Sheba. She is clearly a powerful woman, and Solomon has almost to compete with her, to show he is her equal.[20] She comes to test Solomon with hard questions (1 Kgs 10:1), and goes away convinced by him, though in fact we are never told of any hard questions being asked. At one level, it seems that she is presented as a straightforward supporter of Solomon. But the fact that his wealth is what convinces her of his wisdom is concerning in the light of the warning in Deuteronomy 17:17.[21] If her judgment of Solomon is in terms of a classical monarch of the ANE rather than Israel's model for kingship (which was clearly intended to be different), then such an assessment is inherently suspect. Indeed, that she claims Yahweh has placed Solomon on the throne to 'practise justice and righteousness' (1 Kgs 10:9) generates further concerns, because the extent of his wealth already raises questions about how Solomon sustains it.[22] The narrative thus again prepares readers to understand Solomon negatively, even while using what appears as praise from this foreign queen.

Although it is only fully evident from 1 Kings 11:1, the whole Solomon narrative has thus deployed foreign women, and especially marriages that were also alliances, negatively. But what was a possibility on a first reading to this point becomes a necessary element as we are told of how Solomon loves many 'foreign' (*nokrî*) women, all of whom are initially linked with Pharaoh's daughter. Deuteronomy 17:17,

[20] Gillmayr-Bucher 2007: 138.

[21] If we follow the LXX at 1 Kgs 10:8, it is Solomon's wives (not his men, as per the MT) who are blessed, a note that may well prepare for the ensuing reference to his wives at 1 Kgs 11:1.

[22] Brueggemann (2000: 134) believes the phrase 'constitutes a major critique of the acquisitive aggrandizement embraced by Solomon'.

which has lain in the background of much of this narrative, made clear that a king was not to take many foreign wives because they could turn his heart from following Yahweh. Although 1 Kings 3:3 makes clear that Solomon started from the right place, the hints that have been developing throughout now come together to show the devastating effect of these marriages on his walk with Yahweh. As well as Deuteronomy 17:17, the note about the nations Yahweh specifically indicated Israel was not to marry probably refers to Deuteronomy 7:1–5. This text makes clear that their status as foreign was not itself the problem, but rather that they would lead Israel away from the worship of Yahweh. Rahab has demonstrated that where such women embrace faith in Yahweh, then being foreign is not itself a problem. But Solomon's wives not only failed to embrace Yahweh and continued to worship their own gods, Solomon also enabled such worship. The seeds Solomon sowed before now reap their bitter harvest.

As well as his wives, Solomon maintained other foreign relations that are initially ambiguous. The most important of these was his link with Hiram, something traced back to the link David had established with him (1 Kgs 5:15; ET 5:1). In the MT Hiram responded to news of Solomon's anointing as king, but the LXX suggests that Hiram had anointed him.[23] On balance the MT seems more probable, as the LXX can be read as assuming a model where a king would be honoured to be anointed by another king,[24] though if the LXX is correct it is a further example of the narrator including elements that will emerge more fully as a problem later in the narrative. The connection with David probably dates only to the latter days of his reign, but it does indicate the importance of maintaining such relationships. For David, the association with Hiram was evidence of Yahweh's presence with him (2 Sam. 5:11–12), and initially at least one can interpret Solomon's relationship with him as continuing this pattern. This can be seen in the initial negotiations between them, which focus on building the temple (1 Kgs 5:16–23; ET 5:2–9), reflecting on Yahweh's promise to David (2 Sam. 7:3–17). But it also quickly becomes apparent that this agreement is not cheap – Solomon will pay the Sidonian workers whatever rate Hiram may determine, while Hiram also requires provision of food for his household, though it is not clear exactly how much Solomon is to provide. Already, there is a threat to the idyllic picture painted of his early reign, and the wealth Israel derived from

---

[23] A reading supported by Kuan 1990.
[24] Cf. DeVries 1985: 78.

tribute (1 Kgs 4:20–21). Nevertheless, in the initial presentation it still seems that Solomon is the dominant king, with Hiram acting as a vassal.[25]

Another Hiram was brought from Tyre to complete the temple furnishings (1 Kgs 7:13–51). This man's mother was from Naphtali, but his father was from Tyre, indicating that the boundaries between the northern tribes and the surrounding peoples were porous. This Hiram is introduced in terms reminiscent of Bezalel (Exod. 31:1–11) except that there is no indication of his being filled with the Spirit so that his skill was only with bronze, not gold and silver as well. This could suggest that someone else was responsible for the gold and silver furnishings (1 Kgs 7:48–51), but it might also have been that Hiram was the relevant workman. The temple's furnishings do not, therefore, quite measure up to those of the tabernacle, but it still seems that the work of someone trained outside Israel could be acceptable when it provided for the worship of Yahweh.

An initial reading of King Hiram might reach the same conclusion, but matters become more complex when he is reintroduced into the story (1 Kgs 9:10). Here Hiram came to see twenty settlements in Galilee that Solomon had given him. The circumstances that led to this are never explained.[26] But that Solomon, in addition to the specified timber, received 120 talents of gold from Hiram that were not mentioned in their initial negotiations suggests that he had been building up debt and these settlements were meant to cover this. Exactly why Hiram would be so dismissive of these settlements is unclear since this region would not only have extended his own realm; it represented some of the better farming land in the area.[27] Moreover, in calling Solomon 'my brother' he uses language typical of treaties, but this now implies that whatever the nature of their initial relationship, Solomon is no longer the dominant partner in the relationship. Hiram can now view himself as at least Solomon's equal, and his dismissal of these towns may even suggest that he is in the process of making himself the dominant figure in the relationship, though at the same time there is no indication that he ever received any better

[25] So Wray Beal 2014: 107.

[26] 2 Chr. 8:1–2 has the land transfer going the other way. Although Cogan (2001: 299) dismisses it, there may be value in following Wiseman (1993: 126) and seeing this in terms of a mortgage, which could explain the seeming movement of the towns in two different directions. However, for Kings the key point remains that Solomon had to transfer control of Israelite settlements to Tyre.

[27] 'Cabul' is often thought to come from a root meaning 'worthless', but this is not clear.

territory. Solomon's wisdom might mean he was able to negotiate a doubtful real estate deal, but even if we are to accept that his knowledge of the art of the deal meant he could succeed, we are left in no doubt that such a deal left Israelites as mere pawns in a game between kings. His relationship with Hiram provided much that was necessary for the temple (and his palace), and Tyre's contribution to the temple was something Israel valued. But when Solomon lost sight of the reasons for Israel's existence and engaged in somewhat dubious real estate trades and a subsequent enslavement of continuing Canaanites (1 Kgs 9:20–22) he began to look like the sort of king Deuteronomy 17:14–20 had rejected, and even more like the sort of king about which Samuel had warned the people (1 Sam. 8:10–18).

In his dealings with foreign women and Tyre Solomon demonstrated aspects of his reign where relationships with foreigners had the potential to contribute positively to Israel's life. But by the end of his reign it is apparent that these not only damaged Solomon; they damaged Israel too. That damage then works itself out in 1 Kings 11, where Yahweh raises up various adversaries for Solomon. Two of these, Hadad the Edomite (1 Kgs 11:14–22) and Rezon ben Eliada (1 Kgs 11:23–25), are foreigners who represent a long-term threat to Solomon. But it is Jeroboam ben Nebat, an apparently able Israelite whom Solomon placed over his forced labour, through whom Yahweh will tear away most of the kingdom following Solomon's death. Somewhat remarkably given Solomon's marriage alliance with Egypt, the Egyptians also supported both Hadad and Jeroboam. But Yahweh would not yet give part of the kingdom over to foreigners.

Why then would the narrative take such pains to present Solomon's reign in such ambiguous terms, especially in terms of his dealings with foreigners? It would probably be unwise to trace this back to a single issue, but an important clue is surely to be found in the opening of the temple (1 Kgs 8:1–21) and, more particularly, in the report of Solomon's prayer at that time (1 Kgs 8:22–53). Although there are disputes about the overall structure of 1 Kings 3 – 11, most agree that the construction and dedication of the temple are central.[28] Even Hays, who is perhaps more attuned than most to the implied criticism of Solomon in these chapters, finds comparatively little that is problematic here, and none of his criticisms relate to the prayer.[29] Since much of the prayer is presented as a series of hypothetical cases,

---

[28] See the comparison in D. S. Williams 1999: 50–53.
[29] J. D. Hays 2003b: 169–170.

we may therefore examine it as a text that represents possibilities for Solomon – though we will also note that in the end Solomon fails to live up to the rhetoric of his own prayer, even if it is also 'the high point of his rule'.[30]

In the prayer's presentation we can mark off 1 Kings 8:22–30 as a discrete section, one that introduces the prayer rather than provides its central petitions.[31] It does, however, establish the key theme that Yahweh is not contained by the temple, but that it can be a point of focus for prayer even if God ultimately hears from heaven, which is his real dwelling place,[32] a theme that recurs in the main petitions (1 Kgs 8:32, 34, 36, 39, 43, 45, 49). The initial setting suggests that Yahweh is to hear the prayers of Israel, though as the prayer progresses it becomes clear that the nature of the people of God is more open than this may initially suggest.

The body of the prayer is then presented as a series of seven petitions[33] with a focus on the issue of forgiveness. The significance of this can best be understood by noting that the verb 'forgive' here (slḥ) occurs in qal (as here) only thirty-three times in the Old Testament, and five of these occur in this prayer.[34] Moreover, the pattern of forgiveness here does not depend, as one might have thought, on sacrifice since sacrifice plays no part in the prayer. Instead, forgiveness is Yahweh's gracious response to prayer.[35]

Although six of the seven petitions are concerned with Israel, either individually or corporately, the fifth petition stands out (1 Kgs 8:41–43). Here Solomon considers the case of a 'foreigner' (nokrî) who is expressly not Israelite. This foreigner is not envisaged as someone who necessarily takes up residence within Israel, but who has come because he (or she) has heard of Yahweh's reputation. Indeed, the petition assumes that foreigners from distant nations will

[30] Wray Beal 2014: 132.
[31] Cf. Schmid 2000: 237.
[32] On this theme, see Kamp 2016. Dubovský (2015: 124) sees this idea of divine presence as contrary to the idea of Yahweh as a warrior whose presence is indicated by the ark. But there is no reason why the text cannot view Yahweh's presence from a range of perspectives from which readers build up a view of the whole, with each element being given full weight.
[33] This is part of a general structural element of the Solomon narrative, which frequently divides into groups of seven, noted by Davies (2012). This makes it less likely that petitions six and seven were added later, as proposed by DeVries (1985: 120). On the prayer's overall structure, see Boda 2009: 168–169.
[34] Talstra 1993: 192.
[35] See Knoppers 1995: 230. With Hobbs (1989: 85) we should note that it is prayer and repentance that provide hope.

hear not only of Yahweh's 'reputation' (*šēm*), but also of his mighty hand and outstretched arm. This language echoes some of the key statements of the exodus, and in Deuteronomy 4:34 refers to the process by which Yahweh took a people to himself. In the prayer the identity of this people is now expanded, not so much by Yahweh's going out and finding these foreigners but rather by their responding to reports they apparently hear about Yahweh. This integration with the people of God is perhaps also noted by the opening *wĕgam* of the petition. This could be translated (as in the ESVUK) as 'Likewise' and thus suggest an equivalence between these foreigners and Israel. If so, although the opening petitions focused on Israel, then to the extent that the conditions of the previous petitions applied to foreigners, foreigners too would be covered by them. Many aspects of the covenant curses and blessings from Deuteronomy 28 that lie behind these petitions cannot apply to foreigners who live outside Israel since these focus on life within the land, but this petition still imagines a closer integration between these foreigners and Israel.

Although the fifth petition does not ask for forgiveness for these foreigners, this needs to be understood as at least one possibility for them because the petition emerges out of the preceding ones that had a strong focus on forgiveness. In any case since this petition asks that Yahweh do for them whatever they ask, then forgiveness must be regarded as one possible element. But this petition looks beyond the request of any foreigner, because the reason Yahweh is to answer requests is so that 'all the peoples of the earth may know your name' (*šēm*, 1 Kgs 8:43; cf. 8:60) as well as recognize the validity of the temple as the place known by that name. In making this point, Solomon's prayer is joined with both the cairn at the Jordan (Josh. 4:24) and David's declaration to Goliath (1 Sam. 17:46) in pointing to the fact that Yahweh's work within Israel is linked to his purposes for all peoples.[36] This petition, therefore, demonstrates that foreigners are not an intrinsic threat to Israel and that they can indeed become a part of the people of God, even beyond the boundaries of the land of Israel. In this the petition goes beyond the earlier elements of the Former Prophets, though it is an extension of a trajectory rather than something new. It also explains why, within the Solomon narrative, the element of his association with foreigners is at first introduced in relatively neutral terms that become negative only when we go back

---

[36] Linville (1998: 291) thus sees that through the prayer the temple becomes 'a locus for those seeking piety, not dynastic grandeur'.

and read them again – if these foreigners embrace faith in Yahweh, then even if they never become Israelite they are still a part of the people of God. Foreigners themselves are not a threat – it is the failure to hold to faith in Yahweh that is problematic. In Solomon's story it is his association with foreigners who do not hold this faith that becomes the problem. But the rest of Kings will show that faithful foreigners do indeed exist.

Two kingdoms: 1 Kings 12 – 2 Kings 13

Early kings: 1 Kings 12 – 16

Much of Kings is given over to the account of the kingdoms of Israel (the north) and Judah (the south), with the reigns of their various kings told through a synchronized narrative that moves between them. Because much of the initial attention is given over to problems within Israel, foreigners initially receive comparatively little notice, though the threat of foreign powers continues to be noted in the report of the Egyptian king Shishak who captured Jerusalem in Rehoboam's fifth year (1 Kgs 14:25–28). But the issue of foreignness is noted immediately after the report of Judah under Rehoboam, who introduced foreign worship practices, including the erection of pillars on high places and Asherah (1 Kgs 14:23). In this Judah matches the cult that Jeroboam I introduced in the north and for which the prophet Ahijah already announced Yahweh's punishment (1 Kgs 14:15). Judah had the temple, but this was of no value if the people were not wholly devoted to Yahweh. As such, mention of Shishak's campaign, even though there is no prophetic oracle associated with it, should be understood as an example of the punishment associated with failing to remain faithful to Yahweh,[37] showing that foreign powers were still subject to Yahweh's power. Indeed, the irony here is that Shishak took away the treasures of both the temple and the palace. Admittedly, the 'everything' is hyperbolic since Rehoboam was able to replace golden items with those of bronze, but the result is the same. The glorious house that was meant to draw the nations to Yahweh was diminished by a people who failed to remain true to him. Beyond this, the accounts of both Jeroboam I and Rehoboam introduce a recurring motif that runs through the rest of Kings, showing the problems Israel faced in remaining true to Yahweh alone

[37] So Patterson and Austel 1988: 124.

and thus demonstrating to the nations that Yahweh was truly God. Their actions were the opposite of those reflected in Solomon's prayer, though of course each was continuing the tradition Solomon himself had started when he promoted the worship of other gods.

For the authors of Kings no Israelite king embodied the problem of the promotion of foreign gods more than Ahab. He not only continued the pattern of the northern kings established by Jeroboam I, but extended this by marrying a Sidonian princess, Jezebel, and promoting the worship of Baal and Asherah, as well as triggering the curse Joshua had announced on the one who rebuilt Jericho (1 Kgs 16:29–34; cf. Josh. 6:26). Although it may initially seem that the account of Ahab's reign will be no fuller than that given to his father, Omri (1 Kgs 16:21–28), Kings devotes more space to Ahab than to any other Israelite king, only concluding the report of his reign in 1 Kings 22:40. Much of that space, however, is given to his encounters with various prophets, especially Elijah.

Elijah: 1 Kings 17 – 2 Kings 2:14

Elijah is a crucial figure in this story, not only because of his commitment to Yahweh, but also because of his close association with foreigners. Even his introduction may hint at this (1 Kgs 17:1). Most English Bibles follow the LXX here, suggesting that he is called 'the Tishbite' because he came from a place called Tishbe, even if this place is otherwise unknown.[38] Yet this reading is tautologous. Moreover, the MT would suggest that 'Tishbite' is explained by understanding Elijah as being from 'the settlers of Gilead', taking *tôšāb* here as 'settler, resident alien'.[39] If so, then Yahweh's most trenchant prophet during Ahab's reign[40] was himself a foreigner. However, Elijah's introduction is notable for a degree of narrative reticence.[41] This means that when he first speaks, we do not even know if he is a prophet or simply someone with an inflated view of himself,[42] though we quickly learn that his announcement of a drought is indeed correct (1 Kgs 17:7).[43]

---

[38] Jones 1984: 303.

[39] Cf. Wray Beal 2014: 228; Walsh 1995: 226. Cogan (2001: 425) still prefers the LXX, but his attempt to draw on a Thisbe in Galilee (mentioned in Tob. 1.2) is unpersuasive.

[40] Although not directly relevant to this study, the story of Micaiah (1 Kgs 22:1–28) is just one example that shows that Elijah was not the only prophet to challenge Ahab, even if Elijah was prone at times to think in those terms (e.g. 1 Kgs 19:9–11).

[41] Dharamraj 2011: 9.

[42] Cf. Paynter 2016: 131. On the ambiguity of Elijah's presentation, see Olley 1998.

[43] Moreover, that 1 Kgs 17:16 ties Elijah's word to Yahweh's word further confirms the validity of his message.

This reticence may also mean that we cannot be certain if he is a foreigner. It is, however, notable that whenever Elijah is elsewhere referred to as 'the Tishbite' (1 Kgs 21:17, 28; 2 Kgs 1:3, 8; 9:36) it is in the context of the rejection of foreign worship patterns, particularly those associated with Baal. If so, this may hint at a profound irony – this most vocal spokesperson for the faithful worship of Yahweh (as perhaps implied in his name, which means 'Yahweh is God') was himself a foreigner. Elijah may well represent the sort of inclusion of foreigners suggested by Solomon's prayer except that rather than remaining in their former home, Elijah's family had settled in Israel and demonstrated their faith in the name of their son.

Once the drought has begun, the narrative quickly moves from the brook Cherith east of the Jordan, where Yahweh provides for Elijah through ravens (1 Kgs 17:5–7), to the far north as Elijah is sent to a widow in Zarephath, a town that belonged to Sidon and thus outside Israel's territory. Here, in the heart of territory associated with Baal, who was routinely slain by Mot,[44] it is Yahweh who provides sustenance and life. This is demonstrated in the juxtaposition of two stories from the period when Elijah was there.

In the first of these (1 Kgs 17:8–16) Elijah encounters the widow to whom he was sent when he arrives at the town gate. Just as when he first spoke to Ahab, his opening words can be understood as reflecting an inflated opinion of himself. The woman certainly seems to take them this way when she responds to his request (for water and some bread) that she has nothing baked, pointing out that all she has is a handful of flour and a little oil. She is gathering some sticks so she can prepare what will in effect become a final meal for her and her son. Elijah initially responds by offering encouragement, before again requesting a baked morsel, while also directing her to make something for herself. This directive is expanded by a short salvation oracle which promises that the flour and oil will not run out until Yahweh sends rain. The emphasis here is important, because it stresses that fertility, particularly rain, comes from Yahweh rather than Baal. The validity of this promise is then immediately noted as Elijah, the woman and her household all eat for an extended period, demonstrating that Yahweh indeed spoke through Elijah. Baal was the god whose worship Ahab promoted, particularly through his marriage to Jezebel (who herself came from the same region as the woman). But here, in what some might have regarded as Baal's territory, Baal is already shown

---

[44] Fensham 1980.

as defeated.[45] This defeat is confirmed in Elijah's encounter with the prophets of Baal on Mount Carmel (1 Kgs 18:20–40), but its reality is made clear through a foreign woman receiving the gift of Yahweh while still living in foreign territory.

Although his worship is less prominent in the Old Testament than that of Baal, there are hints of the worship of the chthonic deity Mot.[46] In the Ugaritic Baal cycle[47] there is hostility between Baal (as a storm deity) and Mot (personifying death) in which Mot kills Baal, though Baal is brought back to life. As we do not have the whole text, care must be taken; but there appears to be a link here between the fact that rain is a source of life, perhaps referring to the annual arrival of the wet season, whereas death comes about when the rains do not arrive. The presentation of the stories of the woman at Zarephath in two panels, with the first focused on rain and the second on death, suggests that the Baal cycle lies in the background. In this second panel (1 Kgs 17:17–24) the woman's son becomes ill and dies, leading the woman to complain to Elijah about what he has done. Elijah responds by taking her son and then crying out to Yahweh, complaining that he has killed the boy, before asking that Yahweh restore his life. This time Yahweh responds to Elijah's word, so that he can take the boy back to his mother. This leads to her confession of faith 'Now I know that you are a man of God, and the word of Yahweh in your mouth is true' (1 Kgs 17:24). Reference to Yahweh's word here helps to create a ring structure around the whole of this chapter, tying this event back to Elijah's opening encounter with Ahab (1 Kgs 17:1). Once again Yahweh has worked through his prophet to bring his blessing to a foreign woman in a foreign land, leading to a confession of faith not dissimilar to that anticipated in Solomon's prayer. Israel might have been tempted to worship foreign gods, and especially the gods of Sidon, but this was unnecessary.

Taken whole, 1 Kings 17 has not only introduced Elijah; it has also stressed something that will be a distinctive feature of both his and Elisha's ministry – the prevalence of the miraculous. This is not a feature of all prophetic figures, though it is a feature of those designated 'man of God'.[48] This feature, along with the defeat of the Canaanite gods, has thus prepared readers for the victory over the prophets of

[45] Dharamraj 2011: 13.
[46] See Day 2002: 185–225.
[47] For an accessible version of the text in English, see <http://emp.byui.edu/satterfieldb/ugarit/The%20Epic%20of%20Baal.html>, accessed 30 November 2018.
[48] Petersen 1981: 41.

Baal that dominates 1 Kings 18.[49] This victory, which is set in the context of Elijah's conflict with Ahab, famously culminates in fire from heaven consuming his sacrifice, unlike that of the prophets of Baal, and so to the people confessing, 'Yahweh is God! Yahweh is God!' (1 Kgs 18:39). Only after this does Yahweh send rain on the land (1 Kgs 18:41–46), so that the closing note of this chapter provides an end point to the drought narrative introduced at 1 Kings 17:1. But through these chapters we also see a larger conflict that needed resolving, one hinted at in the introduction of Jezebel into the account of Ahab's reign. The conflict with Baal may seem to have been resolved on Mount Carmel, but in reality it continues into 1 Kings 19.[50] This is because Jezebel was the driving force of Baal worship, another foreign princess who embodied the threat to which Solomon had succumbed.

Jezebel is thus reintroduced as an active figure in the narrative in 1 Kings 19:1–3, and it is her message to Elijah that leads to his fleeing into the wilderness, and ultimately to Horeb (1 Kgs 19:4–18). Even his anointing of Elisha (1 Kgs 19:19–21) is tied back to the threat posed by Jezebel.[51] Much of the chapter shows Elijah's attempting to flee even his role as a prophet. But this is not finally possible, and he finally has to discover a different sense of Yahweh's nature while at Horeb. The mountain is here explicitly called 'the mountain of God', making clear that although Yahweh revealed himself at Mount Carmel, Horeb retained this status. Elijah here has to discover that even though any attributes ascribed to Baal as a storm god truly belong to Yahweh (as the one who provides fertility), Elijah still must not confuse them. This becomes clear as the prophet has to learn that Yahweh is not to be located in the windstorm, the earthquake or the fire. Instead, he hears Yahweh in a thin silence (1 Kgs 19:12). Baal may be associated with dramatic signs, but this is not necessary for Yahweh. Moreover, in Elijah's anointing Hazael as king of Aram and Jehu ben Nimshi as king over Israel along with Elisha, Yahweh will continue the battle with Baal (1 Kgs 19:15–18). Yahweh's victory over the threat posed by Jezebel will not come in something spectacular like that seen on Mount Carmel, but in Yahweh's purposes being worked out in what may otherwise seem to be ordinary historical processes.[52] Yet in these historical processes we

---

[49] Walsh (1995: 262–263) notes important parallels between the widow and her provision for Elijah and Obadiah's provision for the other prophets (1 Kgs 18:3–4).

[50] Cf. Cohn 1982: 334.

[51] Wray Beal 2014: 250.

[52] Cf. Seow 1999: 143.

see Yahweh's goals achieved through foreign kings as well as Israelite ones. Overall, 1 Kings 17 – 19 has thus answered the crucial question of who the true God is,[53] and as such he can continue to achieve his purposes.

Following these events, the report of Ahab's wars with Aram (1 Kgs 20)[54] may seem like an intrusion. Indeed, in the LXX this material occurs after the MT 1 Kings 21, so that the Jezebel materials are kept together, followed by the encounters with Aram.[55] However, it is easier to explain why an editor would join this material rather than separate it, so preference should be given to the MT presentation. As the text now stands, it begins a process of demonstrating the existence of some of the other prophets that Elijah was prone to forget; perhaps some of those previously protected by Obadiah. These prophets also confronted Ahab (1 Kgs 20:13–15, 22, 28, 35–42), offering words of reassurance about Aram's inability to defeat Israel despite their apparent military superiority and challenging him when he failed to take the victory to its logical conclusion. Yahweh is shown to be greater than foreign military powers, but Israel is not to presume on this because they are still to be faithful to the covenant.

Having demonstrated both Yahweh's power over other kings and the continued presence of other prophets in Israel, 1 Kings 21 returns to the conflict with Jezebel, a conflict that is particularly focused through the issue of Naboth's vineyard. With the return of Jezebel to centre stage, we also return to Elijah as the key prophet. As is well known, Naboth owned a vineyard adjacent to Ahab's palace in Samaria. When Ahab offered to buy it, Naboth refused on the basis that it was part of his family inheritance. The exact details are difficult to work out, because it was not impossible to transfer land, but this would usually occur when a family was too impoverished to survive otherwise. Since Ahab's offer is quite fair (in commercial terms), it is important that Naboth's response makes clear that his reason for refusing it is theological. He is not holding out for a better price.[56] Ahab clearly understands that there is no basis for further negotiation;

[53] Schmid 2000: 531. There are, of course, other themes, but this is the one central to our purposes.

[54] Although many English Bibles use 'Syria' here, for this study I have used the transliterated form 'Aram' since 'Syria' refers to a contemporary political construct, not the ancient one. See Younger 2016: 234–235.

[55] This is often associated with a range of historical issues, though none of them are incapable of resolution. See Provan, Long and Longman 2015: 351–354.

[56] Walsh 1995: 319.

and however much he wants the vineyard, it cannot be his. So he goes home and sulks (1 Kgs 21:1–4), acting like a sullen teenager.[57]

Whether or not Ahab fully grasped Naboth's reasoning, he did not see any way of taking this further. But Jezebel did. Wiseman notes an example from a Syrian tablet where the property of a man executed for treachery was forfeited to the palace,[58] and a background like this would certainly explain Jezebel's actions as she arranged for a false accusation to be made against Naboth so he could be put to death on trumped-up charges (1 Kgs 21:5–13). Although Jezebel was clearly the prime mover in this process, Ahab was a willing participant, as he took possession of the land as soon as he heard that Naboth was dead. But it is this that then leads to Yahweh's word coming to Elijah, a phrase that with its echoes of 1 Kings 17 reminds readers that although Yahweh is at work among foreign peoples, and perhaps here even through a foreign prophet, an attempt to impose a foreign model of kingship that echoes the pattern of taking against which Samuel warned (1 Sam. 8:10–18) cannot be accepted. Elijah's encounter with Ahab pulls no punches in declaring Yahweh's judgment on both Ahab and Jezebel (1 Kgs 21:17–24). Ahab might have been incited by Jezebel (1 Kgs 21:25–26), but he could not avoid Yahweh's judgment because of that. Instead, only when Ahab humbled himself before Yahweh did Yahweh send word to Elijah to announce that punishment for his actions would wait for a generation. Despite this, it is clear that although foreigners were welcome to join Israel, and that Yahweh could work among foreigners outside Israel, the patterns of government within Israel were not to follow foreign patterns.

Ahab's demise is then recounted in an account of more warfare with Aram, this time over the key site of Jabesh-gilead (1 Kgs 22:1–40). As with 1 Kings 20 we are introduced to prophets other than Elijah, demonstrating that even if he was a key figure he was not always a reliable one. But unlike 1 Kings 20, where the other prophets are all anonymous, this account focuses on Micaiah as the one who announces Yahweh's word, though as he is first introduced by Ahab readers are led to expect that he will be Elijah.[59] Against the other prophets active in Ahab's court, Micaiah eventually announces a word of judgment on Ahab, though ironically only when Ahab insists that

---

[57] Paynter 2017: 467. The attempt of Napier (1976: 9) to suggest that Ahab was in fact a monarch of 'exceptional stature' is difficult to reconcile with this presentation and can be achieved only through a selective reading of the text.

[58] Wiseman 1993: 181.

[59] Firth 2000: 177–181.

he speak only the truth in Yahweh's name (1 Kgs 22:5–28). That the focus of this chapter is on how that word is worked out, a word that ultimately confirms Elijah's word from the previous chapter, is evident from the fact that Micaiah's story ends as he is taken off to prison, the test of the authenticity of his word being whether or not Ahab returns from battle. Despite Ahab's attempts to subvert this word by disguising himself (unlike Jehoshaphat), he is killed by an arrow drawn at random by one of the Aramean soldiers.[60] Ahab attempted to introduce both foreign worship and a foreign pattern of monarchy, but Yahweh resisted this. This resistance also seems to be evident in the brief note about Jehoshaphat's unsuccessful trading ventures (1 Kgs 22:48–49), as his attempt to follow Solomon's model of wealth acquisition also failed. Yet, in spite of Ahab's failure, his son Ahaziah would also promote Baal worship (1 Kgs 22:53), perhaps because his mother Jezebel continued to be active.

The problems this generated quickly become clear as Moab rebels against Israel (2 Kgs 1:1) and Ahaziah is injured as he falls from an upper level of his house. Unable therefore to respond to Moab, he then sends for an oracle from Baal-Zebub at Ekron (2 Kgs 1:2). Presumably, he viewed this as a different Baal from the one in Sidon, though from the perspective of Kings all Baals are equally worthless.[61] Given that this was an attempt to employ yet more foreign worship, it is no surprise that Yahweh's messenger directs Elijah to confront Ahaziah's messengers and announce Ahaziah's death for his failure to trust Yahweh, a message they duly report back to Ahaziah, who deduces that the prophet they encountered was Elijah (2 Kgs 1:3–8). The balance of the chapter recounts the unfortunate experience of the various groups sent by Ahaziah to arrest Elijah before Elijah finally goes with the third group to repeat directly to the king the message he previously sent by messengers. Once again it is Yahweh's messenger who directs Elijah – the prophet will not listen to Ahaziah's messengers until they begin to disobey Ahaziah.[62] As was the case with his father, Ahaziah promotes the worship of Baal, though presumably in a context where a plurality of deities is possible. But this is a foreign innovation that Elijah, and more importantly Yahweh, will not tolerate.

---

[60] On the correlation between the prophecies of Elijah and Micaiah, see Provan 1995: 164–165.

[61] Nelson 1987: 155.

[62] Cf. Dharamraj 2011: 159.

Elisha: 2 Kings 2:15 – 2 Kings 13:25

Following Elijah's ascension, Elisha becomes the dominant prophetic figure, who continues the patterns established by Elijah, though with some distinctive elements of his own. Nevertheless, the key contours continue since Elisha is clearly Elijah's designated heir. One key distinctive, though, is that even though there are times when Elisha is clearly active outside Israel (2 Kgs 3; 8:7–15), we do not find his miracles occurring outside Israel, even though several closely parallel Elijah's miracles in Zarephath. Where Elijah demonstrated Yahweh's presence outside Israel through Elijah's presence there, the prophet's key encounters with foreigners are principally because of war. Although these are remarkable, the most important for this study is his encounter with Naaman, an Aramean general (2 Kgs 5). In this instance a foreigner came to Israel and discovered the reality of Yahweh, and then continued to worship him after returning to his own land.

Before considering that story, we need briefly to consider the account of the Moabite rebellion and the subsequent campaign against them reported in 2 Kings 3, dated to Jehoshaphat's eighteenth year.[63] As with the battle against Jabesh-gilead (1 Kgs 22:1–40) this involved a joint effort for Israel and Judah, this time with the king of Edom joining them (2 Kgs 3:9). They took a somewhat unusual route to attack Moab, going south of the Dead Sea (rather than crossing the Jordan near Jericho), an area notable for its lack of water. It is no surprise, therefore, that the army found itself without water. But just as Jehoshaphat had previously asked for a prophet, leading to the message from Micaiah, he again proposed seeking a message from Yahweh through one of his prophets. Although previously unmentioned, Elisha was with the group and was approached by the three kings (2 Kgs 3:9–12; cf. 1 Kgs 22:7). The addition of the Edomite king adds an element not present in Ahab's earlier battle against Aram, but just as Micaiah's initial response was rather ambiguous (with his sarcasm revealed only by Ahab's response), so also Elisha's response is laced with both sarcasm and ambiguity.[64] In this instance much depends on the sense of the verb *nkh* since this can mean 'strike [and achieve victory]'[65] or 'strike [but inconclusively]'.[66] As Elisha

---

[63] Wray Beal (2014: 312) notes that earlier this was tied to the second year of Jehoram (of Judah), indicating a co-regency that Jehoshaphat shared with his son.

[64] See R. Westbrook 2005; Firth 2008a: 167–169.

[65] E.g. 1 Sam. 17:35.

[66] E.g. Exod. 21:15.

delivered his oracle, the kings understood it as promising total victory, but the result was inconclusive.[67] Jehoram is presented as less evil than other northern kings because of a reduction in the level of Baal worship (2 Kgs 3:1–3), but the basic problem persists, and the continued presence of foreign worship patterns counted against Israel and Judah, though their need of water was at least addressed.

Although Elisha is also presented as a miracle worker in 2 Kings 4, foreigners do not feature in this aspect of his ministry until 2 Kings 5, where the Aramean general Naaman is introduced. Women play a prominent role in 2 Kings 4, and this provides an important link to the introduction to the Naaman story with its focus on an Israelite slave girl who is able to advise her mistress of the presence in Samaria of an unnamed prophet who can heal Naaman of his skin illness. This story is important because it provides a direct link to Solomon's prayer as Naaman becomes the type of foreigner envisaged there. Perhaps more importantly, just as the word 'forgive' (*slḥ*) is pivotal in the prayer, so it also features here so that Naaman can request forgiveness for the fact that he needed to enter the temple in Damascus even though it was not a centre for the worship of Yahweh (2 Kgs 5:18). When Elisha indicates he can go in peace, it becomes clear that this forgiveness is given. What is perhaps remarkable, though, is that although this was a central theme within Solomon's prayer, this is the only point in Kings in which forgiveness is granted, and it is granted to a foreigner who is in fact the commander of a foreign army.

To appreciate these details, it is necessary to look at this story in more detail. Although 2 Kings 5 is often enough broken up into discrete segments,[68] it is important to read it as a whole, so that both Naaman's healing and Gehazi's illness mutually inform one another. It is notable that the story also uses *šālôm* as a *Leitwort* in verses 19–27, and with verse 19's bridging role in joining the two halves of the story this is a key marker of narrative unity.[69] Along with this, it should be noted that it is Naaman's skin disease that afflicts Gehazi, so that references to this (2 Kgs 5:1, 27) form an envelope for the narrative as a whole, while the money and clothing noted when Naaman set out (2 Kgs 5:5) are also necessary for Gehazi's later

---

[67] The source of the wrath against Israel (2 Kgs 3:27) is unclear, though, as Gilmour (2014: 113–114) points out, if the whole is seen under the sovereignty of God, then he remains the ultimate source.

[68] Usually 2 Kgs 5:1–19 and 5:20–27. For helpful overviews, see Cohn 1983: 171–172 and Gilmour 2014: 144–146.

[69] Ngan 1997: 589.

request (2 Kgs 5:22).[70] The change in status between Naaman and Gehazi is a crucial element within the story as the foreigner comes into the orbit of Israel's life (while yet remaining a foreigner) while the Israelite moves into the pattern of an invalid foreign life, a pattern not dissimilar to that seen in the contrast between Rahab and Achan (Josh. 2, 7).

As he is introduced (2 Kgs 5:1), Naaman seems like the sort of foreigner that Israel would want to avoid. He is a powerful man, a commander of the Aramean king's army with high favour with his master. Yet something strange is also noted – he has this favour because Yahweh gave victory to Aram. We are not told who Naaman defeated, but given the conflicts reported earlier between Israel and Aram we would naturally think that Israel are among those defeated. His might is stressed, yet after noting these elements (almost, it may seem, as an afterthought) we are told he has a serious skin disease.[71] But this issue, which undercuts all the other matters raised in the introduction, is then a central theme for the rest of this story.

That Israel are among those defeated under Naaman is disclosed as we are told of the slave girl taken by the Arameans who, quite unbidden, expresses the wish that Naaman be with an unnamed prophet in Samaria since he will cure him of his illness. In a narrative that focuses on the relationship between Israel and foreigners this girl's mention stands out – narratively, there is no immediate need for this to have been reported like this, but the narrative makes clear that it is a captive Israelite[72] who volunteers this information, and once she has disclosed it the next event reported is Naaman's telling his king, who then promptly tells him to go to Israel, promising a letter to their king in support. Despite the Israelite king's conviction that this is simply the Arameans picking a fight, Elisha intervenes by insisting that Naaman be sent to him 'so he might know there is a prophet in Israel'.

There is no need to think that the narrator approves of every utterance to this point – the girl might have thought that the prophet would heal Naaman, and Elisha wanted him to know there was a

---

[70] Cf. B. O. Long 1991: 67–68. R. D. Moore (1990: 71–84) also points to the prevalence of the word *gādôl*; but as this is such a common word in the OT, it can be considered only in the light of the other points noted.

[71] Traditionally 'leprosy', but this translation confuses this disease with Hansen's disease, and even if we cannot make a formal diagnosis through the biblical term (which may represent a range of different illnesses on modern diagnostic patterns), we can be reasonably certain that it is not what is now known as leprosy.

[72] Cohn (2000: 36) notes that the girl is in most ways an exact opposite to Naaman.

prophet in Israel. Instead, the story will make clear that it is Yahweh who heals Naaman (even if Naaman does not initially approve of Elisha's healing methods). In the end, convinced that he should dip himself in the Jordan as directed, Naaman was healed in accordance with the prophet's word. But it was not the reality of the prophet he came to know. Instead, he realized that 'there is no God in all the world except Israel' (2 Kgs 5:15). He did not know about a prophet; he knew about God. Naaman came to appreciate Israel's key distinctive: they were the only people to know God truly, and therefore he could ask for forgiveness for the fact that in Damascus he would still need to enter the temple of Rimmon. By way of contrast, Gehazi's decision to ask for some of the money and clothing Elisha had declined led to his being afflicted with Naaman's illness. There is a clear echo here of the story of Achan, who had also taken money and clothing not rightly his (Josh. 7:1),[73] so that again it is the foreigner who ended up embodying the life Israel was meant to have and the Israelite who was excluded.[74]

Taken on its own, this is a remarkable story of how Israel's faith was intended to move beyond their boundaries, to redefine the people of God. But within Kings there is evidence that this story has been told with echoes of Solomon's prayer so that this becomes a key intertext, especially petition seven (1 Kgs 8:46–51). There Solomon considered the case of Israel's being defeated in battle and carried off to a foreign land. Although there is no evidence of sin there, that is certainly the context in which the slave girl found herself. Given that this occurred because of an earlier defeat in battle, then petition two (1 Kgs 8:33–34) also is relevant, as also is petition six (1 Kgs 8:44–45). These may all be considered fairly general, but the prevalence of the verbs *slḥ* (forgive) and *šwb* (turn/repent) in this chapter and the prayer provides additional evidence of the extent to which Solomon's prayer is echoed. Most obviously, petition five (1 Kgs 8:41–43), with its emphasis on the foreigner, finds a particular focus in Naaman's experience as he is the foreigner who truly hears, however indirectly, about Yahweh and wants to worship him. Finally, we can note that petition one, with its concern for Yahweh's judging when someone sins against another, has some relevance to Gehazi's condition after he wrongly obtains money and clothing from Naaman. This is not to suggest that

---

[73] Admittedly, the items Gehazi took were not under the ban, but the principle of not claiming things illegitimately still stands.

[74] In 2 Kgs 8:1–6 we encounter Gehazi again, no longer afflicted, but Kings does not report on his healing.

any one situation in this chapter is an exact match for the various petitions – clearly the analogies are relatively general – but because the petitions represent type scenes, this chapter shows different aspects of their working out. Naaman becomes a model of the foreigner envisaged by Solomon's prayer, while in his actions against Naaman Gehazi has typified the pattern established by Achan.

The conflicts between Israel and Aram alluded to in the introduction of the Naaman story are then explored in 2 Kings 6:8 – 7:20.[75] Although there are some features of these accounts that reflect the common pattern of Yahweh's authority over all nations, there are some distinctive features that are of particular relevance to the issue of how Israel relates to foreigners, especially those who are outside the land. As such, these narratives continue to reflect on this matter in a way that extends the insights in the Naaman story. Readers may rightly wonder if, considering the victories Yahweh gave Aram over Israel (2 Kgs 5:2), the relationship with Naaman will change things. Initially, this does not appear to be the case, because although we are informed the Aramean king is complaining about Israel's ability to know where he plans to act (2 Kgs 6:8–13),[76] he is untroubled by the idea of sending troops to Dothan (a major trading town north of Samaria) to capture Elisha after it is revealed that the prophet is the means by which Israel knows Aramean plans. Since the account immediately reports that he sends troops without any intervention from Elisha, we may well wonder if the intelligence he receives is correct. This possibility is exacerbated by the fact that Elisha's servant goes out and sees the extensive Aramean army surrounding the city and cries out in fear. Have these foreigners somehow thwarted Yahweh?

However, Elisha insists that there are more with them than with Aram, and this response immediately changes our perspective. To enable the servant to understand this, Elisha prays for his eyes to open, and as a result he sees the mountains full of horses and chariots of fire, an immediate echo of the story of Elijah's ascension (2 Kgs 2:11). This prayer introduces a motif, opening eyes, that is pivotal for this story since the theme of sight recurs at key points. The servant's

---

[75] There are two separate accounts here, 2 Kgs 6:8–23 and 6:24 – 7:20; but their juxtaposition means they need to be read in the light of each other. See Gilmour 2014: 171–174.

[76] Gray (1964: 464) reckons this must have come about through figures like the captive slave girl in the Naaman story, though how they would have been able to disclose this information is unclear, and in any case involves setting aside the claim of the text.

eyes are opened, and he sees. When the Arameans attack, Elisha again prays, this time that they will be struck with blindness. This prayer is an obvious contrast with his prayer for his servant and is reversed when Elisha prays for the Arameans' eyes to be opened, after he has led them into the city of Samaria (2 Kgs 6:15–21). The opening of their eyes is both a physical regaining of sight and a moment of insight as they discover they are in Samaria.

At this point the narrative sets aside the perspective of the Arameans and instead focuses on the response of the Israelite king who wanted permission from Elisha to kill the captives.[77] Although the exact sense of Elisha's response is difficult to determine, there is no doubt that he prohibited the king from doing so. His point seems to be that the king would not kill prisoners he had taken by more traditional means, and therefore those captured miraculously should not be killed either. However, where such prisoners might more commonly have become slaves, Elisha proposed a much more generous approach – that they be fed and then be allowed to return to their master. As a military strategy this makes no sense. Why should these soldiers be sent back? But of course, the whole story has shown that Yahweh's presence through his prophet made normal military considerations irrelevant. Indeed, it is this that permits an approach of hospitality.[78] More importantly, whereas this story opened with reports of frequent Aramean incursions into Israel, the narrative's conclusion reports the cessation of their raids (2 Kgs 6:23). Foreign powers were subject only to Yahweh's authority; once Israel recognized this, they could take a more positive approach to them. Indeed, considering Solomon's prayer it seems that these Arameans too had the chance to discover the reality of Yahweh.

A second conflict account is introduced with the simple note 'Afterwards' (2 Kgs 6:24). Since the previous verse noted that Aramean raids had ceased, how are we to read this? Setting aside the various source-critical approaches that see this simply as evidence of editorial confusion, it seems better to see it as a note that forces us to reread the end of the previous account to realize that only raiding had

---

[77] R. D. Moore (1990: 90) notes the interchange here plays with the meaning of the verb *nkh* – Elisha had prayed that they be 'struck' with blindness, and the king wants to 'strike' them. This interchange creates a verbal link back to 2 Kgs 3, where this verb's semantic range is also pivotal.

[78] Hobbs (1985: 78) sees this as an attempt to embarrass the Arameans rather than being genuinely humanitarian. But given that they are sent back it is difficult to see that embarrassment was a major issue.

stopped, whereas this was a full-scale invasion.[79] Indeed, reading backwards from this point helps to highlight the important reversals that have taken place, the most important of which is that where the previous narrative concluded with Arameans surrounded by Samaria, this time Samaria was surrounded by Arameans.[80] Going further, there is a comparison here between the men with a skin disease in this story (2 Kgs 7:3–15) and Naaman (2 Kgs 5), for although these men are not healed, they are pivotal in demonstrating the truth of the word of the man of God (2 Kgs 7:16–20), a key motif in Naaman's story too (2 Kgs 5:14). In spite of the challenges, we need to read these accounts as panels that mutually interpret one another.

As with the first account, this one opens by creating a context that may suggest a failing on Elisha's part, as prices for even unclean food and fuel in the city rose rapidly because of the siege. In this context the horror of cannibalism[81] is reported.[82] It is these women who cried out to the king for help, asking for his assistance, something he claimed he could not give.[83] Hearing their story, he swore a self-imprecatory oath to have Elisha executed. But as Elisha is introduced, it is immediately clear that he knows the intentions of Israel's king as well as that of Aram, locking his door against the king's messenger who seems to declare that he can no longer wait for Yahweh (2 Kgs 6:32–33).[84] Elisha's response is to declare that the following day Yahweh will not only lift the siege, but that good food will be available at affordable prices. It is this that triggers the dismissive response of the king's officer, a response that leads to a brief judgment oracle against him.

The balance of the story then works out how this word is fulfilled. This time, the Arameans hear the sound of a great army and flee, concluding that Israel hired the armies of Egypt and the Hittites against them, a literary echo of the heavenly army present at Dothan (2 Kgs 6:17). As a result, Elisha's word is again confirmed, a word

[79] For a helpful overview of critical approaches, see B. O. Long 1991: 91.

[80] Gilmour 2014: 172.

[81] Suggested as an outcome of siege in Deut. 28:53.

[82] Garroway (2018) argues that this indicates a possible (though unintentional) child sacrifice, a factor that contributes to the deliverance of the city. But this seems improbable in a narrative that holds back from sacrificial language.

[83] Cogan and Tadmor (1988: 80) propose reading the king's response as 'No! Let YHWH help you!', whereas most read something like, 'If Yahweh will not help you . . .' (2 Kgs 6:27; cf. ESVUK). Since this breaks the accentuation, preference should probably be given to the more traditional rendering.

[84] The syntax of 2 Kgs 6:33b is ambiguous, and the speaker could be either the messenger or Elisha.

that demonstrates Yahweh's authority over all nations. But it is particularly confirmed through the faithful actions of four men who were
otherwise excluded, men who recognized that (unlike the king) they
could do something.[85] An Israel that had redefined itself through the
inclusion of an Aramean who was also excluded through his illness
now had to redefine itself along the same lines, even while acknowledging that Yahweh continued to work beyond the boundaries
humans set.

Elisha's direct interactions with Aram conclude with the account
of his visit to Damascus (2 Kgs 8:7–15). Ben-hadad was ill, and upon
hearing of the prophet's visit sent an extraordinarily generous gift to
ask him to enquire of Yahweh, a clear contrast with Ahaziah's actions
(2 Kgs 1:2). As the story commences, this seems to be a standard
prophetic enquiry narrative, but by now readers of the Elisha stories
should know that they tend to set up standard expectations only to
subvert them. This subversion is evident in Elisha's rather perplexing
reply – asserting both that he would recover, but also that Yahweh
had shown him that Ben-hadad would die. But there is another hint
of the coming subversion in that the messenger sent to him is none
other than Hazael, the man Elijah had been told to anoint as king of
Aram. Does Elisha lie to him?[86] Not necessarily, though given the
ways in which Micaiah spoke with Ahab (1 Kgs 22:15), or even
Elisha's oracle against Edom (2 Kgs 3:19), there is no reason to think
that everything a prophet says has to be straightforwardly true.[87] In
this instance it is probably better to realize that Elisha was being
deliberately ambiguous, though his subsequent tears became the
means by which Hazael derived more information from him, information that he used to transform Elisha's ambiguity into his own lie
before killing his king. Elisha knew the harm Hazael would do, but
he also knew that Hazael's actions would contribute to the defeat of
Baalism in Israel. Hazael would indeed be a tragic foreign king for
Israel, but also part of the mechanism by which Yahweh would
remove foreign worship.

Elisha's ministry continued as Judah's influence declined (2 Kgs
8:16–29). He finally sent one of his prophetic group to anoint Jehu as
king over Israel (2 Kgs 9:1–13), thus completing a matter left over
from Elijah's ministry (1 Kgs 19:16). Although this is set within the

---

[85] R. D. Moore 1990: 103–104.

[86] Kethib seeks to resolve this, but the presence of the contradiction in Qere indicates
that this is the preferred reading.

[87] Cf. Wray Beal 2014: 362.

context of war between Aram and Israel (and Judah), the main focus in the Jehu story (2 Kgs 9 – 10) is on Israel's internal politics. Where foreigners (such as Jezebel, 2 Kgs 9:10, 30–37) feature, they are presented as a continuation of the Elijah story, demonstrating the fulfilment of his word concerning Naboth (1 Kgs 21:20–24). Jehu did indeed bring an end to Baal worship (2 Kgs 10:18–27), and this brings commendation, but it is a commendation tinged with condemnation (2 Kgs 10:31–32) because he did not remove Israel's fundamental sin of the golden calves. Once this point is noted, it is also possible to reread his bloody story and see that even as he claimed loyalty to Yahweh he did not hold to Yahweh's standards.[88]

One result of Jehu's coup was the establishment of a foreign monarchy in Jerusalem as Athaliah seized the throne there (2 Kgs 11:1–3),[89] and only with her removal and the restoration of the temple could Elisha's death be reported. Athaliah was already noted as a threat since she was a descendant of Omri (2 Kgs 8:26), though of course this still meant she was Israelite. Whether or not she was a descendant of Jezebel too, she apparently was influenced by the models of monarchy she represented, seizing the throne after her son Ahaziah had been killed by Jehu and putting to death his sons, excepting Joash who was saved by the actions of Ahaziah's sister Jehosheba (2 Kgs 11:2). The rebellion against Athaliah, led by the priest Jehoiada, not only removed her and installed Joash as king; it was the point at which the Baal altar was torn down so that (for a period at least) foreign worship was removed from Jerusalem (2 Kgs 11:18). This, along with temple reforms, clearly shows that Jehoiada (and Joash) need to be seen as reformers, but their reforms occur within the context of the continued conflict with Aram under Hazael, conflicts that affected both Judah (2 Kgs 12:17–19) and Israel (2 Kgs 13:1–13).

Given the context of Hazael's anointing (even if this anointing itself is never recounted), it is possible to see his continued success as showing that Aram was Yahweh's instrument for disciplining Israel. But Elisha's reappearance in the narrative (2 Kgs 13:14–21)[90] shows that it was not necessary that Aram continue to dominate. Elisha was

[88] See ibid. 382–384.

[89] For why the text need not be divided on a source analysis, see Dutcher-Walls 1996: 23–25.

[90] This account poses several difficulties that cannot be addressed here. At a literary level, though, there is good reason for including this account here, as this provides a key boundary with the directives to Elijah (1 Kgs 19:15–18), which have shaped so much of the subsequent narrative, including the introduction of Jehu's dynasty.

by now old and frail, but the Israelite king Joash still consulted him, twice calling him 'My father' (2 Kgs 13:14). It is not clear that when he continues by saying 'The chariot of Israel and its horsemen' that this is a title he gives to Elisha,[91] since Elisha's response to this is to direct him to take a bow and arrows. The term certainly connects Elisha to Elijah since it occurs in the final scene for each (2 Kgs 2:12),[92] but it seems best to understand it as an expression of the difficulty faced by Israel's army. This would make sense of Elisha's directing Joash to shoot the bow and then declaring it to be the arrow of Yahweh's victory over Aram (2 Kgs 13:17), a statement that evokes the earlier reference to a deliverer for Israel from Aram (2 Kgs 13:5). Where the earlier deliverer had been unnamed, a context for deliverance from Aram is established with the promise of victory at Aphek. This victory would not, however, be as complete as it might have been because when directed by Elisha to strike the ground with the remaining arrows, Joash stopped after striking the ground three times, something Elisha seemingly interpreted as rather half-hearted, meaning Aram would be defeated three times, but not more. In spite of this, and Hazael's continued harrying of Israel after Elisha's death, Yahweh was gracious and compassionate towards Israel, a phrase that occurs nowhere else in Kings, but that evokes Yahweh's self-declaration in Exodus 34:6–7.[93] Even as life was still possible after Elisha's death (2 Kgs 13:20–21), so also there was hope for Israel because nations such as Aram remained under Yahweh's authority.

The fall of the kingdoms: 2 Kings 14 – 25

To the fall of Israel: 2 Kings 14 – 17

In spite of the signs of grace with which 2 Kings 13 ended, the rest of Kings recounts the decline and fall of the kingdoms of Israel and Judah. The accounts of Israel and Judah are synchronized until the fall of Israel, after which the narrator presents a reflection on the causes of Israel's fall (2 Kgs 17:7–23). Outside battle accounts, almost all of which can be understood as reports of either sin or its effects, foreigners do not play a significant role in these chapters. Moreover, their presentation is accordingly through stock figures. There are brief

---

[91] As proposed by Weingart 2018.
[92] Gilmour (2014: 201–203) notes that this account connects with a wider range of Elijah stories, notably Ahab's encounters with Aram in 1 Kgs 20:33–34.
[93] Olley 2013: 208.

moments that look a little beyond this, such as Amaziah's defeat of Edom (2 Kgs 14:7) or Jeroboam II's expansion of Israel's borders (2 Kgs 14:25), but these are not developed.

The most important element for these chapters is undoubtedly the rise of Assyria.[94] Kings is not particularly interested in the politics behind this, seeing their pressure on Menahem (2 Kgs 15:19)[95] and the subsequent kings of Israel and Judah as evidence of these kings' sin (2 Kgs 15:23–38). More directly, Kings focuses on Ahaz's reign in Judah (2 Kgs 16) as one that was particularly influenced by Assyria. Brueggemann has rightly observed that Ahaz was placed in a position with no good choices, one in which his resolution of willingly accommodating himself to Assyrian practice must have seemed obvious at the time, but that looking back could be seen as great folly.[96] But even before his decision to accommodate himself to Assyrian practice, the text reports that he engaged in the worship practices[97] of the nations Yahweh drove out before Israel (2 Kgs 16:3).[98] That is, Ahaz, like Achan, had already begun a process towards embodying foreign practices inconsistent with faith in Yahweh. This basic inconsistency is then demonstrated by his decision to send a 'present' to the Assyrian king to assist him when he is under pressure from the combined forces of Aram and Israel (2 Kgs 16:5–9). Politically, this must have seemed astute, but Ahaz went beyond this, choosing to demonstrate his commitment to Assyria by making a copy of an altar he had seen when he met Tiglath-Pileser at Damascus (2 Kgs 16:10–16). The details of how this worked out are not clear, but it is likely that it meant that Yahweh was worshipped as a vassal deity in the temple.[99] Somewhat surprisingly, Kings makes no comment on these actions. But, as Seow has observed, this is because it is content to demonstrate that Yahweh's sovereign purposes are being worked out through these choices, purposes that will see both kingdoms exiled, and yet also ultimately protected.[100]

---

[94] For a helpful overview of Assyria in this period, see Hays with Machinist 2016: 44–57.

[95] 'Pul' here refers to Tiglath-Pileser III.

[96] Brueggemann 2000: 463.

[97] To pass someone 'through the fire' may not refer to formal sacrifice, but is clearly something prohibited by Deut. 18:10, which would suggest this was considered a divinatory practice.

[98] A similar comment will be made on Manasseh, 2 Kgs 21:2, 6.

[99] McKay 1973: 8.

[100] Seow 1999: 251.

The restraint shown in 2 Kings 16 is, however, only temporary, because 2 Kings 17 not only reports Israel's fall; it offers an extended theological reflection on the reasons for it. Even though Israel's last king, Hoshea, can be said to have done evil 'but not like the kings of Israel before him' (2 Kgs 17:2), Israel has reached a point of no return. Hoshea initially submitted to Shalmaneser, but Shalmaneser was subsequently offended and invaded Israel, laying siege to Samaria before capturing and then exiling the kingdom (2 Kgs 17:4–6), and subsequently bringing in other peoples to live in their land along with those who remained (2 Kgs 17:24–41). This conforms to normal Assyrian practice, and laid the template that would later be followed by Babylon.

Although historians might discuss the reasons for Israel's fall from the perspective of the politics of the time, Kings takes a different route. Its opening statement lays out its basic thesis – the exile of the northern kingdom was because they had sinned against Yahweh, the one who had brought them out of Egypt in the exodus (2 Kgs 17:7). The balance of this section (2 Kgs 17:7–23) is effectively an expansion of this. That Israel are here referred to as 'the children of Israel' is probably an initial hint of the fact that although most of this discussion is concerned with the northern kingdom, Judah is not exempt (2 Kgs 17:19). Strikingly, although numerous foreigners continue to live within Israel, they are not stated as the cause of Israel's fall. Rather, the problem is traced back to the decision to engage in worship of foreign gods (Asherah and Baal) and the worship of the calves that Jeroboam I established.

Not only was a substantial part of Israel exiled by Assyria, but other peoples were brought in to possess the north (2 Kgs 17:24). As noted above, this was consistent with normal Assyrian practice; but from the perspective of Kings this was a practice doomed to failure because it did not acknowledge Yahweh's authority. So, although much of the book has demonstrated that foreigners could enjoy the blessing of Yahweh, here the commentary offers a somewhat sarcastic take on Assyrian practice. In response to Yahweh's sending lions, the Assyrian king was persuaded that this was because the resettled people did not know the law of that land's god, and he accordingly sent a priest back to Bethel so the people could fear Yahweh (2 Kgs 17:25–28). Although this might be regarded positively, the commentary here goes on to reflect on the fact that these peoples continued to worship other gods, and so lived contrary to Yahweh's purposes for Israel, a practice that had continued to the point where this chapter (at least) was written (2 Kgs 17:29–41).

To the fall of Judah: 2 Kings 18 – 25

As with the period preceding Israel's fall, there is little engagement with foreigners in these chapters apart from the continued inter-action with (mostly hostile) foreign powers. This continues the pattern seen throughout Kings, where such powers are subject to Yahweh's authority. Nevertheless, within this there are also some distinctive elements that require reflection, showing that concern for those outside Israel remained important even in the face of crisis.

Perhaps the most notable element here is the encounter between Judah and Assyria that dominates the report of Hezekiah's reign (2 Kgs 18 – 20). Much of the discussion here has focused on a range of historical problems that have led to source-critical analyses that have divided the text into different sources,[101] and compared this to various material in Isaiah,[102] though more 'literary' readings of the narrative have also been proposed.[103] I cannot unravel all these issues here beyond noting that our concern is with the presentation of foreigners in the final form of Kings, though in doing so it should become evident that a coherent reading of these chapters is possible.

Within the framework of Kings it is immediately evident that Hezekiah stands out in comparison with the previous kings of Judah in being given considerably more narrative space. To this it can be added that he is the first king to receive a wholly positive evaluation in comparison with David, something replicated only for Josiah (2 Kgs 18:3; cf. 2 Kgs 22:2). Hezekiah also receives the additional commendation that he trusted in Yahweh, so there was no king like him either before or after in Judah (2 Kgs 18:5). In spite of this, Hezekiah continued to face the challenge of dealing with pressure from Assyria. There is thus an immediate paradox introduced for his reign, one that largely governs the whole of this report, when it is noted that Yahweh was with him so he prospered wherever he went, but also that he was under pressure from the king of Assyria, even if he rebelled against him (2 Kgs 18:7). Politically, anyone who rebelled against Assyria could expect only one outcome: military reprisals; and it is this that dominates 2 Kings 18:13 – 19:37.[104] This passage effectively works out how it can be said that Yahweh was with

---

[101] See Childs 1967: 67–103.

[102] Along with Childs, see also Clements 1980; Y.-K. Kim 2008; Thomas 2014: 374–393.

[103] E.g. Nolan Fewell 1986; P. S. Evans 2009.

[104] Largely paralleled in Isa. 36 – 39.

Hezekiah in a context which can also report that Sennacherib was able to come against all of Judah's fortified cities and take them (2 Kgs 18:13), though as the narrative continues it becomes clear that Jerusalem at least remained.

At first blush the statement that Yahweh was with Hezekiah seems hard to substantiate, since he paid substantial tribute to Sennacherib (2 Kgs 18:14–16). But instead of withdrawing as one might expect after such a payment, the balance of 1 Kings 18 reports on the Assyrians' laying siege to Jerusalem, complete with a speech from the Rabshakeh (2 Kgs 18:19–25),[105] one of three Assyrian officials (along with Tartan and Rab-saris). One might expect the Tartan, as the senior figure, or even the Rab-saris ('chief eunuch', though perhaps 'chief official' might be better) to be the speaker, but instead it is the Rabshakeh (chief cupbearer) who speaks, perhaps because of his facility with Hebrew.[106] Certainly, Hezekiah's officials will complain about the use of Hebrew, preferring to use Aramaic in order to avoid spreading panic among the inhabitants of Jerusalem (2 Kgs 18:26–27), though of course this was obviously the goal of the Rabshakeh's speech.[107] This is evident from the fact that though his initial speech (2 Kgs 18:19–25) was formally directed to Hezekiah (2 Kgs 18:19), it was clearly meant to be heard by all. By his second speech he is speaking directly to the population of Jerusalem more generally (2 Kgs 18:28–35). In both he argues that there is no value in Judah's resisting Assyria, even claiming that Yahweh has brought the Assyrians up to destroy Jerusalem (2 Kgs 18:25). Readers may note an element of hubris in his speech when he compares Yahweh with the gods of the nations the Assyrians previously defeated (2 Kgs 18:33–35), since Kings has consistently demonstrated that all nations are under Yahweh's authority.[108] In a narrative so strongly marked by speech, the silence commanded by Hezekiah is rhetorically important, though the torn clothing of those who heard the Rabshakeh when reporting to him speaks clearly too (2 Kgs 18:36–37).

---

[105] Nolan Fewell (1986: 80–81) points to the disproportionate amount of space given to speeches in this narrative as a mechanism for demonstrating its interpretative importance.

[106] Wray Beal 2014: 467.

[107] See Höffken 2008, though his Greek parallels probably represent an enduring trope rather than key comparative material for this speech.

[108] P. S. Evans (2009: 348) also points to an internal inconsistency in his speeches – first claiming Yahweh brought up the Assyrians and then claiming Yahweh was not to be trusted. There is, however, no need to regard this as an example of Bakhtinian dialogism since propaganda has seldom needed to be internally consistent – in instances like this it simply needs a mechanism for generating fear.

The torn clothing of his messengers is quickly matched by Hezekiah, but where the Rabshakeh's speech was marked by triumphal boasting, Hezekiah's response was to go to the temple while also sending messengers to Isaiah. His message to Isaiah already notes the possible weakness in the Rabshakeh's position, though in so doing his words also begin to reflect David's in 1 Samuel 17.[109] There, just as Goliath had sought to 'mock' (*ḥrp*) Israel but David had seen this as defiance of the living God (1 Sam. 17:26), so also Hezekiah recognizes that the Rabshakeh was sent by Sennacherib to 'mock' (*ḥrp*) the living God (2 Kgs 19:4). David's task there had been to reframe Goliath's language, and this role falls to Hezekiah here, though with the notable change that this time Hezekiah raises this as a question taken up by Isaiah when he assured Hezekiah that the Assyrians had reviled Yahweh, and Sennacherib would therefore be sent back to his own land and die (2 Kgs 19:6–7). Just as the initial report of Sennacherib's campaign (2 Kgs 18:13–16) had provided an initial summary, so Isaiah's speech here provides a summary of the events that follow.

The pattern established by the Rabshakeh's previous speeches is repeated in a letter sent to Hezekiah by Sennacherib that again warned against trusting in Yahweh on the basis that none of the gods of the nations were able to deliver them from being placed under the ban by the Assyrians. Once again Hezekiah's response is to go to the temple, this time with his prayer reported (2 Kgs 19:14–19). The prayer draws on the language of the ark as the place of Yahweh's enthronement. Where the Assyrian position was that Yahweh was like the gods of the other nations, Hezekiah's prayer insists that as creator, Yahweh alone is God of all kingdoms. The Assyrians could defeat the gods of the nations, but only because they were not really gods. Hezekiah's prayer climaxes in its closing verse, an appeal that echoes David's encounter with Goliath in its determination that all the earth should come to know Yahweh through his saving work for his people (2 Kgs 19:19; cf. 1 Sam. 17:46–47). This statement also picks up on the theme in Solomon's prayer of all the peoples coming to know Yahweh (1 Kgs 8:43, 60), while also echoing the reason for the cairn at the Jordan (Josh. 4:24). Hezekiah's prayer, placed near the end of the Former Prophets, thus picks up a key theme from near the beginning while also drawing on David as the pattern for Hezekiah, a pattern that Solomon understood in his prayer even if his actions did not always follow through on it. Israel's existence, and especially through

---

[109] On the importance of the David–Hezekiah pattern, see Provan 1988: 91–132.

Yahweh's saving acts for them, was to point to all the greatness of Yahweh, inviting all to come to a meaningful point of acknowledging him. Within Kings there is the additional note that foreigners might remain foreigners while making this acknowledgment.

The balance of this story then demonstrates how Isaiah's summary message (2 Kgs 19:6–7) is worked out, though this response is specifically in terms of Hezekiah's prayer (2 Kgs 19:19). But interaction with foreigners at this point is not resolved by the removal of the Assyrians since Hezekiah then became ill,[110] with Isaiah initially expecting that Hezekiah would die, until Yahweh again responded to prayer, granting Hezekiah an additional fifteen years.[111] Following his recovery, Hezekiah received envoys from the Babylonians,[112] even showing them his treasures and military equipment. Whereas his encounter with the Assyrians was marked by an excess of dialogue, this time no dialogue is reported. Instead, we must wait for Isaiah to question him and so draw out the significance of this event. Hezekiah only confirmed what the narrator had reported, though even this appears to be given unwillingly. For this he was rebuked by Isaiah, who anticipates the Babylonian exile in his answer. Hezekiah's response is hardly presented as his finest moment, as he was seemingly content with the success of the immediate generation, unlike the earlier announcement of longer-term deliverance (2 Kgs 20:16–19; cf. 20:6). Yahweh is greater than the nations, and Israel's function (as Hezekiah's own prayer recognized) was to be the means of Yahweh's being known by all. An alliance (of sorts) with Babylon was not how this would be achieved.

The final presentation of Hezekiah thus demonstrated the problem of being too closely aligned with a foreign power, and this issue then comes to prominence in the account of Manasseh (2 Kgs 21:1–18).[113] Manasseh has the distinction of being Judah's longest-reigning king, but whereas his father received the best assessment possible for a king in Judah, Manasseh joins Ahaz in receiving a wholly negative rating. For such a lengthy reign the account in Kings is remarkably sparse, offering no stories, and focusing instead on a report of actions that

---

[110] Indeed, the events here probably predate the events of Sennacherib's invasion, but narratively need to be considered after them. See Wray Beal 2014: 479.

[111] 2 Kgs 20:1–11. On the use of this as a patterning device specific to Kings, see Cohn 1985, though the key variation here is that Hezekiah does not die.

[112] Their arrival is closely patterned on that of the Assyrians, with both bringing 'letters' (2 Kgs 19:14; 20:12). Cf. Cohn 2000: 144.

[113] His son Amon (2 Kgs 21:19–26) appears to have continued with his policies, but as foreigners are not mentioned in his reign he is not considered here.

demonstrate the assessment of Manasseh as having done 'evil in Yahweh's eyes' (2 Kgs 21:2). This is to prepare for the direct announcement of the upcoming exile (2 Kgs 21:10–15),[114] something that is traced back to his reign. In this he contrasts with Hezekiah, whose actions anticipated the exile, but who was not regarded as causing it. Kings is careful not to provide any information that might provide an alternative reading of Manasseh, so we hear the assessment of him quite directly. He has done evil, and that evil is traced wholly to the patterns of worship he introduced, worship that was consistent with the Canaanite pattern that had been rejected. In this way Manasseh led the nation astray so that they were worse than the Canaanites (2 Kgs 21:9). Only when we know of Manasseh's failures in worship can we learn that his practice of violence had an impact on the whole of Judah, as if to say that this emerged because of the worship patterns he established. The presentation of Manasseh evokes the introduction to Solomon's prayer (1 Kgs 8:22–30) in that it is a reversal of all that the temple was meant to be. Instead of making Israel's faith something that was to be known by all, by swamping Judah's life with Canaanite practice he becomes another example of the Achan typology that runs through the Former Prophets, exploring what happens when Israel lose their distinctiveness. Foreigners are not a problem, but a foreign faith is. This is why Manasseh's sin is the one that Yahweh will not forgive (2 Kgs 24:3–4). Unlike Naaman, who could be forgiven because he wanted to serve Yahweh, Manasseh made forgiveness impossible precisely because he removed himself, and led the nation, away from the context of prayer that made forgiveness possible. Manasseh is the anti-type, not only to David and Hezekiah in terms of kingship, but also to the Aramean general Naaman in terms of possible forgiveness.

Following Manasseh and his son Amon, Kings focuses on Josiah as the other king who did what was right and so could be considered to have done right before Yahweh (2 Kgs 22:2). Where the faults of Ahaz and Manasseh could be traced back to their worship practices, so also Josiah's achievements are centred on the theme of worship, which is why he too can be compared with David.[115] However,

---

[114] This passage is regarded as an addition to the text by those committed to the theory of a double redaction of a Deuteronomistic History, though even Nelson (1981: 23) regards mention of the exile as a weak argument (while still regarding this as an exilic text). Although my rejection of the Deuteronomistic History does not prohibit the possibility of editing of the text, it makes less likely the sort of redaction history suggested by Joseph (2015: 189–193), in which Manasseh was gradually made worse.

[115] Cf. Joseph 2015: 148.

although the account of Josiah's reign is relatively lengthy, it too can be compared with Manasseh's in that we are told relatively little of what he did. Even the longest element, the finding of the book of the Torah (2 Kgs 22:3–20), focuses more on the actions of those who found the scroll, though the fact that Josiah had begun repairs to the temple at least enabled this. Josiah's achievements are shaped by his response to the discovery of this scroll, which means that (in contrast to Hezekiah) foreigners are of relatively little interest for the report of his reign. However, the contrast with Manasseh is certainly clear – where he promoted foreign worship, Josiah acted to remove it, though without the excesses that had marked Jehu's reign (2 Kgs 23:4–14). Josiah can thus be regarded as a king without comparison in Judah (2 Kgs 23:25), though, because of Manasseh, this was not enough to remove Yahweh's anger (2 Kgs 23:26–27).

That Josiah could not himself change Judah's fate then introduces a series of accounts that show Judah's interacting with the major powers of the day, something triggered by the emergence of Babylon as the new empire that swept across the Fertile Crescent, claiming the former Assyrian territory for themselves. Like Hezekiah, Josiah seems to have been caught up in the politics of this, and so was killed by Pharaoh Neco in an unnecessary battle (2 Kgs 23:28). This in turn triggered a series of puppet kings being placed on the throne in Jerusalem (2 Kgs 23:31 – 24:17). Although Josiah was initially succeeded by his son Jehoahaz (2 Kgs 23:31), Neco replaced him shortly afterwards with his brother Eliakim, changing Eliakim's name to Jehoiakim (2 Kgs 23:32–35). When Nebuchadnezzar arrived, Jehoiakim initially served him; but after rebelling, Judah was under constant pressure from the nations around them. Although this might be interpreted as these peoples seeing the need to pacify Babylon, Kings sees this as Yahweh's expressing his sovereignty over all the nations (2 Kgs 24:2–3). Following Jehoiakim's death, his son Jehoiachin briefly reigned (2 Kgs 24:8–9), before he too was deposed, this time by Nebuchadnezzar, and replaced by his uncle Mattaniah, who was in turn renamed Zedekiah by Nebuchadnezzar (2 Kgs 24:10–17). In turn, Zedekiah rebelled against Babylon, and so triggered the final tragic fall of Jerusalem (2 Kgs 25:1–21). This saw the removal of a significant portion of the population of Jerusalem along with many valuables from the temple. The place that was meant to signify the hope provided for all by Yahweh was ruined because of a persistent pattern of rebellion and sin. Yet even in exile there was a hint of hope as Jehoiachin was given a place of prominence, though Kings appears to have been written too close to this event to offer a final interpretation of it (2 Kgs 25:27–30). But in closing, the book continues to affirm that all nations are ultimately under Yahweh's rule, even if there is no clarity as to what this may mean.

Conclusions: kings and foreigners beyond the borders of Israel

As with the previous books of the Former Prophets, foreigners play an important role in Kings. Some aspects of Israel's relationship with foreigners continue here much as before, most notably that some foreign powers continued to oppose Israel, and these were therefore resisted. But this opposition is not seen in specifically political or ethnic terms. For Kings, the central issues revolve around the worship of Yahweh and how he is known in the nations. This, in part at least, explains why so much attention is given to the Assyrian crisis in 2 Kings 18 – 20: it is here that Yahweh's exaltation relative to the so-called gods of the nations becomes particularly clear. But in this narrative we also see once again the key element of the importance of all peoples seeing the reality of Yahweh (2 Kgs 19:19). Yahweh's acting for Israel when they face hostile powers is a key means by which all peoples will know him. But Yahweh may also use these foreign powers to discipline a disobedient Israel because all such nations are ultimately under Yahweh's reign (2 Kgs 17:7–23).

But Kings does go beyond the earlier books in the Former Prophets in its focus on foreigners who live beyond the boundaries of Israel. This emerges in Solomon's prayer at the dedication of the temple as he prays for such foreigners (1 Kgs 8:41–43) and in his statement on the purpose of the temple (1 Kgs 8:60). This statement is also tied to Hezekiah's prayer in the Assyrian crisis and points to the pivotal role of the prayer for the whole of Kings. Within Kings this concern for foreigners who come to believe in Yahweh while living outside the land comes to its clearest focus in the Naaman story (2 Kgs 5); though, as we have noted, there are also elements in the Elijah cycle that point to this concern. Alongside this, Kings continues to demonstrate that when Israel (or an individual Israelite) turn from Yahweh, they effectively lose their status. Once more, therefore, the people of God are defined not by ethnicity, but on the basis of a faith relationship to Yahweh.

Chapter Six

Foreigners and the people of God

Initial orientation: key themes from the Former Prophets

Reading the Former Prophets through the grid of foreigners opens up several key themes within them. At this point it is helpful to step back and draw these together. Having done this, we will then briefly consider how these themes fit within the larger witness of the Bible before considering some implications that emerge from them.

Although there is value in treating each book as a distinctive witness since each has its own emphases, there are also good reasons for seeing the Former Prophets as a collection intended to be read together. As we have noted, Judges specifically links itself to Joshua, while Kings is closely tied to Samuel. Although the initial links between Judges and Samuel are not quite as strong, perhaps why the tradition represented in the LXX, which continues in English Bibles today, felt comfortable in including Ruth at this point, we also saw there were important links between them. How each book relates to the previous one differs, but their final composition and collection indicates that they need to be read together.[1]

Foreigners are important across the collection, and Israel experienced them in different ways. Nevertheless, it is possible to trace three main threads through the whole of the Former Prophets.

Foreigners as enemies of Israel

The first thread is perhaps the least contentious, and so can be dealt with briefly. Across this collection Israel encounters foreigners who are their enemies. Such enemies are rarely identified with an individual and are more typically considered in terms of non-Israelite nations who oppose Israel for some reason. As we progress through the

---

[1] See Koorevaar 2012 and Peterson 2014 for models of reading these texts closest to that followed here.

Former Prophets, the nature of Israel's enemies changes from nations within the land to peoples outside it. This change can be mapped against the shape of Israel at a given point in time – in Joshua Israel are presented as a group working together while aware that they have disparate interests (notably, in the case of those east or west of the Jordan, with Manasseh as a bridge people). The enemies are within the land, opposing Israel's claiming the land. But in Judges Israel functions as a set of more or less discrete 'tribes',[2] and although their enemies are national, these enemies tend to affect only a given part of Israel. These enemies are not major powers but other groups settling in the region about the same time. Although these enemies attack Israel, it is clear that they do so as an expression of Yahweh's purposes for Israel – those who remained in the land were a test for Israel; while others attacked because they were the means Yahweh used to discipline Israel for their sin. Although much falls under the category of 'sin' in Judges,[3] the primary focus of the narrative is the sin of Israelite worship of gods other than Yahweh. It is this that triggers Israel's encounters with foreign powers.

Samuel and Kings do not relate to foreign powers in quite the same way. In part, this may be because once we reach Kings the major powers that came to dominate the ANE have emerged, and Israel therefore has to deal with the expansionist goals of these peoples. Nevertheless, although there is no longer an immediate correlation between Israel's sin and their encounter with a hostile foreign power, this element is not lost. It is particularly evident in the summary of why the northern kingdom fell to Assyria (2 Kgs 17:7–23); but it is not the only reason why such invasions might happen, as becomes clear in the subsequent encounter between Judah and Assyria (2 Kgs 18 – 19). This shift had already happened in Samuel, where encounters with the Philistines are presented within a context of peoples competing for the same land, without necessarily implying that Israel had sinned before any one encounter with these foreigners. Although Samuel and Kings present Israel's encounters with foreign powers differently, the theme that unites them with Joshua and Judges is that such nations always remain under Yahweh's authority. Foreigners can be a threat to Israel, but they are never an absolute threat, only one that is related to what Yahweh permits.

---

[2] The traditional designation is retained here, though it is not particularly helpful in the light of modern sociology, which might suggest that 'clans' is a better translation of the main terms.

[3] Cf. Boda 2009: 137–144.

Israel's life as a witness to foreigners

The second thread is particularly important for our purposes, though it is closely related to the third. Although Joshua commences the Former Prophets by preparing Israel for battle (Josh. 1), the book immediately problematizes the idea that all foreigners are to be regarded negatively through the story of Rahab (Josh. 2). A Canaanite prostitute, she demonstrates loyalty to Israel and is in turn integrated into Israel following Jericho's capture (Josh. 6:22–25). Her importance cannot be overstated, even if first-time readers of Joshua do not know if the oath sworn by the scouts there is a great mistake or evidence that Israel's relationship to foreigners is complex and determined by faith in Yahweh rather than by ethnicity.

Rahab's two appearances are carefully structured around the account of Israel's crossing the Jordan (Josh. 3 – 4). For much of the year crossing the Jordan is not particularly difficult, though in the spring thaw it can be. That Israel crossed the river at this time is a miracle that evokes the crossing of the Sea from the exodus and provides important background, showing that exodus and eisodus belong together. But the important element for our purposes is to note the cairn established at Gilgal at the end of the crossing, a cairn that points to the fact that all peoples are meant to know Yahweh (Josh. 4:21–24). This is the first occurrence of a key refrain that occurs three more times in the Former Prophets, though the variations that occur between them mean we should avoid thinking of this as a formula that has only one function. Rather, it is a refrain that can be applied to a range of contexts. Here in Joshua the focus is on Israel's remembering that their existence is a pointer to all the peoples to know that Yahweh is mighty and that they should fear him. That is, the main application of the refrain here is to remind Israel of Yahweh's might; though, in a context where an oath has been sworn to Rahab, it leaves open the possibility that foreigners may well join Israel, something that gradually emerges as more of a possibility as the book of Joshua continues.

The refrain's second occurrence is found in David's encounter with Goliath (1 Sam. 17:46–47). This time it is uttered by David in the midst of taunts between him and Goliath. As the last of the taunts before the combat, it is clearly the focus to which the whole narrative has been building, so as in Joshua it is placed at a point of narrative climax. Here the witness moves in two directions. David's victory over Goliath bears witness to all the earth that there is a God in Israel while also reminding Israel that Yahweh does not win battles by normal means of combat. The refrain here is applied equally to foreigners and Israel, something that emerges naturally enough given the context of combat between Israel and the Philistines.

The refrain occurs a third time in Solomon's blessing of Israel after his prayer of dedication for the temple (1 Kgs 8:60). The larger context here makes clear that Yahweh gave Israel rest in the land and has been faithful to all his promises. The goal of this therefore is that Israel should be careful to walk in Yahweh's ways (1 Kgs 8:54–61). In this context the use of the refrain also builds on the concern for the foreigner expressed in Solomon's prayer, but is now a reminder to Israel that the goal of their faithfulness is not for themselves alone but also for those outside Israel. Israel's faithfulness is their testimony to the nations that Yahweh alone is God.

The refrain's final occurrence is in Hezekiah's prayer during the Assyrian crisis (2 Kgs 19:19). In this instance Hezekiah asks that Yahweh's act of delivering Israel may enable all the earth to know that Yahweh alone is God. The prayer has clear echoes of Solomon's prayer, but also of David's encounter with Goliath. Judah at this time had no mechanism for defeating Assyria, but the echo from the earlier conflict is a reminder of the fact that Yahweh's victories were not won on the basis of traditional military strength. Where David's encounter stressed the reality of Yahweh's presence within Israel, Hezekiah's prayer joins with Solomon's in asking that all may know that Yahweh alone is God.

We should not isolate the occurrences of this refrain from their wider contexts, because it is notable that each contributes to the major concern with foreigners encountered in each book of the Former Prophets. Nevertheless, it is a key feature across the collection as a whole for demonstrating the concern for peoples beyond Israel while matching Israel's developing awareness that they exist not only to worship and serve Yahweh, but also to point all peoples to a knowledge of this.[4] It should be noted that the refrain does not occur in Judges, but this is not in itself problematic if we first approach each book on its own terms. Nevertheless, the absence of the refrain here is balanced by an equivalent but opposite concern in Judges 2:10, where a generation arose who did not know Yahweh. As such, Judges functions as the counterexample, the story of what happens to an Israel that is no

---

[4] Even the partial acknowledgment of this by the Gibeonites (Josh. 9; 2 Sam. 21:1–14) is a step towards this.

longer living in faithfulness and that therefore offers no witness to others.

Israel as foreigners

Closely related to the issue of Israel's witness to foreigners is the possibility that Israel may themselves become (in effect) foreigners. Although Israel can be defined ethnically, throughout the Former Prophets they can also be understood as a faith community; and an Israel that ceases to remain faithful to Yahweh can lose its status. So, just as foreigners who commit themselves to Yahweh can become part of Israel, so also Israelites who abandon Yahweh lose their status as his people.

The key figure for understanding this is Achan (Josh. 7) since there are numerous allusions to him in the balance of the Former Prophets. Achan himself was an 'Israelite of the Israelites' (cf. Phil. 3:5) but he also took from the items placed under the ban at Jericho. His sin had an impact on the whole nation, as they were unable to capture the relatively small city of Ai, demonstrating that sin was damaging to the nation as a whole. Achan is treated, in effect, as a Canaanite and is thus contrasted with Rahab. Within the opening chapters of Joshua Canaanites become Israelites, and Israelites become Canaanites. A typology based on Achan begins to develop in Joshua 22, where the possible division over the altar frequently alludes to and ultimately references Achan, even if in that instance the conflict is resolved. This typology is explored in each of the subsequent books of the Former Prophets. The story of the rape of the concubine at Gibeah and the ensuing conflict in Judges 19 – 21 frequently evokes this story, showing that the problem was not only individual but could manifest itself across whole tribes. The presentation of Saul in Samuel has many echoes of Achan,[5] while both Gehazi (2 Kgs 5) and Manasseh (2 Kgs 21:1–18) also provide a number of allusions to Achan. Throughout the Former Prophets there are instances of foreigners who become Israelites (even while remaining outside the land by the time we reach Kings) while Israelites become foreigners.

Taken as a whole, while also allowing for distinctive elements within each book, we can note that the Former Prophets are concerned with the formation of Israel as a faith community. The starting point for this is certainly the ethnic group that can be called 'Israel', but they are ultimately not defined on the basis of ethnicity. The Israel that

[5] Cf. Michael 2013.

matters is the one that is continually reminded that their existence is for others, for foreigners, who can be welcomed into the nation or even share Israel's faith while remaining where they are. An Israel that forgets this reality places itself under Yahweh's discipline and can lose its status, and that discipline can involve other nations since they too are under Yahweh's sovereignty.

Echoes in the Old Testament

Tracing these elements across the whole of the Old Testament would require a major study in its own right, so a few summary comments are offered here to demonstrate that later periods in Israel's life saw them following this same pattern. Given that the Former Prophets probably reached their final form in the exile[6] we will note only a couple of examples from books after the exile that seem to reflect back on these accounts.[7]

Ezra is perhaps not a book that many would turn to in this regard given the fact it reports the exclusion from the community of those who married inappropriately (Ezra 10). Nevertheless, there are points where it seems to reflect on the themes traced in the Former Prophets so that even the situation of the marriages is understood in the light of the events there.

As a first point in Ezra we can consider the celebration of the Passover after the dedication of the second temple (Ezra 6:19–22). The account comes as the climax of the report on the initial returnees. Given their struggles to build the temple and the ambivalence expressed by many on the conditions of the initial return to Jerusalem,[8] it demonstrates that God continued to work among them, particularly through the ministries of Haggai and Zechariah. That Passover could be celebrated therefore places the return to the land within the setting of the exodus, seeing this celebration in continuity with what had gone before. Undoubtedly, this reaches back to Exodus 12,[9] but there are also echoes here of narratives from the Former

[6] This is a heavily contested observation that cannot be defended here, but see Hubbard and Dearman 2018: 116, though with the caveat that there is evidence that each book may have existed apart from the others.

[7] Although Ruth could be considered here, debates about its date mean we cannot be sure it reflects on the whole of the Former Prophets.

[8] See Bänziger 2014.

[9] Admittedly, the slaughter of the lambs by priests is not envisaged there, but as H. G. M. Williamson (1985: 85) notes, this appears to have become the established practice by the Second Temple period.

Prophets. This Passover was eaten not only by those Israelites who had returned from the exile, but also by all those who had joined them. Those who had joined them were apparently proselytes, and are defined as those who had separated themselves from the uncleanness of the peoples of the land (Ezra 6:21). Earlier this group had rejected the offer of help from others already in the region (Ezra 4:2–3), but in that case they were defined as those who had been settled in the region by Assyria, alluding back to 2 Kings 17:24–41 and the mixed worship that had developed with this. But now the worshipping community is joined by non-Israelites, the only criterion being that these people devote themselves to the worship of Yahweh. Although there are numerous points where foreigners join Israel, such accounts are more typical of the Former Prophets than Chronicles, the historical books more closely linked to Ezra–Nehemiah. Indeed, it is the Former Prophets with their accounts such as that of Rahab which establish the pattern here, so that foreigners can join Israel.[10] Just as the celebration of Passover marked Israel's entry into the land (Josh. 5:1–12), so their return to the land is finally marked by the same celebration here.[11] Israel's life has here in some way witnessed to foreigners, so that they join themselves to Yahweh and then to Israel.

But Ezra also reports a situation with echoes of the Achan story, and the closeness of this account to the Passover report may also indicate a conscious echo of the Joshua account. In this case we meet the issue of inappropriate marriages that was a major concern for the post-exilic community (Ezra 9:1–4). In this instance the problem was that the Israelites, and especially some of the leaders, had not separated themselves from the abominations of the peoples of the land.[12] This is a clear reverse from those at the Passover who had separated themselves. The issue is not that these people had married foreigners but rather that they had not separated themselves from their abominations – Ezra knows that it was possible for foreigners to join themselves to Yahweh and thus not be a problem for Israel. There is here an immediate and general link to the Achan story because it is clear that these leaders have begun to associate with Canaanite practice. But more specifically, the term used to describe

[10] Cf. Lorein 2010: 126.
[11] Bänziger 2014: 156.
[12] The peoples listed begin with the Canaanites but continue with others who more obviously continued in the period. The listing, however, is a deliberate echo of the accounts from Joshua even as it updates the list to the then current conditions.

Israel's 'treachery' (*ma'al*, Ezra 9:2) is the same as that used in Joshua 7:1. That is, the summary term used here is the same as that in the Achan story. By their intermarriage, and more specifically their failure to separate themselves from the abominations of the land, these leaders brought Israel back to the status of being Canaanite. The patterns established in the Former Prophets thus continued among the post-exilic community as they too wrestled with the challenge of remaining faithful to Yahweh while remaining a community that was open to foreigners but not to foreign worship.

We may note a further example in an even less expected place. The book of Esther is often regarded as an almost secular text, and is perhaps best known as the only book of the Old Testament that definitely does not mention God.[13] Esther is, however, a text that deliberately alludes to large parts of the Old Testament so that it needs to be read intertextually if we are to appreciate its theology.[14] Although there is no direct allusion to the Achan traditions, the possibility of losing Israel's distinctiveness seems to lie behind Mordecai's challenge to Esther to intervene on behalf of her people following the publication of Haman's decree for the destruction of the Jews (Esth. 4). The danger for Esther here was that she could not survive even if she remained in the palace, and this despite the fact that she had been careful not to divulge her ancestry. Survival was not to be gained by failing to identify with her people, and effectively becoming Persian. The Persians are generally viewed positively within the Old Testament, but that did not mean that Israel could become Persian. By contrast, after Esther's intervention and introduction of Mordecai to the king (Esth. 8:1–2), and the subsequent issuing of a counter-edict (Esth. 8:3–14), we are told that many from the peoples of the country 'declared themselves to be Jews' (Esth. 8:17). The exact sense of this phrase is not clear since the participle here could have the sense of 'pretended to be Jews'. But even if full conversion to Judaism is not in view, 'became Jews' is still a probable interpretation.[15] This probability becomes stronger when we note that the dread which is said to have fallen on these peoples echoes the experience Rahab had previously described for the inhabitants of the land (Josh. 2:9).[16] Hence even Esther shows

---

[13] Song of Songs may mention Yahweh (Song 8:6), but this depends on the meaning of a suffix there.

[14] Firth 2010: 19–22.

[15] Allen and Laniak 2003: 252; Breneman 1993: 356.

[16] The terminology is not identical, but there is a conceptual match.

awareness of these patterns from the Former Prophets and weaves them into its story.

Echoes in the New Testament

As with echoes in the Old Testament, my comments here need to be brief. At one level this is because the New Testament no longer understands the people of God as one nation, but rather they are drawn from all peoples (Acts 15:13–14). Nevertheless, some specific points are worthy of reflection. Although there are many texts here, three brief soundings from Matthew will demonstrate how these themes are picked up in the New Testament.[17]

We may begin by noting the visit of the Magi to the infant Jesus (Matt. 2:1–12). These are pagans from the east who engage in astrology, and yet seek the one born 'king of the Jews' (Matt. 2:2). Herod, though not Jewish himself, was still king in Jerusalem and so was troubled by this news. He therefore called together the priests and scribes to find where the Messiah would be born. On discovering that he was to be born in Bethlehem, he sent the Magi there, trying to use them to find out the information he needed to kill the child. In this there is a neat reversal of David's encounter with Uriah (2 Sam. 11) – there, the anointed king sent a foreigner back to his death, carrying the message that would lead to this. But here foreigners are sent to the true anointed king, yet are guided away, through a dream, from providing the information that will lead to his murder. As the Magi would probably have represented the Persian court,[18] there is also an echo of the events that triggered the Ammonite war (2 Sam. 10:1–4). There David's attempt to offer greetings to the new king were rebuffed, leading to considerable death. Here, although Herod pretends to receive them, his goal is the Messiah's death, so that what was a friendly greeting between kings is a trigger to violence. Along with this it is notable that the Magi clearly follow religious practices that lie outside those of Israel, and yet the validity of their worship of Jesus can be affirmed. The refrain of the Former Prophets thus finds expression in the worship offered here, even if these foreigners do not become a recognizable part of the people of God.

[17] Luke's presentation of Jesus' Nazareth sermon (Luke 4:16–30) includes reference to some of the key texts from the ministry of Elijah and Elisha with foreigners, so the texts noted from Matthew do not stand outside a wider tradition of Jesus' ministry and teaching.

[18] Morris 1992: 36.

Matthew's interest in foreigners can also be seen in the account of the healing of a centurion's servant (Matt. 8:5–13).[19] This account is in a group of healings reported after the conclusion to the Sermon on the Mount that demonstrate the reality of the kingdom in Jesus. Approached by the centurion, Jesus seems initially reluctant to act on his behalf, a pattern repeated in the encounter with the Canaanite woman (Matt. 15:21–28).[20] But the centurion, though clearly a member of the Roman forces that controlled the region at the time, gave a response that accepted that he was not worthy for Jesus to enter his house, but at the same time continued to believe that Jesus could heal, even though to this point in Matthew's Gospel there have been no healings at a distance. The man's faith is sufficient to astonish Jesus, something that otherwise happens only in the unbelief he encounters in Nazareth (Mark 6:6). What is remarkable is that this centurion is defined as someone who is foreign, because the contrast Jesus makes is between his faith and the faith Jesus has found in Israel – and in this contrast it is the foreigner's faith that exceeds all that Jesus has found within Israel. As a result, it is this foreigner who sets the pattern for those who will feast at the messianic banquet (cf. Isa. 25:6–9), with many coming from east and west and joining, while Israelites are excluded. Reference here to the east naturally evokes the visit of the Magi, while as a Roman[21] the centurion has come from the west. The potential exclusion of the 'sons of the kingdom' echoes the exclusion of Achan and those in the Former Prophets who have followed his pattern, while the presence of many from elsewhere again follows the pattern of the refrain.

As a final sounding, we can note Jesus' encounter with the Canaanite woman (Matt. 15:21–28).[22] That these events happen in the region of Tyre and Sidon evokes Elijah's ministry in that same area (1 Kgs 17:8–24).[23] The term 'Canaanite' occurs nowhere else in the New Testament, but might also raise negative expectations on the part of

[19] If this account is parallel to John 4:46–53, then *pais* could mean 'son'; but with Carson (1984: 200) the extent of the differences makes it more likely that these are independent stories.

[20] Most English Bibles render Jesus' response in v. 7 as an offer to come to heal him, but with Nolland (2005: 355) it is better to understand this as a question (or perhaps an exclamation with questioning intent).

[21] The man did not have to come from Rome itself, but the empire spread out to the west.

[22] In Mark's parallel (Mark 7:24–30) her Gentile status is noted, but Matthew sharpens this by calling her a Canaanite.

[23] It is possible that 'and Sidon' is an addition Matthew makes to the text at this point, as the term is textually uncertain in Mark.

some readers, except that the Former Prophets consistently showed the possibilities that existed for Canaanites within Israel when these foreigners embraced Israel's faith. This woman approaches Jesus, and immediately expresses herself in terms that indicate familiarity with this faith (and thus echoes Rahab) by calling Jesus 'son of David' as she asks for mercy because of the demonic oppression of her daughter (Matt. 15:22). As with the centurion, Jesus is initially unwilling to respond, and his disciples want to send her away because of her persistence. Even when Jesus addresses her by pointing out that he has been sent only to the lost sheep of Israel, she persists, calling him 'Lord' as she asks for help (Matt. 15:23–25). Again Jesus tries to dissuade her, but she persists and debates with him, eventually convincing him to act, once again on the basis of her faith. As with the centurion's servant, this healing also happened at a distance. Although the main focus of Jesus' ministry was on Israel (cf. Matt. 10:6), this encounter with a Canaanite woman represents an important point in establishing the fact that the ultimate goal of this ministry was to all peoples (Matt. 28:16–20). Moreover, it is a Canaanite woman who saw what the disciples could not, repeating the pattern seen in Samuel where foreigners, especially those of Canaanite descent, see more clearly than many Israelites what God is doing. Within Matthew and the rest of the New Testament this pattern ultimately looks beyond ethnicity to form a new people that knows and serves God in Christ.

Pointers for an ethic towards foreigners

In the light of the discussion to this point, a few summary points can be offered.

First, unlike the negative views expressed in many popular treatments of the Old Testament in general, and the Former Prophets in particular, the attitude towards foreigners is quite positive. This is because within these texts ethnicity itself is never a problem. Israel's life was meant to point to the reality of God, and various elements within their life were intended to sustain this. This would include the cairn by the Jordan and the temple in Jerusalem, as both witnessed to the reality of God. Although the cairn functioned more to remind Israel of this reality, such a reminder was necessary only if Israel was liable to forget this key element of their mission. Alongside this, the temple witnessed both to Israel and to foreigners of the reality that Yahweh alone was God. Israel's worship, both in its less structured and more formal expressions, was intended to look beyond Israel and be the means by which God's presence was recognized. This means that the idea that God was somehow a petty ethnic cleanser[24] is to be rejected. It also suggests that Christians who take these elements seriously need to reflect on how it is that our worship and communal life are open to including the stranger, and that indeed our structures continue to remind us of this.

Second, the positive attitude towards foreigners also recognized that the people of God were not defined on the basis of ethnicity but rather on the basis of faith. Coming from the perspective of the New Testament, this statement does not seem particularly significant. But this idea has deep roots within the Old Testament itself. Even Canaanites, seemingly the most despised of people, have a future within the people of God when they commit themselves to him (or even when they choose not to oppose him). The integration of Rahab and the Gibeonites, along with other continuing Canaanites in Joshua, finds a focus in the accounts from David's reign, where continuing Canaanites usually understand Yahweh and his purposes much better than Israelites do. Even before this, the accounts in Judges have shown that Yahweh worked through foreigners for the benefit of his people. All of this is contrasted with the varying expressions of the Achan typology we have noted running through the Former Prophets. Each of these elements is also expressed in the New Testament, as we have noted within Matthew's Gospel. It is worth noting that even the commission with which the Gospel ends can be understood in the light of the refrain that runs through the Former Prophets, albeit as one that represents a more deliberately outward movement than we find there. Here once again we are reminded that God's saving work is for all the peoples of the earth. God is not a petty racist, but a God whose purposes have always included all peoples, irrespective of ethnicity. Indeed, even those whom God's people might be inclined to reject remain central to his purposes.

Such positive attitudes towards foreigners lead to a third reflection. My own experience as a foreigner is largely positive, but this is far from common as many societies wrestle with issues of migration and how they are to be formed. It goes beyond the goals of this study to explore the implications of this material for contemporary discussions of migration and how the church might wrestle with them, though it can contribute to such reflections. It is certainly true that the church as a whole has recognized the importance of welcoming foreigners,

---

[24] Dawkins 2006: 51.

though whether this is always expressed in local contexts is less clear. But the church is called to be a people of faith that models God's ultimate purposes in which all peoples are gathered within the kingdom, a purpose alluded to in Jesus' response to the centurion (Matt. 8:11–13). How the local church deals with foreigners within it becomes a context in which to live out this ethic, while also pointing to the greater goal of inclusion that the church as a whole should demonstrate. In doing this we may also live out the refrain from the Former Prophets, and declare to all the world the reality of God who, in Christ, is made known to us.

One way in which we might helpfully think about this is in terms of an issue noted in the first chapter, the idea that someone might be the 'wrong kind' of foreigner. Unlike our time in the UK, where my family and I are usually the 'right kind of foreigner' (or at least not the 'wrong kind' being complained about), when my wife and I worked in Zimbabwe we were often conscious of being the 'wrong sort of foreigner'. We lived and worked in a country that was redefining its identity, a process that continues today, and where white foreigners could be viewed as particularly problematic. Those with whom we worked closely were usually appreciative of our work, but there were places where it was considered unsafe for us to go on our own because of resistance to what the former colonial administration (and the later post-Unilateral Declaration of Independence government) had done. We were undoubtedly, for many, the 'wrong kind' of foreigner. But one of my most treasured memories is of our last Sunday in the country. There we attended a worship service in the high-density township on the edge of Bulawayo where we had done much of our work. We were the only white family there. But in the meeting an ANC freedom fighter who was in exile from South Africa (Nelson Mandela was still in prison) spoke. She announced that she had spent the whole of her life attempting to drive white people from Africa, but that day for the first time ever she wanted at least some white people to stay. There were, no doubt, many complex factors involved, and of course this addresses issues of race as well as ethnicity. But in that service as we shared with our friends we were reminded that even in as divided a country as that, there was no such thing as 'the wrong sort' of foreigner. That church had welcomed us and made us part of their life, and in doing so modelled precisely the ethic we have traced through the Former Prophets, one that can include even strangers like us. In a world that builds walls between communities, or makes the environment hostile for foreigners, this was an example of what the people of God can be: a community that does not discriminate on the basis of ethnicity, because we serve a God who does not do so. This is an ethic that is easily talked down in political discourse, but therefore one that is more important than ever for the church, as the people of God, to live out and show a different way of life.

Bibliography

Achenbach, R., R. Albertz and J. Wöhrle (2011), *The Foreigner and the Law: Perspectives from the Hebrew Bible and the Ancient Near East*, Wiesbaden: Harrassowitz.

Ackroyd, P. R. (1977), *The Second Book of Samuel*, CBC, Cambridge: Cambridge University Press.

—— (1981), 'The Succession Narrative (So-Called)', *Int* 35: 383–396.

Allen, L. C., and T. Laniak (2003), *Ezra, Nehemiah and Esther*, Peabody: Hendrickson.

Amit, Y. (1987), 'Judges 4: Its Contents and Form', *JSOT* 39: 89–111.

Anderson, A. A. (1989), *2 Samuel*, WBC, Dallas: Word.

Arnold, B. T. (1989), 'The Amalekite's Report of Saul's Death: Political Intrigue or Incompatible Sources?', *JETS* 32: 289–298.

Aster, S. Z. (2003), 'What Was Doeg the Edomite's Title? Textual Emendation Versus a Comparative Approach', *JBL* 122: 353–361.

Auld, A. G. (2011), *I & II Samuel: A Commentary*, OTL, Louisville: Westminster John Knox.

Awabdy, M. A. (2014), *Immigrants and Innovative Law: Deuteronomy's Theological and Social Vision for the* גר, Tübingen: Mohr Siebeck.

Bailey, R. C. (1990), *David in Love and War: The Pursuit of Power in 2 Samuel 10–12*, Sheffield: JSOT Press.

Baker, R. (2018), 'Double Trouble: Counting the Cost of Jephthah', *JBL* 137: 29–50.

Bal, M. (1992), *Murder and Difference: Gender, Genre and Scholarship on Sisera's Death*, Bloomington: Indiana University Press.

Ball, E. (1977), 'The Co-Regency of David and Solomon (1 Kings 1)', *VT* 27: 268–279.

Bänziger, T. (2014), *'Jauchzen und Weinen': Ambivalente Restauration in Jehud. Theologische Konzepte der Wiederherstellung in Esra–Nehemia*, Zürich: TVZ.

Bauer, U. F. W. (2000), 'Judges 18 as an Anti-Spy Story in the Context of an Anti-Conquest Story: The Creative Use of Literary Genres', *JSOT* 88: 37–47.

Beldman, D. J. H. (2017), *The Completion of Judges: Strategies of Ending in Judges 17–21*, Winona Lake: Eisenbrauns.

Bergen, R. D. (1996), *1, 2 Samuel*, NAC, Nashville: Broadman & Holman.

Birch, B. C. (1998), 'The First and Second Books of Samuel', in L. E. Keck (ed.), *The New Interpreter's Bible*, Nashville: Abingdon, 949–1383.

Block, D. I. (1999), *Judges, Ruth*, NAC, Nashville: Broadman & Holman.

Boda, M. J. (2009), *A Severe Mercy: Sin and Its Remedy in the Old Testament*, Winona Lake: Eisenbrauns.

——— (2012), 'Judges', in T. Longman III and D. E. Garland (eds.), *The Expositor's Bible Commentary*, rev. edn, Grand Rapids: Zondervan, 2: 1043–1288.

Bodner, K. (2002), 'Is Joab a Reader-Response Critic?', *JSOT* 27: 19–35.

——— (2005), *David Observed: A King in the Eyes of His Court*, Sheffield: Sheffield Phoenix.

——— (2014), *The Rebellion of Absalom*, New York: Routledge.

Boling, R. G. (1982), *Joshua: A New Translation with Notes and Commentary*, with an introduction by G. E. Wright, AB, Garden City: Doubleday.

Breneman, M. (1993), *Ezra, Nehemiah, Esther*, NAC, Nashville: Broadman & Holman.

Brenner, A. (1990), 'A Triangle and a Rhombus in Narrative Structure: A Proposed Integrative Reading of Judges IV and V', *VT* 40: 129–138.

Briggs, R. S. (2010), *The Virtuous Reader: Old Testament Narrative and Interpretive Virtue*, Grand Rapids: Baker Academic.

Brown, J. K. (2008), 'Genre Criticism and the Bible', in D. G. Firth and J. A. Grant (eds.), *Words and the Word: Explorations in Biblical Interpretation and Literary Theory*, Nottingham: Apollos, 111–150.

Brueggemann, W. (1990a), '1 Samuel: A Sense of Beginning', *ZAW* 102: 33–48.

——— (1990b), *Power, Providence and Personality: Biblical Insight into Life and Ministry*, Louisville: Westminster John Knox.

——— (2000), *1 & 2 Kings*, Macon: Smyth & Helwys.

——— (2002), *Ichabod Toward Home: The Journey of God's Glory*, Grand Rapids: Eerdmans.

Budde, K. (1902), *Die Bücher Samuel erklärt*, Tübingen: Mohr.

Bultmann, C. (1992), *Der Fremde in antiken Juda: Eine Untersuchung zur sozialen Typenbegriff 'ger' und seinen Bedeutungswandel in der alttestamentlichen Gesetzgebung*, Göttingen: V&R.

Butler, T. C. (2009), *Judges*, WBC, Nashville: Thomas Nelson.

—— (2014a), *Joshua 1–12*, WBC, Grand Rapids: Zondervan.

—— (2014b), *Joshua 13–24*, WBC, Grand Rapids: Zondervan.

Campbell, A. F. (1975), *The Ark Narrative (1 Sam 4–6; 2 Sam 6): A Form Critical and Traditio-Historical Study*, Missoula: Scholar's Press.

—— (1986), *Of Prophets and Kings: A Late Ninth-Century Document (1 Samuel 1–2 Kings 10)*, Washington: Catholic Biblical Association.

Campbell, K. M. (1972), 'Rahab's Covenant: A Short Note on Joshua ii 9–21', *VT* 22: 243–244.

Carroll R., M. D. (2008), *Christians at the Border: Immigration, the Church and the Bible*, Grand Rapids: Baker.

Carson, D. A. (1981), *Divine Sovereignty and Human Responsibility: Biblical Perspectives in Tension*, London: Marshall, Morgan & Scott.

—— (1984), 'Matthew', in F. E. Gaebelein (ed.), *The Expositor's Bible Commentary*, vol. 8, Grand Rapids: Zondervan, 3–599.

Chambers, N. (2015), 'Confirming Joshua as the Interpreter of Israel's *Tôrah*: The Narrative Role of Joshua 8:30–35', *BBR* 25: 141–153.

Childs, B. S. (1967), *Isaiah and the Assyrian Crisis*, London: SCM.

Chisholm Jr, R. B. (2007), 'Yahweh Versus the Canaanite Gods: Polemic in Judges and 1 Samuel 1–7', *BibSac* 164: 165–180.

—— (2009), 'What's Wrong with This Picture? Stylistic Variation as a Rhetorical Technique in Judges', *JSOT* 34: 171–182.

—— (2013), *A Commentary on Judges and Ruth*, Grand Rapids: Kregel Academic.

Clements, R. E. (1980), *Isaiah and the Deliverance of Jerusalem: A Study of the Interpretation of Prophecy in the Old Testament*, Sheffield: JSOT Press.

Cogan, M. (2001), *1 Kings: A New Translation with Introduction and Commentary*, AB, New Haven: Yale University Press.

Cogan, M., and H. Tadmor (1988), *II Kings*, AB, Garden City: Doubleday.

Cohn, R. L. (1982), 'The Literary Logic of 1 Kings 17–19', *JBL* 101: 333–350.

—— (1983), 'Form and Perspective in 2 Kings V', *VT* 33: 171–184.

———— (1985), 'Convention and Creativity in the Book of Kings: The Case of the Dying Monarch', *CBQ* 47: 603–616.

———— (2000), *Berit Olam: Studies in Hebrew Narrative and Poetry. 2 Kings*, Collegeville: Liturgical Press.

Conroy, C. (1978), *Absalom! Absalom! Narrative and Language in II Sam 13–20*, Rome: Pontifical Biblical Institute.

Coote, R. B. (1998), 'Joshua', in L. E. Keck (ed.), *The New Interpreter's Bible*, Nashville: Abingdon, 2: 553–719.

Copan, P., and M. Flanagan (2014), *Did God Really Command Genocide? Coming to Terms with the Justice of God*, Grand Rapids: Baker Academic.

Cowles, C. S. (2003), 'The Case for Radical Discontinuity', in S. N. Gundry (ed.), *Show Them No Mercy: Four Views on God and Canaanite Genocide*, Grand Rapids: Zondervan, 11–46.

Creach, J. F. D. (2012), 'Joshua 13–21 and the Politics of Land Division', *Int* 66: 153–163.

———— (2013), *Violence in Scripture*, Louisville: Westminster John Knox.

Crowell, B. L. (2013), 'Good Girl, Bad Girl: Foreign Women of the Deuteronomistic History in Postcolonial Perspective', *BibInt* 21: 1–18.

Cundall, A. E., and L. Morris (1968), *Judges and Ruth: An Introduction and Commentary*, Leicester: Inter-Varsity Press.

Davies, J. A. (2012), 'Heptadic Verbal Patterns in the Solomon Narrative of 1 Kings 1–11', *TynB* 63: 21–34.

Davis, D. R. (2002), *1 Kings: The Wisdom and the Folly*, Fearn: Christian Focus.

Dawkins, R. (2006), *The God Delusion*, London: Black Swan.

Day, J. (1993), 'Bedan, Abdon or Barak in 1 Samuel xii 11?', *VT* 43: 261–264.

———— (2002), *Yahweh and the Gods and Goddesses of Canaan*, Sheffield: Sheffield Academic Press.

DeVries, S. J. (1985), *1 Kings*, WBC, Waco: Word.

Dharamraj, H. (2011), *A Prophet Like Moses? A Narrative-Theological Reading of the Elijah Stories*, Milton Keynes: Paternoster.

Drews, R. (1989), 'The "Chariots of Iron" of Joshua and Judges', *JSOT* 45: 15–23.

Driver, S. R. (1913), *Notes on the Hebrew Text and Topography of the Books of Samuel*, Oxford: Clarendon.

Dubovský, P. (2015), *The Building of the First Temple: A Study in Redactional, Text-Critical and Historical Perspective*, Tübingen: Mohr Siebeck.

Dutcher-Walls, P. (1996), *Narrative Art, Political Rhetoric: The Case of Athaliah and Joash*, Sheffield: Sheffield Academic Press.

Earl, D. S. (2003), 'Moving Beyond Grammatico-Historical Methods: The Value and Application of a Literary-Poetic Approach with Specific Reference to 2 Kings 6:24–7:20', *Evangel* 21: 66–76.

—— (2010a), *The Joshua Delusion? Rethinking Genocide in the Bible*, with a response by C. J. H. Wright, Cambridge: James Clarke.

—— (2010b), *Reading Joshua as Christian Scripture*, Winona Lake: Eisenbrauns.

Edelman, D. (1986), 'Saul's Battle Against Amaleq (1 Sam 15)', *JSOT* 35: 71–83.

Ederer, M. (2017), *Das Buch Josua*, Stuttgart: Katholisches Bibelwerk.

Endris, V. (2008), 'Yahweh Versus Baal: A Narrative-Critical Reading of the Gideon/Abimelech Narrative', *JSOT* 33: 173–195.

Evans, M. J. (2017), *Judges and Ruth: An Introduction and Commentary*, TOTC, London: Inter-Varsity Press.

Evans, P. S. (2009), 'The Hezekiah–Sennacherib Narrative as a Polyphonic Text', *JSOT* 33: 335–358.

Fensham, F. C. (1980), 'A Few Observations on the Polarisation between Yahweh and Baal in 1 Kings 17–19', *ZAW* 92: 227–236.

Finkelstein, I. (2017), 'Major Saviors, Minor Judges: The Historical Background of the Northern Accounts in the Book of Judges', *JSOT* 41: 431–449.

Firth, D. G. (2000), 'Backward Masking: Implicit Characterisation of Elijah in the Micaiah Narrative', *OTE* 13: 174–185.

—— (2001), 'Shining the Lamp: The Rhetoric of 2 Samuel 5–24', *TynB* 52.2: 203–224.

—— (2005a), 'Play It Again Sam: The Poetics of Narrative Repetition in 1 Samuel 1–7', *TynB* 56.2: 1–17.

—— (2005b), 'Speech Acts and Covenant in 2 Samuel 7:1–17', in J. A. Grant and A. I. Wilson (eds.), *The God of Covenant: Biblical, Theological and Contemporary Perspectives*, Leicester: Apollos, 79–99.

—— (2005c), '"That the World May Know." Narrative Poetics in 1 Samuel 16–17', in M. Parsons (ed.), *Text and Task: Scripture and Mission*, Milton Keynes: Paternoster, 20–32.

—— (2007), 'The Accession Narrative (1 Samuel 27–2 Samuel 1)', *TynB* 58.1: 61–82.

—— (2008a), 'Ambiguity', in D. G. Firth and J. A. Grant (eds.), *Words and the Word: Explorations in Biblical Interpretation and Literary Theory*, Nottingham: Apollos, 151–186.

——— (2008b), 'David and Uriah with an Occasional Appearance by Uriah's Wife: Reading and Re-Reading 2 Samuel 11', *OTE* 21: 310–328.

——— (2009), *1 & 2 Samuel*, AOTC, Nottingham: Apollos.

——— (2010), 'When Samuel Met Esther: Narrative Focalisation, Intertextuality, and Theology', *STR* 1: 15–28.

——— (2011), 'The Spirit and Leadership: Testimony, Empowerment and Purpose', in D. G. Firth and P. D. Wegner (eds.), *Presence, Power and Promise: The Role of the Spirit of God in the Old Testament*, Nottingham: Apollos, 259–280.

——— (2014), 'The Historical Books', in T. J. Burke and K. Warrington (eds.), *A Biblical Theology of the Holy Spirit*, London: SPCK, 12–23.

——— (2015), *The Message of Joshua: Promise and People,* BST, Nottingham: Inter-Varsity Press.

——— (2017a), *1 & 2 Samuel: A Kingdom Comes*, London: Bloomsbury T&T Clark.

——— (2017b), 'Disorienting Readers in Joshua 1.1–5.12', *JSOT* 41: 413–430.

——— (2017c), 'Models of Inclusion and Exclusion in Joshua', in H. Hagelia and M. Zehnder (eds.), *Interreligious Relations: Biblical Perspectives*, London: T&T Clark, 71–88.

——— (2018), 'Joshua 24 and the Welcome of Foreigners', *AcT* 38: 69–85.

Flanagan, J. W. (1983), 'Social Transformation and Ritual in 2 Samuel 6', in C. L. Meyers and M. O'Connor (eds.), *The Word of the Lord Shall Go Forth: Festschrift for D. N. Freedman*, Winona Lake: Eisenbrauns, 361–372.

Fokkelman, J. P. (1981), *Narrative Art and Poetry in the Books of Samuel: A Full Interpretation Based on Stylistic and Structural Analyses*, vol. 1: *King David (II Sam. 9–20 & I Kings 1–2)*, Assen: van Gorcum.

——— (1984), 'A Lie Born of Truth, Too Weak to Contain It: A Structural Reading of 2 Sam 1:1–16', *OTS* 23: 39–55.

——— (1986), *Narrative Art and Poetry in the Books of Samuel: A Full Interpretation Based on Stylistic and Structural Analyses*, vol. 2: *The Crossing Fates (I Sam. 13–31 & II Sam. 1)*, Assen: van Gorcum.

——— (1989), 'Saul and David: Crossed Fates', *BRev* 5.3: 20–32.

——— (1990), *Narrative Art and Poetry in the Books of Samuel: A Full Interpretation Based on Stylistic and Structural Analyses*, vol. 3: *Throne and City (II Sam. 2–8 & 21–24)*, Assen: van Gorcum.

——— (1993), *Narrative Art and Poetry in the Books of Samuel: A Full Interpretation Based on Stylistic and Structural Analyses*, vol. 4: *Vow and Desire (1 Sam. 1–12)*, Assen: van Gorcum.

Ford, W. (2015), 'What About the Gibeonites?', *TynB* 66: 197–216.

Frisch, A. (2004), '"And David Perceived" (2 Samuel 5,12): A Direct Insight into David's Soul and Its Meaning in Context', *SJOT* 18.1: 77–92.

Frolov, S. (2013), *Judges*, Grand Rapids: Eerdmans.

García-Alfonso, C. (2010), *Resolviendo: Narratives of Survival in the Hebrew Bible and in Cuba Today*, New York: Peter Lang.

Garroway, K. (2018), '2 Kings 6:24–30: A Case of Unintentional Elimination Killing', *JBL* 137: 53–70.

Garsiel, M. (1983), *The First Book of Samuel: A Literary Study of Comparative Structures, Analogies and Parallels*, Jerusalem: Rubin Mas.

Genette, G. (1980), *Narrative Discourse: An Essay in Method*, Ithaca: Cornell University Press.

George, M. K. (1999), 'Constructing Identity in 1 Samuel 17', *BibInt* 7: 389–412.

Gillmayr-Bucher, S. (2007), '"She Came to Test Him with Hard Questions": Foreign Women and Their View of Israel', *BibInt* 15: 135–150.

——— (2009), 'Framework and Discourse in the Book of Judges', *JBL* 128: 687–702.

Gilmour, R. (2014), *Juxtaposition and the Elisha Cycle*, London: Bloomsbury T&T Clark.

Gitay, Y. (1992), 'Reflections on the Poetics of the Samuel Narrative: The Question of the Ark Narrative', *CBQ* 54: 221–230.

Glanville, M. (2018), *Adopting the Stranger as Kindred in Deuteronomy*, Atlanta: SBL.

Gorringe, T. (1998), 'Political Readings of Scripture', in J. Barton (ed.), *The Cambridge Companion to Biblical Interpretation*, Cambridge: Cambridge University Press, 67–80.

Gray, J. (1964), *I & II Kings*, London: SCM.

Green, B. (2003), *How Are the Mighty Fallen? A Dialogical Study of King Saul in 1 Samuel*, London: Sheffield Academic Press.

Grønbæk, J. (1971), *Die Geschichte vom Aufstieg Davids (1. Sam. 15–2. Sam. 5): Tradition und Komposition*, Copenhagen: Prostant apud Munksgaard.

Gundry, S. N. (2003), *Show Them No Mercy: Four Views on God and the Canaanite Genocide*, Grand Rapids: Zondervan.

Gunn, D. M. (1974), *Narrative Pattern and Oral Tradition in Judges and Samuel*, *VT* 24: 286–317.

—— (2005), *Judges*, Oxford: Blackwell.

Hall, A. L. (2003), 'Prophetic Vulnerability and the Strange Goodness of God: A Reading of Numbers 22 and 1 Kings 17', *Sewanee Theological Review* 46: 340–348.

Halpern, B. (2001), *David's Secret Demons: Messiah, Murderer, Traitor, King*, Grand Rapids: Eerdmans.

Hamilton, V. P. (2001), *Handbook on the Historical Books*, Grand Rapids: Baker Academic.

Hamley, I. M. (2015), 'What's Wrong with "Playing the Harlot"? The Meaning of זנה in Judges 19:2', *TynB* 66: 41–62.

—— (2019), *Unspeakable Things Unspoken: Otherness and Victimisation in Judges 19–21: An Irigaryan Reading*, Eugene: Pickwick.

Hamlin, E. J. (1990), *At Risk in the Promised Land: A Commentary on the Book of Judges*, Grand Rapids: Eerdmans.

Han, S. (2015), *Der 'Geist' in den Saul-und Davidgeschichten des 1. Samuelbuches*, Leipzig: Evangelische Verlagsanstalt.

Hauser, A. J. (1975), 'The "Minor Judges" – A Re-evaluation', *JBL* 94: 190–200.

Hawk, L. D. (1991), *Every Promise Fulfilled: Contesting Plots in Joshua*, Louisville: Westminster John Knox.

—— (2000), *Joshua*, Collegeville: Liturgical Press.

—— (2010), *Joshua in 3-D: A Commentary on Biblical Conquest and Manifest Destiny*, Eugene: Cascade.

Hawkins, R. K. (2013), *How Israel Became a People*, Nashville: Abingdon.

Hays, C. B., with P. Machinist (2016), 'Assyria and the Assyrians', in B. T. Arnold and B. A. Strawn (eds.), *The World Around the Old Testament: The People and Places of the Ancient Near East*, Grand Rapids: Baker Academic, 31–106.

Hays, J. D. (2003a), *From Every People and Nation: A Biblical Theology of Race*, Leicester: Apollos.

—— (2003b), 'Has the Narrator Come to Praise Solomon or to Bury Him? Narrative Subtlety in 1 Kings 1–11', *JSOT* 28: 149–174.

Hays, N. (2018), 'Family Disintegration in Judges 17–18', *CBQ* 80: 373–392.

Heffelfinger, K. M. (2009), '"My Father Is King": Chiefly Politics and the Rise and Fall of Abimelech', *JSOT* 33: 277–292.

Hentschel, G., and C. Nießen (2008), 'Der Bruderkrieg zwischen Israel und Benjamin (Ri 20)', *Bib* 89: 17–38.

Hill, A. E. (2006), 'On David's "Taking" and "Leaving" Concubines (2 Samuel 5:13, 15:16)', *JBL* 125: 129–139.

Hobbs, T. R. (1985), *2 Kings*, WBC, Dallas: Word.

—— (1989), *1, 2 Kings*, WBC, Dallas: Word.

Höffken, P. (2008), 'Der Rede des Rabsake vor Jerusalem (2 Kön. Xviii / Jes xxxvi) im Kontext anderer Kapitulationsforderungen', *VT* 58: 44–55.

Hoffmeier, J. (2009), *The Immigration Crisis: Immigrants, Aliens and the Bible*, Wheaton: Crossway.

Houston, F. S. (2015), *You Shall Love the Stranger as Yourself: The Bible, Refugees and Asylum*, London: Routledge.

Houston, W. J. (2008), *Contending for Justice: Ideologies and Theologies of Social Justice in the Old Testament*, London: T&T Clark.

Houten, C. van (1991), *The Alien in Israelite Law: A Study of the Changing Legal Status of Strangers in Ancient Israel*, Sheffield: Sheffield Academic.

Howard Jr, D. M. (1998), *Joshua*, Nashville: Broadman & Holman.

Hubbard Jr, R. L. (1984), 'The Hebrew Root *PG'* as a Legal Term', *JETS* 27: 129–133.

—— (2001), '"What Do These Stones Mean?": Biblical Theology and a Motif in Joshua', *BBR* 11: 1–26.

Hubbard Jr, R. L., and J. A. Dearman (2018), *Introducing the Old Testament*, Grand Rapids: Eerdmans.

Jacobson, H. (1992), 'The Judge Bedan (1 Samuel xii 11)', *VT* 42: 123–124.

—— (1994), 'Bedan and Barak Reconsidered', *VT* 44: 108–109.

Janzen, W. (1994), *Old Testament Ethics: A Paradigmatic Approach*, Louisville: Westminster John Knox.

Järlemyr, S. (2016), 'A Tale of Cross-Dressers, Mothers, and Murderers: Gender and Power in Judges 4–5', *SEÅ* 81: 49–62.

Jones, G. H. (1984), *1 and 2 Kings*, NCBC, 2 vols., Grand Rapids: Eerdmans.

Joseph, A. L. (2015), *Portrait of the Kings: The Davidic Prototype in Deuteronomistic Poetics*, Minneapolis: Fortress.

Kallai, Z. (1996), 'Samuel in Qumrān: Expansion of a Historiographical Pattern (4QSamᵃ)', *RB* 103: 581–591.

Kamp, A. (2016), 'The Conceptualization of God's Dwelling Place in 1 Kings 8: A Cognitive Approach', *JSOT* 40: 415–438.

Kent, G. J. R. (2011), *Say It Again, Sam: A Literary and Filmic Study of Narrative Repetition in 1 Samuel 28*, Cambridge: Lutterworth.

Keys, G. (1996), *The Wages of Sin: A Reappraisal of the 'Succession Narrative'*, Sheffield: Sheffield Academic Press.

Kim, J.-S. (2007), *Bloodguilt, Atonement and Mercy: An Exegetical and Theological Study of 2 Samuel 21:1–14*, Bern: Peter Lang.

Kim, U. (2008), *Identity and Loyalty in the David Story: A Postcolonial Reading*, Sheffield: Sheffield Phoenix.

Kim, Y.-K. (2008), 'In Search of the Narrator's Voice: A Discourse Analysis of 2 Kings 18:13–16', *JBL* 127: 477–489.

Klein, L. R. (1989), *The Triumph of Irony in the Book of Judges*, Sheffield: Almond.

Klein, W. W., C. L. Blomberg and R. L. Hubbard Jr (2017), *Introduction to Biblical Interpretation*, 3rd edn, Grand Rapids: Zondervan.

Klement, H. H. (2000), *2 Samuel 21–24: Context, Structure and Meaning in the Samuel Conclusion*, Bern: Peter Lang.

Knoppers, G. N. (1993), *Two Nations Under God: The Deuteronomistic History of Solomon and the Dual Monarchies*, vol. 1: *The Reign of Solomon and the Rise of Jeroboam*, Atlanta: Scholar's Press.

——— (1995), 'Prayer and Propaganda: Solomon's Dedication of the Temple and the Deuteronomists' Program', *CBQ* 57: 229–255.

Ko, G. (2018), '2 Samuel 20–24: A Theological Reflection on Israel's Kingship', *OTE* 31: 114–134.

Koopmans, W. T. (1990), *Joshua 24 as Poetic Narrative*, Sheffield: Sheffield Academic Press.

Koorevaar, H. J. (1990), *De Opbouw van het Boek Jozua*, Heverlee: Centrum voor Bijbelse Vorming-België.

——— (2012), 'The Book of Joshua and the Hypothesis of the Deuteronomistic History: Indications for an Open Serial Model', in E. Noort (ed.), *The Book of Joshua*, Leuven: Peeters, 219–232.

Krause, J. J. (2012), 'Vor wem soll die Auskundschaftung Jerichos geheim gehalten werden? Eine Frage zu Josua 2:1', *VT* 62.4: 454–456.

——— (2014), *Exodus und Eisodus: Komposition und Theologie von Josua 1–5*, Leiden: Brill.

——— (2015a), 'Aesthetics of Production and Aesthetics of Reception in Analyzing Intertextuality: Illustrated with Joshua 2', *Bib* 96.3: 416–427.

——— (2015b), 'The Book of the Torah in Joshua 1 and 23 and in the Deuteronomistic History', *ZAW* 127: 412–428.

Kuan, J. K. (1990), 'Third Kingdom 5:1 and Israelite–Tyrian Relations During the Reign of Solomon', *JSOT* 46: 31–46.

Laha Jr, R. R. (2012), 'Joshua 20', *Int* 66: 194–196.

Lau, P. H. (2011), *Identity and Ethics in the Book of Ruth: A Social Identity Approach*, Berlin: de Gruyter.

Lau, P. H., and G. Goswell (2016), *Unceasing Kindness: A Biblical Theology of Ruth*, London: Apollos.

Lebhar Hall, S. (2010), *Conquering Character: The Characterization of Joshua in Joshua 1–11*, London: T&T Clark.

Lee, K.-J. (2017), *Symbole für Herrschaft und Königtum in den Erzählungen von Saul und David*, Stuttgart: Kohlhammer.

Lilley, J. P. U. (1967), 'A Literary Appreciation of the Book of Judges', *TynB* 18: 94–102.

—— (1993), 'Understanding the *ḤEREM*', *TynB* 44: 160–177.

Lindars, B. (1995), *Judges 1–5: A New Translation and Commentary*, Edinburgh: T&T Clark.

Linville, J. R. (1998), *Israel in the Book of Kings: The Past as a Project of Social Identity*, Sheffield: Sheffield Academic Press.

Long, B. O. (1991), *2 Kings* (Grand Rapids: Eerdmans, 1991).

Long, V. P. (1989), *The Reign and Rejection of King Saul: A Case for Literary and Theological Coherence*, Atlanta: Scholars Press.

—— (1994), *The Art of Biblical History*, Leicester: Apollos.

Lorein, G. W. (2010), *Geschriften over de Perzische Tijd: Daniël, Esra-Nehemia, Esther, Haggai, Zacharia, Maleachi*, Heerenveen: Groen.

McCann, J. C. (2002), *Judges*, Louisville: John Knox.

McCarter Jr, P. K. (1980a), *1 Samuel: A New Translation with Notes and Commentary*, AB, Garden City: Doubleday.

—— (1980b), 'The Apology of David', *JBL* 99: 489–504.

—— (1984), *II Samuel: A New Translation with Notes and Commentary*, AB, Garden City: Doubleday.

McConville, J. G. (2017), *Joshua: Crossing Divides*, London: Bloomsbury T&T Clark.

McKay, J. W. (1973), *Religion in Judah Under the Assyrians*, London: SCM.

McKenzie, S. L. (2000), *King David: A Biography*, New York: Oxford University Press.

McKeown, J. (2015), *Ruth*, Grand Rapids: Eerdmans.

Mann, T. W. (2011), *The Book of the Former Prophets*, Eugene: Cascade.

Marcus, D. (1986), *Jephthah and His Vow*, Lubbock: Texas Tech Press.

Martin, L. R. (2008a), 'Power to Save?! The Role of the Spirit of the Lord in the Book of Judges', *JPT* 16: 21–50.

—— (2008b), *The Unheard Voice of God: A Pentecostal Hearing of the Book of Judges*, Blandford Forum: Deo.

Massey, J. E. (1994), 'Reading the Bible from Particular Social Locations: An Introduction', in L. E. Keck (ed.), *The New Interpreter's Bible*, vol. 1, Nashville: Abingdon, 150–153.

Matthews, V. H., and D. C. Benjamin (1993), *Social World of Ancient Israel: 1250–587 BCE*, Peabody: Hendrickson.

Merrill, E. H. (2011), 'The Samson Saga and Spiritual Leadership', in D. G. Firth and P. D. Wegner (eds.), *Presence, Power and Promise: The Role of the Spirit of God in the Old Testament*, Nottingham: Apollos, 281–293.

Michael, M. (2013), 'The Achan/Achor Traditions: The Parody of Saul as "Achan" in 1 Samuel 14:24–15:35', *OTE* 26: 730–760.

Miller Jr, P. D., and J. J. M. Roberts (1977), *The Hand of the Lord: A Reassessment of the 'Ark Narrative' of 1 Samuel*, Baltimore: Johns Hopkins University Press.

Mitchell, G. (1993), *Together in the Land: A Reading of the Book of Joshua*, Sheffield: JSOT Press.

Mommer, P. (1991), *Samuel: Geschichte und Überlieferung*, Neukirchen-Vluyn: Neukirchener Verlag.

Moore, G. F. (1903), *A Critical and Exegetical Commentary on Judges*, 2nd edn, Edinburgh: T&T Clark.

Moore, R. D. (1990), *God Saves: Lessons from the Elisha Stories*, Sheffield: Sheffield Academic Press.

Morris, L. (1992), *The Gospel According to Matthew*, PNTC, Grand Rapids: Eerdmans; Leicester: Inter-Varsity Press.

Napier, D. (1976), 'Inheritance and the Problem of Adjacency: An Essay on 1 Kings 21', *Int* 30: 3–11.

Neef, H.-D. (1989), 'Der Sieg Deboras und Baraks über Sisera; Exegetische Beobachtungen zum Aufbau und Werden von Jdc 4, 1–24', *ZAW* 101: 28–49.

Nelson, R. D. (1981), *The Double Redaction of the Deuteronomistic History*, Sheffield: JSOT Press.

—— (1987), *First and Second Kings*, Louisville: John Knox Press.

—— (1997), *Joshua: A Commentary*, Louisville: Westminster John Knox.

—— (2007), 'Ideology, Geography and the List of the Minor Judges', *JSOT* 31: 347–364.

Ngan, L. L. E. (1997), '2 Kings 5', *RevExp* 94: 589–597.

Nolan Fewell, D. (1986), 'Sennacherib's Defeat: Words at War in 2 Kings 18:13–19:37', *JSOT* 34: 79–90.

Nolland, J. (2005), *The Gospel of Matthew*, Grand Rapids: Eerdmans.

Noort, E. (ed.) (2012), *The Book of Joshua*, Leuven: Peeters.

Noth, M. (1981), *The Deuteronomistic History*, 2nd edn, Sheffield: JSOT Press.

Oeste, G. K. (2011a), 'Butchered Brothers and Betrayed Families: Degenerating Kinship Structures in the Book of Judges', *JSOT* 35: 295–316.

—— (2011b), *Legitimacy, Illegitimacy, and the Right to Rule: Windows on Abimelech's Rise and Demise in Judges 9*, London: T&T Clark.

Olley, J. W. (1998), 'Yahweh and His Zealous Prophet: The Presentation of Elijah in 1 and 2 Kings', *JSOT* 80: 25–51.

—— (2003), 'Pharaoh's Daughter, Solomon's Temple and the Palace: Another Look at the Structure of 1 Kings 1–11', *JSOT* 27: 355–369.

—— (2013), '2 Kings 13: A Cluster of Hope in God', *JSOT* 36: 199–218.

Olson, D. T. (1998), 'The Book of Judges', in L. E. Keck (ed.), *The New Interpreter's Bible*, Nashville: Abingdon, 2: 721–888.

Ortlund Jr, R. C. (1996), *God's Unfaithful Wife: A Biblical Theology of Spiritual Adultery*, Leicester: Apollos.

Parker, K. I. (1992), 'Solomon as Philosopher King? The Nexus of Law and Wisdom in 1 Kings 1–11', *JSOT* 53: 75–91.

Parry, R. (2004), *Old Testament Story and Christian Ethics: The Rape of Dinah as a Case Study*, Milton Keynes: Paternoster.

Patterson, R. D., and H. J. Austel (1988), '1, 2 Kings', in F. E. Gaebelein (ed.), *The Expositor's Bible Commentary*, Grand Rapids: Zondervan, 4: 1–300.

Paynter, H. (2016), *Reduced Laughter: Seriocomic Features and Their Functions in the Book of Kings*, Leiden: Brill.

—— (2017), 'Ahab – Heedless Father, Sullen Son: Humour and Intertextuality in 1 Kings 21', *JSOT* 41: 451–474.

—— (2018), '"Revenge for My Two Eyes": Talion and Mimesis in the Samson Narrative', *BibInt* 26: 133–157.

Petersen, D. L. (1981), *The Roles of Israel's Prophets*, Sheffield: JSOT Press.

Peterson, B. N. (2014), *The Authors of the Deuteronomistic History: Locating a Tradition in Ancient Israel*, Minneapolis: Fortress.

Pitkänen, P. (2017), 'Ancient Israelite Population Economy: *Ger, Toshav, Nakhri and Karat* as Settler Colonial Categories', *JSOT* 42: 139–153.

Prouser, O. H. (1994), 'The Truth About Women and Lying', *JSOT* 61: 15–28.

Provan, I. W. (1988), *Hezekiah and the Books of Kings: A Contribution to the Debate About the Composition of the Deuteronomistic History*, Berlin: de Gruyter.

——— (1995), *1 and 2 Kings*, Peabody: Hendrickson.

Provan, I. W., V. P. Long and T. Longman III (2015), *A Biblical History of Israel*, 2nd edn, Louisville: Westminster John Knox.

Robinson, G. (1993), *Let Us Be Like the Nations: A Commentary on the Books of 1 and 2 Samuel*, ITC, Edinburgh: Handsel.

Römer, T. (2006), 'Das doppelte Ende des Josuabuches: einige Anmerkungen zur aktuellen Diskussion um "deuteronomistisches Geschichtswerk" und "Hexateuch"', *ZAW* 118: 523–548.

Rösel, H. N. (2011), *Joshua*, Leuven: Peeters.

Rost, L. (1982), *The Succession to the Throne of David*, Sheffield: Almond.

Routledge, R. (2008), *Old Testament Theology: A Thematic Approach*, Nottingham: Apollos.

Rowe, J. Y. (2011), *Michal's Moral Dilemma: A Literary, Anthropological and Ethical Interpretation*, London: T&T Clark.

——— (2012), *Sons or Lovers: An Interpretation of David and Jonathan's Friendship*, London: T&T Clark.

Satterthwaite, P. E. (1992), 'Narrative Artistry in the Composition of Judges XX 29FF', *VT* 42: 80–89.

——— (1994), '"No King in Israel": Narrative Criticism and Judges 17–21', *TynB* 44.1: 75–88.

Schenker, A. (1982), *Der Mächtige im Schmelzofen des Mitleids*, Freiburg Schweiz: Universitätsverlag; Göttingen: Vandenhoeck & Rupprecht.

Scherer, A. G. (2005), 'Gideon – ein Anti-Held? Ein Beitrag zur Auseinandersetzung mit dem sog. 'Flawed Hero Approach' am Beispiel Jdc. VI 36–40', *VT* 55: 269–273.

Schmid, H. (2000), *Das Erste Buch der Könige*, Wuppertal: Brockhaus.

Seebass, H. (2012), 'Das Buch Josua als literarisch nicht zu erwartende Fortsetzung des Buches Numeri', in E. Noort (ed.), *The Book of Joshua*, Leuven: Peeters, 249–258.

Seiler, S. (1998), *Die Geschichte von der Thronfolge Davids (2 Sam 9–20; 1 Kön 1–2): Untersuchungen zur Literarkritik und Tendenz*, Berlin: de Gruyter.

Seitz, C. R. (2011), *The Character of Christian Scripture: The Significance of a Two-Testament Bible*, Grand Rapids: Baker Academic.

Selman, M. J. (1994), *1 Chronicles: An Introduction and Commentary*, TOTC, Leicester: Inter-Varsity Press.

Seow, C.-L. (1999), 'The First and Second Books of Kings', in L. E. Keck (ed.), *The New Interpreter's Bible*, Nashville: Abingdon, 3: 1–295.

Sherwood, A. (2006), 'A Leader's Misleading and a Prostitute's Profession: A Re-examination of Joshua 2', *JSOT* 31: 43–61.

Short, J. R. (2010), *The Surprising Election and Confirmation of King David*, Cambridge, Mass.: Harvard University Press.

Simon, L. T. (2000), *Identity and Identification: An Exegetical and Theological Study of 2 Sam 21–24*, Rome: Gregorian University.

Sjöberg, M. (2006), *Wrestling with Textual Violence: The Jephthah Narrative in Antiquity and Modernity*, Sheffield: Sheffield Phoenix.

Sklar, J. (2013), *Leviticus: An Introduction and Commentary*, TOTC, Nottingham: Inter-Varsity Press.

Smith, H. P. (1899), *A Critical and Exegetical Commentary on the Books of Samuel*, ICC, Edinburgh: T&T Clark.

Snaith, N. H. (1978), 'Altar at Gilgal: Joshua xx 22–29', *VT* 38: 330–335.

Soggin, J. A. (1972), *Joshua: A Commentary*, London: SCM.

———— (1987), *Judges: A Commentary*, 2nd edn, London: SCM.

Spina, F. A. (1991), 'A Prophet's "Pregnant Pause": Samuel's Silence in the Ark Narrative (1 Sam 4:1–7:2)', *HBT* 13.1: 59–73.

———— (2005), *The Faith of an Outsider: Exclusion and Inclusion in the Biblical Story*, Grand Rapids: Eerdmans.

Steinmann, A. E. (2016), *1 Samuel*, St. Louis: Concordia.

Stek, J. H. (2002), 'Rahab of Canaan and Israel: The Meaning of Joshua 2', *CJT* 37: 28–48.

Sternberg, M. (1985), *The Poetics of Biblical Narrative: Ideological Reading and the Drama of Literature*, Bloomington: Indiana University Press.

Strawn, B. A. (2017), *The Old Testament Is Dying: A Diagnosis and Recommended Treatment*, Grand Rapids: Baker Academic.

Sutherland, R. K. (1992), 'Israelite Political Theories in Joshua 9', *JSOT* 53: 65–74.

Talstra, E. (1993), *Solomon's Prayer: Synchrony and Diachrony in the Composition of 1 Kings 8, 14–61*, Kampen: Kok Pharos.

Thomas, B. D. (2014), *Hezekiah and the Compositional History of the Book of Kings*, Tübingen: Mohr Siebeck.

Toczyski, A. (2018), *The 'Geometrics' of the Rahab Story: A Multi-Dimensional Analysis of Joshua 2*, London: T&T Clark.

Vaal-Standon, M. de (2015), 'The Meaning and Implications of Ruth 4:5 – A Grammatical, Socio-Cultural and Juridical Investigation', PhD thesis, University of Pretoria.

Vannoy, J. R. (1978), *Covenant Renewal at Gilgal: A Study of 1 Samuel 11:14–12:25*, Cherry Hill: Mack.

Walsh, J. T. (1995), *Berit Olam: Studies in Hebrew Narrative and Poetry. 1 Kings*, Collegeville: Liturgical Press.

———— (2009), *Old Testament Narrative: A Guide to Interpretation*, Louisville: Westminster John Knox.

Walton, J. H., and J. H. Walton (2017), *The Lost World of the Israelite Conquest: Covenant Retribution and the Fate of the Canaanites*, Downers Grove: IVP Academic.

Way, K. C. (2018), 'The Meaning of the Minor Judges: Understanding the Bible's Shortest Stories', *JETS* 61: 275–285.

Webb, B. G. (2008), *The Book of the Judges: An Integrated Reading*, repr., Eugene: Wipf & Stock (original, 1987).

———— (2012), *The Book of Judges*, Grand Rapids: Eerdmans.

Weingart, K. (2018), '"My Father, My Father! Chariot of Israel and Its Horses!" (2 Kings 2:12 // 13:14): Elisha's or Elijah's Title?', *JBL* 137: 257–270.

Wenham, G. J. (1979), *The Book of Leviticus*, NICOT, Grand Rapids: Eerdmans.

———— (2000), *Story as Torah: Reading Old Testament Narratives Ethically*, Grand Rapids: Baker Academic.

Wénin, A. (2012), 'Josué 1–12 comme récit', in E. Noort (ed.), *The Book of Joshua*, Leuven: Peeters, 109–138.

Westbrook, A. D. (2015), *'And He Will Take Your Daughters . . .' Woman Story and the Ethical Evaluation of Monarchy in the David Narrative*, London: Bloomsbury T&T Clark.

Westbrook, R. (2005), 'Elisha's True Prophecy in 2 Kings 3', *JBL* 124: 530–532.

Williams, D. S. (1999), 'Once Again: The Structure of the Narrative of Solomon's Reign', *JSOT* 86: 49–66.

Williams, J. G. (1991), 'The Structure of Judges 2:6–16:31', *JSOT* 49: 77–85.

Williamson, H. G. M. (1985), *Ezra–Nehemiah*, Waco: Word.

Williamson, P. R. (2007), *Sealed with an Oath: Covenant in God's Unfolding Purpose*, Nottingham: Apollos.

Willis, J. T. (1971), 'An Anti-Elide Narrative Tradition from a Prophetic Circle at the Ramah Sanctuary', *JBL* 90: 288–308.

Winther-Nielsen, N. (1995), *A Functional Discourse Grammar of Joshua*, Stockholm: Almqvist & Wiksell.

Wiseman, D. J. (1964), 'Rahab of Jericho', *TynB* 14: 8–11.

——— (1993), *1 and 2 Kings*, TOTC, Leicester: Inter-Varsity Press.

Wolde, E. van (1995), 'Ya'el in Judges 4', *ZAW* 107: 240–246.

Wong, G. T. K. (2006), *Compositional Strategy of the Book of Judges*, Leiden: Brill.

Wood, B. G. (2011), 'Hittites and Hethites: A Proposed Solution to an Etymological Conundrum', *JETS* 54: 239–250.

Wozniak, J. (1983), 'Drei verschiedene literarische Beschreibungen des bundes zwischen Jonathan und David', *BZ* 27: 213–218.

Wray Beal, L. M. (2014), *1 & 2 Kings*, AOTC, Nottingham: Apollos.

——— (2017), 'The Past as Threat and Hope: Reading Joshua with Numbers', *BBR* 27: 461–483.

——— (Forthcoming), *Joshua: Story of God Commentary*, Grand Rapids: Zondervan.

Wright, C. J. H. (2004), *Old Testament Ethics for the People of God*, Leicester: Inter-Varsity Press.

Wright, S. I. (2000), 'An Experiment in Biblical Criticism: Aesthetic Encounter in Reading and Preaching Scripture', in C. Bartholomew, C. Green and K. Möller (eds.), *Renewing Biblical Interpretation*, Carlisle: Paternoster, 240–267.

Wünch, H.-G. (2014), 'The Stranger in God's Land – Foreigner, Stranger, Guest: What Can We Learn from Israel's Attitude Towards Strangers?', *OTE* 27: 1129–1154.

Yee, G. A. (1988), '"Fraught with Background", Literary Ambiguity in II Samuel 11', *Int* 42: 240–253.

——— (1993), 'By the Hand of a Woman: The Metaphor of the Woman Warrior in Judges 4', *Semeia* 61: 99–132.

Youngblood, R. F. (1992), '1, 2 Samuel', in F. E. Gaebelein (ed.), *The Expositor's Bible Commentary*, Grand Rapids: Zondervan, 3: 553–1104.

Younger Jr, K. L. (1990), *Ancient Conquest Accounts: A Study in Ancient Near Eastern and Biblical History Writing*, Sheffield: JSOT Press.

——— (2016), 'Aram and the Arameans', in B. T. Arnold and B. A. Strawn (eds.), *The World Around the Old Testament: The People and Places of the Ancient Near East*, Grand Rapids: Baker Academic, 229–265.

Zehnder, M. (2005), *Umgang mit Fremden: Ein Beitrag zur Anthropologie des 'Fremden' im Licht antiker Quellen*, Stuttgart: Kohlhammer.

—— (2013), 'The Annihilation of the Canaanites: Reassessing the Brutality of the Biblical Witness', in M. Zehnder and H. Hagellia (eds.), *Encountering Violence in the Bible*, Sheffield: Sheffield Phoenix, 263–290.

Zyl, A. H. van (1988, 1989), *1 Samuël*, 2 vols., Nijkerk: G. F. Callenbach.

Index of authors

Index of Scripture references

209

Index of ancient sources

Titles in this series:

An index of Scripture references for all the volumes may be found at
http://www.thegospelcoalition.org/resources/nsbt.